Performance and F

Performance and Participation

Practices, Audiences, Politics

Edited by

Anna Harpin
&
Helen Nicholson

First published 2017 by
PALGRAVE

Palgrave in the UK is an imprint of Macmillan Publishers Limited,
registered in England, company number 785998, of 4 Crinan Street,
London, N1 9XW.

Palgrave Macmillan in the US is a division of St Martin's Press LLC,
175 Fifth Avenue, New York, NY 10010.

Palgrave is a global imprint of the above companies and is represented
throughout the world.

Palgrave® and Macmillan® are registered trademarks in the United States,
the United Kingdom, Europe and other countries.

ISBN 978–1–137–39317–3 hardback
ISBN 978–1–137–39316–6 paperback

This book is printed on paper suitable for recycling and made from fully
managed and sustained forest sources. Logging, pulping and manufacturing
processes are expected to conform to the environmental regulations of the
country of origin.

A catalogue record for this book is available from the British Library.

A catalog record for this book is available from the Library of Congress.

Table of Contents

List of Illustrations

Notes on Contributors

Adam Alston is a lecturer in theatre and performance studies at the University of Surrey, specialising in immersive and participatory theatre practices, with a particular focus on the aesthetics and politics of audience engagement. More recently he has been addressing the histories, aesthetics and phenomenology of partial and complete darkness in avant-garde and contemporary theatre and performance. His first monograph, *Beyond Immersive Theatre: Aesthetics, Politics and Productive Participation*, was published with Palgrave Macmillan, and he is currently working on a co-edited collection with Martin Welton (QMUL), contracted with Methuen, titled *Theatre in the Dark: Shadow, Gloom and Blackout in Contemporary Theatre*.

Stephen Bottoms is professor of contemporary theatre and performance at the University of Manchester, UK. His books include *Sex, Drag and Male Roles: Investigating Gender as Performance* (with Diane Torr, 2010), *Small Acts of Repair: Performance, Ecology and Goat Island* (with Matthew Goulish, 2007), and *Playing Underground: A Critical History of the 1960s Off-Off-Broadway Movement* (2004), among others. He has guest edited themed editions of the journals *Performance Research* ('Performing Literatures', 2009; 'On Ecology', 2012) and *Contemporary Theatre Review* ('Tim Crouch, *The Author* and the Audience', 2011; 'Electoral Theatre', 2015). Steve has been engaged for several years with practice-based research into the use of sited performance in contexts of environmental change: see www.performancefootprint.co.uk and www.multi-story-shipley.co.uk.

Colette Conroy is a senior lecturer in drama at the University of Hull. She is the author of *Theatre & The Body* (Palgrave, 2010) and has published work on the connections between politics, bodies and performance. Most recently, she has published work about disability cultures and sport and about her own engagement in sport as a disabled person. She has a background as a theatre-maker, including time spent as the associate director of Graeae Theatre Company, the UK's foremost professional theatre company of disabled people. She is co-editor of the international refereed journal *RiDE: the Journal of Applied Theatre and Performance*. She is currently working on a book project about the philosopher Jacques Rancière and the implications of his thought for applied and social theatre practices.

Dawn Fowler is a lecturer and researcher who has taught at the University of York and the University of the West of England. Her research interests include theatre and war, marginalized writing and children's theatre. She has published chapters on radical theatre in Bristol, militant suffrage in the work of Marie Jones and the treatment of war in plays by David Greig and Charles Wood. She holds a PhD from the University of York.

James Frieze is the author of *Naming Theatre: Demonstrative Diagnosis in Performance* (Palgrave, 2009) and of essays on contemporary performance in various journals and collections. He is a senior lecturer in drama at Liverpool John Moores University, and his work focuses on devising, improvisation, performance theory and contemporary performance. He has collaboratively devised and directed numerous site-responsive performances, including theatrical adaptations of nonfiction prose, poems, online virtual worlds and other kinds of source-text. His current research focuses on theatre, participation and the forensic turn – a monograph on this subject is in progress under contract with Routledge. He is also the editor of a forthcoming collection (Palgrave, 2016) titled *Reframing Immersive Theatre: The Politics and Pragmatics of Participatory Performance*.

Anna Harpin is associate professor of theatre and performance studies at the University of Warwick. Her research explores cultural histories of madness and trauma. She has recently published an edited collection titled *Performance, Madness, Psychiatry: Isolated Acts* (Palgrave) and is completing her monograph *Disordered: Madness and Cultural Representation* with Routledge. She is also developing a new project on cultural portraits of shame. In addition to her academic work, she is a theatre-maker with her company, Idiot Child, who are making a new piece about fear, titled *What if the plane falls out of the sky?*

Deirdre Heddon is professor of contemporary performance practice at the University of Glasgow. She is a series co-editor of *Performing Landscapes* (Palgrave Macmillan), for which she is writing *Performing Landscapes: Forests*. She is also the author of *Autobiography and Performance* (Palgrave Macmillan, 2008), co-author of *Devising Performance: A Critical History* (Palgrave Macmillan, 2005) and co-editor of a number of anthologies, including *Histories and Practices of Live Art* (Palgrave Macmillan, 2012) and, most recently, *It's All Allowed: The Performances of Adrian Howells*

(Intellect/LADA, 2016). Her research has been published in various journals and editions, from *Performance Research* to *Cultural Geographies*, and emerges also in practice-based outputs (*The Walking Library* and *40 Walks*). Dee is the founding dean of the Scottish Graduate School for Arts & Humanities.

Liam Jarvis is a lecturer in drama in the Department of Literature, Film and Theatre Studies at the University of Essex. He co-founded Analogue, with whom he has created award-winning devised work from stage shows to interactive performance events that have toured the UK and toured internationally. The work of the company has included *Mile End* (toured in 2007–08, winning a Scotsman Fringe First and the Arches Brick Award), *Beachy Head* (toured in 2009–10, co-produced with The New Wolsey (Ipswich)), *2401 Objects* (toured in 2011–12, co-produced with Oldenburgisches Staatstheater and The New Wolsey (Ipswich), winning a Scotsman Fringe First Award), *Lecture Notes on a Death Scene* (a one-on-one show that toured in 2011), *Re-enactments* (a headphone piece developed through a fellowship at Hanse-Wissenschaftskolleg (Germany), short-listed for the Oxford Samuel Beckett Theatre Trust Award and commissioned by Shoreditch Town Hall in 2013–14), *Transports* (an interactive installation staged at Shoreditch Town Hall, Forest Fringe and the Science Museum's Dana Centre in 2014), *Living Film Set* (commissioned by Theatre Royal Plymouth 2016–17) and *Sleepless* (co-produced with Staatstheater Mainz and Shoreditch Town Hall – touring in 2016). His AHRC-funded PhD research at Royal Holloway, University of London examined immersive performance practices that are integrative of neuroscientific body transfer illusions as an applied tool for audiences to feel with the body of another.

Alison Jeffers is a full-time lecturer and researcher in drama at the University of Manchester. Having worked in community arts and actor training, she began her academic career as a PhD researcher on the *In Place of War* project in Manchester (2004–08) which was set up to investigate relationships between war, theatre and performance. Alison's research concerns theatre and performance practices made about and by both refugees and asylum seekers in the UK. She has published *Refugees Theatre and Crisis: Performing Global Identities* (2011) in addition to an extensive body of other writing about refugees and performance, verbatim theatre, performances of citizenship and the ethics of social archiving in Belfast. She is currently researching the British community arts movement of the 1970s and early 1980s and working on a co-edited book titled *Culture, Democracy and the Right to Make Art: the British Community Arts Movement*.

Helen Nicholson is professor of theatre and performance at Royal Holloway, University of London, where she is also associate dean (research) for the Faculty of Arts and Social Sciences. Helen has been co-editor of *RiDE: The Journal of Applied Theatre and Performance* since 2004 and author of several books in the field, including *Applied Drama: The Gift of Theatre* (2005, second edition 2014), *Theatre & Education* (2009) and *Theatre, Education and Performance: The Map and the Story* (2011), for which she was awarded the Distinguished Book Award by the American Alliance for Theatre and Education in 2012. Helen is currently leading a major research project on amateur theatre, funded by the Arts and Humanities Research Council, grant references: AH/K001922/1 and AH/N001567/1.

1   Performance and Participation

Anna Harpin and Helen Nicholson

Getting stuck in

In September 2015 the labyrinthine corridors of the Queen Elizabeth Hall on London's South Bank were opened for *Memory Point(s)*, an interactive performance developed by Platform 4 that documented and evoked the lives of people living with dementia in an assemblage of beautiful vignettes and installations. As part of the Secret Southbank Centre programme, audiences were led underground through the concrete corridors of its brutalist architecture to witness fragmented shards of memories almost forgotten, to rediscover the joys of a dressing-up box and to join a tea-dance, each experience capturing and framing the multi-sensory qualities of everyday life. In one of the theatres above, an audience was sitting in the dark, watching Timberlake Wertenbaker's *Our Country's Good*, a play set in Botany Bay in 1788 that represents the redemptive power of participating in theatre. In nearby Shoreditch Town Hall, audiences were invited into dreamthinkspeak's *Absent* at 15-minute intervals throughout the day to experience a haunting narrative of loss and soullessness, a journey that was played out in the old town hall's atmospheric basement rooms.

This snapshot of three performances illustrates some of the different approaches to theatre-making and modes of participation that are shaping contemporary theatre. Audiences who attend the theatre in the twenty-first century are often asked to wear outdoor clothing or don masks or blindfolds; they may find themselves on tours through basements, being costumed in backstage areas, lured into atmospheric city spaces not designed for theatregoing or handed electronic devices with which to vote or play. Contemporary theatre-makers are grappling with innovative methods of participation, finding that the appetite for new forms of cultural engagement presents creative opportunities. Yet audiences who prefer to remain seated in more conventional theatre buildings are also, of course, participants in the live event; their attention is felt by actors and affects the experience of the performance. All audiences – whether they are walking through tunnels or siting on upholstered seats – might be swept along by the emotion and atmosphere of the performance or find themselves resistant or immune to its contagious affects. However construed, the relationship between performance and participation is intricate and multifaceted, and it increasingly raises questions about how contemporary theatre-makers and audiences are negotiating this complex interplay. If performance is always already participatory, and if participation itself is an inherently performative notion, how might this conceptual terrain be understood without reducing participation to another *theatra mundi*, bounding imprecisely across all cultural milieu?

Performance and Participation: Audiences, Practices, Politics reflects our shared perception that the twenty-first century is redefining the political relationship between performance and participation, with profound and sometimes contradictory consequences for theatre-makers and audiences. Historically, participation in performance was widely associated with democracy, with agency and with protest, or with the popular, the unruly and the countercultural. For much of the twentieth century, participatory forms of performance were regarded as a rebellious counterpoint to the disciplinary spaces of conventional theatre by the modernist avant-garde, and in industrial economies, popular theatres of the Left harnessed the energy of collective participation to resist to the constraints of a hierarchical society. Across the world, applied theatre has used participatory strategies to encourage a whole range of social benefits, such as grassroots activism, health education and development activities, where it is assumed that 'bottom-up' or 'people's participation' in decision-making processes automatically ensures greater representation and extends civic engagement and community involvement. The assumption of the de facto value of joining in has been tenaciously held. The significance of cultural participation (and non-participation) in theatre has often been expressed as binary divisions between active / passive, liberated / constrained, democratic / hierarchical, mobile/fixed, empowered / oppressed and so on, with clear judgements made about their egalitarianism or emancipatory potential. Our contention in this book is that these dichotomies reproduce patterns of thought that were associated with a previous industrial era and that new forms of creative engagement reflect a deeper cultural shift evident in post-industrial networked societies, challenging tired debates about the instrumental or intrinsic value of participatory performance and extending far beyond the contemporary fashion for actor and audience interactivity. This book thus investigates a broader contextualisation for participation, engaging with the contemporary moment by considering how the cultural and political vocabularies at stake in the term 'participation' are entangled.

In theatre and performance studies, the implications of this cultural shift have been widely observed. Shannon Jackson, Jen Harvie and Claire

Bishop are influential voices in this debate, all of whom respond to the ways in which different forms of participation and engagement are curated as part of what Jackson memorably described as the 'social turn' in contemporary performance art. Jackson's analysis of the ways in which performers become 'fabricators' of shared real-time events demonstrates the multiplicity of aesthetic registers that have become harnessed to socially engaged art (2011: 12–13). Harvie contributes to the debate by placing contemporary performance in the context of neoliberalism, observing cultural trends in London that frequently require audiences to engage in different forms of 'devolved' collaboration (2013). Claire Bishop's critique of participatory performance as a form of impoverished and manipulative social work (described as 'artificial hells') resonates throughout this book, and many authors gathered in this collection respond directly or indirectly to her call for a 'more nuanced language' to discuss socially engaged art-making (Bishop 2012: 18). What emerges from all these perspectives – and from debates between the relational aesthetics furthered by art critic Nicolas Bourriaud and by Grant Kester's communitarian dialogic art – is that participation in the theatrical event inhabits a paradox (Bourriaud 2002; Kester 2011). Participation is politically pliable, and it can no longer be taken for granted that its dramaturgical strategies carry specific political meanings or social imperatives. Nor can it be assumed that to participate is to claim space and voice in ways that might be considered 'empowering' or anti-authoritarian. Gareth White has responded thoughtfully to this impulse, considering audience participation as an aesthetic 'invitation' that is experienced in multiple ways (White 2012: 221–235). Others are more polemical, including Ben Fletcher-Watson, who has observed that the liberating potential of participation in theatre with very young children swerves towards a tyrannical mode of hegemonic practice (Fletcher-Watson 2015: 24–38).

One of the central interventions of this volume is to (temporarily) dispense with distinctions of dramatic form (immersive theatre, live art, scripted play) or participant group (amateur, professional, community) as primary navigational tools for theatre and performance practice. By uniting playwriting, marathon running, ecological one-to-one performances and immersive theatre through the mechanic of felt experience, the authors gathered in this book seek to understand the agency of participation as an embodied practice rather than a thing that is done to, or by, others. Rather than analysing the power in terms of its resistance or acquiescence to specific disciplinary structures, this way of thinking acknowledges that the sensing subject is also a priori a participant in the networks and flows of power that shape everyday life. Cultural geographer Hayden Lorimer, writing about the relationship between performance and cultural theory, summarises the implications of this new attention to affective subjectivities for the politics of representation:

> [T]o more traditional signifiers of identity and difference (class, gender, ethnicity, age, sexuality, disability), have been added another order of abstract descriptors: instincts, events, auras, rhythms, cycles, flows and codes. (2007: 92)

Thus understood, rather than positioning participation on the positive side of fixed binaries, this conceptual framework suggests that it makes no sense to make sharp distinctions between participation (active, rebellious, critical) and non-participation (passive, receptive, docile). This book seeks, therefore, to contest the binary between participation and non-participation in an attempt to expand the horizons of perception and thought about the business of cultural 'doing'. Across the spectrum of practices investigated in this book, the creative negotiation between participation and performance rearranges aesthetic registers and theatrical codes, dismantling oppositions and making power not only visible but audible, tangible, felt.

The book is curated into three sections: Recognising Participation, Labours of Participation and Authoring Participation. Rather than developing a general theory of participation that might constitute a new strand of audience studies, each section critically engages with productive questions about how different forms of performance speak to the political dynamics of participation. Chapters might be read sequentially or, because there are many shared motives and recurring themes, as a conversation across and between the sections. In this introduction, we shall outline some of the broader conceptual and political questions that recur in this book. We shall begin by considering questions of recognition and move to address labours of participation and authorship. When woven together, these three themes capture the social and the aesthetic possibilities of theatre and articulate some of the conceptual dynamics between participation and performance.

Acts of recognition: Do you see what I mean?

Is participation an action or a way of seeing and perceiving? How far does the act of participation necessitate a witness? What systems of meaning make an individual or group behaviour visible or invisible as participatory? What social gestures fall silently outside the echo chamber of modes of doing and being that might be considered 'ordinary'? In short, how is participation recognised, and who or what conditions the terms of this *doing*? This book is interested not only in acts of participation, but also in how they are recognised and felt as such, by whom they are recognised and why that may matter. This seam within the volume is studded with questions of making space for who or what may not be immediately heard, sensed or seen, and there is also an interest in how artistic practices seek to redistribute power by dismantling and troubling terms of participation that have become mundane or quotidian. In thinking through if and how one might recognise participation, the authors collectively move beyond a transactional reading of bodies and behaviours and towards a messier ecology of senses and sensing. That is to say, rather than simply arguing that there is a better way to 'see things', these essays embrace a more unsteady, intersectional understanding of participation. In this sense, as opposed to thinking about how participation might be represented and clearly recognised in a given performance, this book looks down the opposite end of the telescope in the hope of glimpsing a constellation of practices that together comprise a political ecology of participation.

By trying to excavate a new territory of thinking with respect to political action, the authors consider the relationship between resistance, participation and non-participation. Recognition is inherently political, and gestures that recognise those who have been historically marginalised or disenfranchised are potent symbolic acts. Following the analysis of the politics of recognition led by the philosopher Charles Taylor towards the end of the twentieth century, Nancy Fraser argued for a 'new constellation' of the political, in which cultural recognition is not considered separate from material inequalities; both economic redistribution and cultural recognition are necessary for social justice. She argues for 'parity of participation' based on an awareness of the political force of misrecognition:

> From this perspective, recognition is a remedy for injustice, not a generic human need. Thus, the form(s) of recognition justice requires in any given case depend(s) on the form(s) of misrecognition to be redressed. Everything depends in other words on precisely what currently misrecognized people need in order to be able to participate as peers in social life. (Fraser 1998: 5)

Dawn Fowler's anxieties about the dismissal of 'women's work' speak to this concern to dismantle culturally defined hierarchies and re-shape social relations. Alison Jeffers is similarly concerned with the political implications of what she describes as 'long-held and cherished community narratives' in Northern Ireland, suggesting that recognising different forms

5

of authorship through the process of play-making can shift perceptions. The dislocation of participation from the individual to the collective (in its broadest meaning), from belonging to diffusion and from the past to the present, has significant implications for what it means to act politically.

An interest in the practice of reflexivity runs throughout the book, and it is often harnessed to a political sensitivity to the wider environment. Some authors capture this impulse by careful attentiveness to listening and by analysing how performance can encourage attunement to the human and nonhuman worlds and sensory alertness to its flow and rhythms. For Deirdre Heddon, the intricacy, intimacy and silence of one-to-one performance with artist Adrian Howells' inspired deep attentiveness, a labour of love that she describes as a kind of 'entangled listening' to the vital forces of the world that are both human and more-than-human. Similarly, there is Stephen Bottoms' acute awareness of the river's agency in Shipley, Yorkshire, where he wove local residents' stories into a performance designed to raise awareness of the risks of flooding. In common with Colette Conroy's concern with participants, onlookers and environments in the context of marathon running, Bottoms, drawing on the work of Gilles Deleuze, also attends to the plural registers of participation involved in performative journeys. Arguing that all three ecologies of 'the environment, social relations and human subjectivity' have meaning-making force, he explores how the river asserted its vitality in performance. Throughout this book, there is a recurring interest in how patterns of participation conjoin the artistic with the social and temporal, in which the materialities of landscape, place, objects and performance are not just props or a backdrop to the dramatic action, but integral to it, casting an assertive presence.

The chapters gathered in the section Recognising Participation explore how participation, in varied activities – live art, marathon running, immersive theatre-making and playwriting – occurs in the intervals between things. Participation is, then, less an action than an encounter and a perception. As Heddon demonstrates in her encounters with Howells and as Conroy argues in relation to long-distance running, the political imperative to reconceive participation along sensual and sentient lines is urgent. Indeed, both Conroy and Heddon make cases for an expanded perception of recognition that takes account of the full range of environmental registers immanent in performance. Challenging the idea that intimate performance with one other participant constitutes a one-to-one encounter, Heddon suggests that the experience of listening offers opportunities to become attuned to the more-than-human world. Likewise, Conroy lingers in the hinterlands between opposition and relationality and between difference and interdependence. Here she broadens the aperture and invites one to look through, rather than at, participation.

A second thread that swerves through this thematic cluster is an interest in moments of misrecognition. Where is the locus of power situated when participatory actions are read and (mis)understood? Whose judgements about understanding or misunderstanding are recognised? For both Colette Conroy and Anna Harpin, it is politically important to disentangle intention and reception. Whether it is the running body or the non-verbal body, there is a pertinent question to be asked about how difference and resistance are framed and narrated. If alterity is too readily perceived as a form of protest (whether intended or not), what are the consequences for the notion of non-participation? That is to say, are bodies that appear different (wilfully or otherwise) read as somehow non-participatory in and of themselves? If so, and if difference becomes constrained by the very legitimation of some forms of participation, does this paradoxically render non-participation a nonsense and impossibility? Jarvis's exploration of Analogue's *Re-enactments* also articulates the dramaturgical impossibility of non-participation and reflects upon the consequences of this for the theatrical offer that the piece makes. How much does this theatrical management of participation by the company invisibly erase or mask the actions of those participants opting out of the encounter?

Debates about recognition call, then, for a move away from participation as the practice of joining in and instead towards a radical presumption of participation and an attendant, hospitable and curious embrace of the political terms of such encounters. Radically, this book responds to the contemporary call to attend to affect – not as a subset of human sensibility but as a relational force that exists between bodies, objects and technologies. Participation, as affective encounters, brings together the sentient with the spatial and environmental. This dance between the affective agency of environments, social relations and subjectivities is evident throughout this collection, offering insights into an expanded meaning of perception and recognition. Many authors recognise the potency of environmental agency. This complements human-centred narratives of participation, capturing an urgent need to recognise not only interpersonal political subjectivities but also nonhuman and more-than-human relationalities.

Labours of participation: Working it out

A central debate in this book attends to how participation, as a mode of audience engagement, disrupts conventional divisions of labour between audience and artist and how, in the process, agency – as a political act – is experienced, denied or exercised. Throughout this collection, authors are concerned with the ways in which participation brings social and artistic labour into dialogue and how practices of participation might disrupt or affirm social relations or political antagonisms. Participatory performance demands a reassessment of how far the labour of social criticism that has been so long associated with the arts has been lost or redistributed and of whether some forms of immersive theatre-making are becoming little more than a commercial theme park.

There are two key perspectives on labour debated in this book, both of which connect to our discussion of the political dynamic between the aesthetic strategies and social implications of participatory performance. First, there is a consistent perception that the performative qualities of participation reflect wider social changes in which the value of creative labour is being redefined, and in a climate in which the political has become increasingly aestheticised. As the philosopher Chantal Mouffe points out, this way of thinking has political implications for the relationship between art and politics. Writing about the radical potential for the arts in what she describes as an era of 'post-political consensus', Mouffe argues that

> I do not see the relation between art and politics in terms of two separately constituted fields, art on one side and politics on the other, between which a relation would need to be established. There is an aesthetic dimension in the political and there is a political dimension in art. ... [It] is not useful to make a distinction between political and non-political art. (2007: 11)

The essays in this book critically interrogate this proliferation of the political, offering new appreciations of the customary labour of the artist as social critic. Second, many authors critically read the creative relationality between participation and performance by engaging with theoretical positions that trouble conventional distinctions between subject and object, human and nonhuman, and dismantle narratives of cause-and-effect.[1] There is a strong post-phenomenological current running through this book, where the everyday labour of participating in the world is understood as part of a broader political ecology, framed by multiple, contested and material assemblages, flows and networks.

Authors in this book respond, either implicitly or explicitly, to the ways in which twenty-first century economies are redefining links between creative labour and political agency. The new spirit of post-industrial capitalism, as Luc Boltanski and Eve Chiapello describe, has appropriated the energy of the countercultural movements of the 1960s, a time when

8

cultural participation became particularly associated with social freedom and personal liberty. They argue that the anti-hierarchical aesthetic
strategies associated with the brave new world of the mid-twentieth
century have been used in the twenty-first century to support modes of
self-regulation required by contemporary capitalism:

> [C]reativity, unbridled self-fulfilment; the authenticity of a personal
> life as against hypocritical, old-fashioned social conventions – these
> might seem, if not definitely established, at least widely acknowledged
> as essential values of modernity. (Boltanski and Chiapello 2005: 419)

This pattern of beliefs has not only changed ways of living; it has also
altered patterns of labour, replacing the disciplinary practices of the Fordist
period with more fluent and participatory forms of self-management,
autonomy and creative entrepreneurship. Repetitive labour of the industrialised workforce has been eroded in the affluent West, leaving not only
an increased commercial demand for creative labour, but also greater work-
place precarity. In this political climate, creativity is becoming increasingly
commodified, and the arts have become associated with urban regeneration and gentrification as well as social criticism. Noting this trend, Mouffe
argues that in a society in which political questions have been reduced to
solving technical issues, the criticality of the arts still has strong potential
to 'disrupt the smooth image that corporate capitalism is trying to spread,
bringing to the fore its repressive character' (2007: 13). In relation to theatre, Adam Alston elegantly summarises the political ambiguity surrounding participatory performance in his chapter in this collection. He writes
that participation tends to be seen 'either as an intervention in the material networks of capitalism, or as a complicit feature or effect of the political ideologies that facilitate capitalist hegemony' (150).

It might be tempting to respond to this apparent aporia by reasserting
traditional binaries that defined the relationship between participation and
non-participation in performance, adding subcategories to further distinguish
between forms of participation: commodified/consumerist versus politically
disruptive/communitarian. Authors in this book resist this approach. Instead
they offer readings of how the commercial imperatives associated with some
forms of participatory theatre can be recognised and reimagined, as well as
aesthetic strategies framed in ways that offer social and political agency. James
Frieze navigates this paradox in his discussion of dreamthinkspeak's immersive performance *One Step Forward, One Step Back* in Liverpool Cathedral.
Recognising that the performance took place against a backdrop of urban
regeneration, Frieze argues that the process of participating in this promenade

performance encouraged contemplation, a mode of engagement that has often been neglected in favour of more visible forms of activity.

The chapters gathered in the section Labours of Participation demonstrate explicitly different ways in which participation works. Helen Nicholson's chapter addresses participatory practices in which conventional divisions of labour are reassessed and where clear-cut distinctions between professional, amateur and community artists are contested and eroded. Her chapter examines the affective labour of non-professional performers, raising questions about how the social and communitarian ambitions of professional theatre-makers can be aligned with innovative contemporary performance practices. Dawn Fowler's chapter takes up the debate by addressing the labours of activism, and she attends to the performative qualities of craft activists, known as 'craftivists'. In her examination of the gender politics of quiet and slow craftivism, Fowler unbinds some of the established hierarchies of silence and voice, political doing and political being, activism and pacifism. Fowler's concern with the dynamic between political activism and craft opens questions about the authority of anonymity and how an unsigned or unacknowledged creative intervention can carry political weight. Adam Alston takes debates about agency in a different direction, demonstrating that the marketing strategies of immersive theatre use secrecy as an alluring commodity to tempt audiences to buy tickets, but he also argues that in the hands of innovative theatre-makers, secrecy can also be politically progressive. Revitalising the cultural labour of artists as social critics, Alston directs his attention to Erving Goffman's frame analysis as a strategy to think through the politics of participation. He applies Goffman's concept of 'keying' to performances that invoke secrecy, suggesting that performative activities that are temporarily 'bracketed' from everyday life might shape and alter perceptions. When put in conversation, this section throws into relief how the labour of audiences and artists is reciprocally and mutually embedded in their commercial, political and social environments. In each of these chapters and elsewhere, authors offer a rich set of debates that show how the materiality of performance engages the immaterial labour of audience members, suggesting that the political is not only discursively constructed but also found in gaps and silences and in the rhythms and flows of the performed event.

Authorship and authority: Who's doing what?

Participation promises authorship. It is marked, sometimes erroneously, by the offer of impacting on the affective shape, atmosphere or political direction of the performance. Authorship may construct an illusion of audience autonomy that operates to serve the spectacle of a highly controlled or choreographed experience. Similarly, the technologies of performance may mask tacit hierarchies of knowledge, power, labour and cultural value. In such transactional exchanges, audiences are permitted an illusion of being *with*, rather than *at*, a performance. Audience members sometimes describe having 'done' a certain performance: Have you done *The Drowned Man*? The question implies agency. Even in applied theatre and socially engaged performance, participants' contributions are often carefully curated. So what is at stake when artists hand over aspects of authorship to their audiences? How does this distribute authority?

While working in markedly distinct theatre forms, each chapter in this book puts authorship in recession. A central strand of the debate does not simply replace the authorial vision of artists with participation-as-authorship; rather, questions of authorship are placed in the context of wider political debates about agency, refusing stale distinctions between collective or communitarian forms of participation as authentic and emancipatory, and authorial artistic vision as necessarily manipulative and authoritarian. Authors in this book are remarkably consistent in their refusal of this stereotype, asking pivotal questions about how the dynamic between authority, authorship and participation might be reimagined in the material relationality of performance. This ambition relates to Jean-Luc Nancy's analysis of community, whose work is invoked by Heddon in this book. In *Being Singular Plural*, Nancy questions the ways in which authorship implies an ontological separation between human agency and the nonhuman world – a position that, he argues, places particular stress on the world as it is represented by humanity. Instead, as Heddon notes, Nancy proposes a social ontology in which 'being-with', as a relational force, replaces the apparent autonomy of individual authorship. The relationality of authorship is similarly debated by Helen Nicholson, who finds both fragile hierarchies and productive tensions between the authorial vision of professional artists and the non-professional performers they sought to engage. As Liam Jarvis points out in his reflections on his work with his company Analogue, it is often the case that the shared creative labour of participants – however understood – invites responses that are multi-perspectival. Rather than defining audiences as heterogenic or curating responses that depend on a generic 'we', he suggests that there is a precise and detailed analysis of how participation is nuanced and perceived in multiple ways.

The authors gathered in the collection cumulatively interrogate the day-to-day manner in which ideas of 'I', 'We', 'You', 'Them', 'Human' and 'Nonhuman' are constituted as relational entities, perceived emotionally and affectively, as well as experienced cognitively. Writing in her volume *The Cultural Politics of Emotion*, Sara Ahmed argues that emotions do not really belong to anyone:

> So emotions are not simply something 'I' or 'We' [the crowd] have. Rather, it is through emotions, or how we respond to objects and others, that surfaces or boundaries are made: the 'I' and 'We' are shaped by, and even take the shape of, contact with others. (2014: 10)

Ahmed proposes a direct relationship between feelings and citizenship, arguing that citizenship is, in many ways, 'a technology for deciding whose happiness comes first' (2014: 225). The political constellation sketched here of affect, emotion, citizenship and participation strikes at the heart of the political concerns of this volume. Following Ahmed's suggestion that emotion is not individualised as a 'thing' that belongs to an individual but rather as an interrelational connection, this book raises questions about how far participation might be understood along similar lines – not as an action or activity but as an assemblage of peoples, objects and environments. Moreover, if there is a moral register to emotional governance, then perhaps the ability to *feel right* or feel *the right way* conditions an ability to participate politically in a wide ecological field. This concern is picked up by Harpin in her interrogation of the disciplinary structures and institutional practices that govern apparently acceptable modes of being in the world. In her exploration of mutism, she invites the reader to reflect upon how we might tune in to embodied practices of listening in new ways. Here and elsewhere, the volume investigates how the performative practice of participation necessarily attends to notions of agency, autonomy and authority.

In the section Authoring Participation, authors Stephen Bottoms, Alison Jeffers and James Frieze consider various theatrical and performative strategies through their multifaceted interrogations of 'doing', both as individual and collective modalities of engagement. Bottoms' exploration of a Batesonian understanding of humility cracks open the conversation about what might constitute participation. In this chapter, a hospitable letting go of notions of authorship and authority serves to shore up, perhaps paradoxically, a more robust sense of meaning and political purpose in the community in which he is a visitor, a guest and sometimes an interloper. Perhaps the greatest sense of unease about the promise of authorship lies in debates about immersive theatre, where participatory practices can be experienced at their most obviously coercive. James Frieze tackles this unease by turning his attention to the 'forensic turn' in the interactivity of promenade performance, arguing that following a 'story-trail' of clues as part of an immersive theatrical experience constructs a misplaced perception that knowledge of the world is 'all-deducing'. In the work of dreamthinkspeak, Frieze finds a lacuna in which new forms of authorship might be perceived.

Alison Jeffers' analysis of authority as potential for positive articulation of power strikes at the heart of many of the debates about authorship in this book. The politics of authorship and authority operate in a very tangible way in Jeffers' chapter about community plays in Northern Ireland, where she considers the contribution of 'non-specialist' members of the locality to performance-making. By bringing their local knowledge of Northern Ireland's troubled history to the process, participants redefined orthodox understandings of the past, finding new confidence in their identities and reshaping temporal relationships with their communities. For Jeffers, a reworked concept of authority challenges the 'cause-and-effect narratives' that dominated community arts in the late twentieth century, providing a refreshing opportunity to shape and authorise community stories in performance. By unhooking authorship from creativity here – and elsewhere in the book – authors consider how participants are invited to rethink the political implications of when and why they might choose to act. Taken together, this book documents how the extraordinariness of the theatrical event frames everyday relational encounters between people, places, artefacts and histories, as well as where holding the theatrical moment long enough enables participants to attend to new political imaginings.

Practising politics

At the heart of this book lies an interest in how the political is being redefined in performance and how different forms of participation are reshaping questions of agency as relational practices rather than as individualised acts. Questions of authorship, creative labour and cultural recognition are all situated in the political realm, and this book offers insights into how they are mutually embedded in diverse and performative practices of participation. The book does not advance a unified position or land upon a coherent definition of the term; rather we seek to expose the degree to which participation is a contested practice.

One of the recurring debates in this volume questions what counts as politics, and unsurprisingly, the essays draw currency from different theoretical positions. Invoked in this book is the work of Gilles Deleuze,

Gregory Bateson and Jean-Luc Nancy, brought into the analysis of the political to assess questions of authorship and relationality within and across human agency and nonhuman actants. For other authors, the work of Jacques Rancière, Erving Goffman and Chantal Mouffe offers opportunities to inflect the political with new frames of analysis that address the homogenising 'we' of consensual politics, replacing its drive for sameness with a respect for the open-handed representation of antagonism and recognition of difference and alterity. What is missing here, crucially, is the deterministic view that power and control are always exerted externally, and as a consequence, there is an understanding that everyone is somehow implicated in participating in the biopolitical flows and networks of political power. The political philosopher William Connolly captures this impulse in ways that resonate with the political debates articulated in this book:

> [T]o alter the networks in which you participate is eventually to alter the relational mode of desire coursing through you. … [W]hen the next round of action by you or your assemblage expresses that altered quality either or both may be poised to take a more adventurous political stance or accept a new level of ethical responsibility than before. You may be ready to listen to a new mode of inspiration to which you were previously tone-deaf. This is how, on the positive side, spirals of involvement between desire, action, ethics and politics work. (2010: 116)

What is at stake here is an awareness that such 'spirals of involvement' articulate with *the* political, but they do not carry *specific* political meanings or imperatives. It makes the labour of participation explicitly political, but also and always paradoxical and ambiguous. It is this very ambiguity that makes it all the more important to exercise vigilance, as Mouffe warns, over what, and who, is considered legitimate or welcome participants and who is left outside or excluded.

Performance and Participation: Audiences, Practices, Politics marks a paradigm shift in that there is a palpable move away from understanding participation as an invitation and a response and towards a recognition of participation as an ecology of mutual doings and beings. This not only shifts attention away from a cause-and-effect structure but also deliberately and radically redistributes the conditions of social and cultural engagement. By sweeping a diverse set of debates regarding participation and performance into a shared arena, this book encourages a more politically charged and nuanced debate about what we – as academics, theatre-makers and audience members – actually all mean when we talk of participation.

Indeed, a central intervention that the book makes is to render the diversity of conceptualisations associated with participation legible, and open for critical scrutiny. The book has, therefore, attempted to linger over the question of what is at stake when participation is used as a conceptual tool. Alongside its decentring of the individual as the locus of action and agency, the book illuminates the ways in which participation is an interpretive encounter rather than a self-evident action. Noting the significant resurgence of critical and cultural interest in notions and practices of participation, the book forms a reflective response to why the contemporary moment appears somehow to *need* participation. The chapters offer, of course, not the conclusion but rather the beginning of an entangled conversation about the politics of getting stuck in.

Endnote

1. For a more detailed analysis of this concept, see Helen Nicholson, 'A Good Day Out: Applied Theatre, Relationality and Participation' in Hughes, Jenny and Nicholson, Helen, *Critical Perspectives on Applied Theatre* (Cambridge: Cambridge University Press, 2016), pp. 248–268.

SECTION I

RECOGNISING PARTICIPATION

2 The Cultivation of Entangled Listening

An Ensemble of More-Than-Human Participants

Deirdre Heddon

In this chapter, I return to the work – and the words – of performance maker Adrian Howells (1962–2014). The intention of this return is twofold: to listen again in order to listen better and differently; and, through listening out for listening, to move analyses of Howells' work on from a sedimented focus on its apparent one-to-one form towards a recognition of its more-than-one structure. This move, I suggest, is implicit in Howells' later work, particularly *The Garden of Adrian* (2009), where the artist cultivates a careful attending – a stretching towards – which is also an invitation to attend. Turning my attention – my listening – to Howells' frequently stated commitment to listening, a listening beyond oral-aural communication, I identify what I refer to as an 'entangled listening' practice. I propose entangled listening as resonant listening – a listening which depends on touching; Howells' work also prompts me to conceive of touch as listening – that is, a resonant touching. Such resonance, I argue, is central to the instantiation of being-with-others and, significantly, others beyond the human. This proposed extension from the one-to-one to the more-than-human is crucial in our time of environmental crisis and is a move that displaces the exceptionalism of the human (as) actor. Environmental critic Val Plumwood asserted that one of the most important virtues of communication is listening to the other, which demands an attentiveness that is open and receptive (2002: 194). This is a participatory listening; listening is part of the practice of participation. Newly open and receptive to Howells' work and words, in the face of his untimely death, I create my own deliberate dialogical entanglement here, a dialogue about listening which knots together interdisciplinary threads drawn from diverse fields of environmental politics, philosophy and performance in order to ask, What sort of participation does an entangled listening afford and to whom?

Prompts to listening

The prompt towards me listening again and better – more openly – to the words and work of Adrian Howells emerges from an unexpected environment. In 2013, I participated in a research project funded by the Arts and Humanities Research Council (AHRC) under its *Connected Communities* theme. 'In conversation with …: co-designing with more than human communities' was both a response to and intervention into presumptions implied by the AHRC's iteration of communities within its funding call.[1] The community composition figured by the AHRC appeared wholly human, rendering invisible the vast and varied contributions made by nonhumans to community formations and practices.[2] Also unrecognised were the ways in which more-than-humans are deeply enmeshed in research processes and projects. 'In conversation with …' sought first to widen notions of 'community' and second to make explicit the contributions that nonhumans made to research endeavours. As project initiator Michelle Bastian asked, how might both research and community 'be rethought within a "more-than-human" framework?'[3] This question was approached through structured attempts at conducting research *with* nonhuman co-participants, namely animals (dogs), plants (trees), insects (bees) and elements (water).

The third workshop of the project focused my attention, inadvertently, on listening practices. Staged in the Forest of Dean, the intention of this workshop was to explore how arts-based experiential methods might engender embodied responses to trees, proposing affective attunement as a method of conversation.[4] Attunement opens a space for communication beyond anthropocentric attachments to purely vocal exchanges. Two days in duration, the workshop was held mostly outdoors, amidst – with – the forests and trees of the Wye Valley. Our team of academic researchers was joined by Nikki Moore from InsideOUT, a community organisation working in partnership with the Forestry Commission to increase access by underrepresented groups to the landscape of the Wye Valley, and Sarah Sawyer, community links officer with the Wye Valley Area of Natural Beauty. Workshop activities ranged from carving wooden spoons to creating bio-diversity balls of clay. Notably, one activity – simply sitting alone in the forest – initially planned to last for just five minutes, was extended to more than 15 following the very vocal requests made by the human participants. Lying on the forest floor, in this extended time, I felt myself stretch into listening.[5]

At the end of the two days, sitting on a circle of logs in the forest, we reflected on 'conversations with trees'. Ironically, though, conversations failed to take place because very little listening was in evidence. Speakers were interrupted, talked over, ignored or denied as perspectives were presented with the force of categorical certainty. How, I worried, could we converse with trees when we still didn't know how to converse with – attend to – each human other? How could we cultivate better listening habits? As the only performance theorist and practitioner in our interdisciplinary group of researchers, I found myself – then and now – stretching, backwards and forwards, to the work of Adrian Howells, a master crafter of occasions for listening and a model for attentive listening practice. In his performance, *Salon Adrienne* (2005), for example, I was ensconced in an actual salon, though its doors were shut to all but me. Adrian washed my hair gently, talked about his past, massaged my head and then, as we both looked at my reflection in the mirror, asked me what I saw there and how I felt about getting older. In another performance, *Held* (2006), Adrian sat opposite me at a kitchen table, holding both my hands in his as he asked me about handholding: whose hands do I hold? Why? How does that feel? As I talked, he squeezed my hands gently. As a participant in Adrian's work, I always felt that he was listening, really listening. I felt heard.

Feeling heard but not listening

From 2006 to 2009, I was academic mentor to Howells, supporting him in his role as an AHRC creative fellow at the University of Glasgow. Howells' fellowship allowed him to undertake extensive practice-based research into the use of risk in intimate and site-responsive performance practice. Over the course of the three years of funding, he developed a number of research-informed works. To date, his performance catalogue has been categorised and understood singularly as 'one-to-one' – that is, one performer performing for/with one spectator-participant. Indeed, Howells has rightly been claimed as a leading artist in the one-to-one genre (Zerihan 2009; Machon 2013: 17). However, describing Howells' work as simply or only one-to-one risks neglecting a host of other relations mobilised in the work. Listening again and listening differently allows these other relations and interrelations to become audible. Through listening, defined as both an ontological position and a material practice, it becomes clear that I am not the only participant in the work; more precisely, 'I' am not the only participant in the work, because 'I' am never 'only'.

In an article that Howells and I co-authored in 2011, he introduces himself and his practice:

> [M]y work has been motivated by the sense that in this age of mass-mediation and technological advancement there is a necessity to prioritize opportunities for audiences to have intimate face-to-face, one-to-one encounters in real-time with real people. My work prioritizes interpersonal connectedness and what I refer to as an authentic experience between two people (though the question of 'authenticity' in the field of performance is always vexed). (Heddon and Howells 2011: 2)

Gven this introduction to his work, it is not surprising that Howells is located as a one-to-one practitioner. He draws specific attention here to the experiences rendered between two people. However, rereading this paragraph in 2015, I am troubled by its parentheses. In it, I hear not Howells but myself, or at least an echo of my critical certainty and heavy-handed intervention. In fact, it is entirely possible that this parenthetical material, though attributed to Howells, was inserted into the text by me during the process of co-authorship (an entangled business if ever there was one). I perform a similar intervention in another article when I reflect that 'claims of authenticity … are tricky to define in an environment of roles and masks, of script and improvisation, of being a performer and playing at being one' (Heddon et al. 2012: 121). Such critical interventions are not unique to me. Dominic Johnson, in the introduction to his interview with Howells, seems to distance himself critically from Howells' terms, too:

> For Howells, the form provides a unique possibility for what he terms authenticity, communion, connectivity, confession or revelation. Such terms are clearly loaded. They suggest questions and provocations concerning authenticity, honesty, agency and compliance, truth and fakery, and distinctions between art and life. (2014: 174)

As I listen again now, I can hear that, in spite of repeated mediations performed by his interlocutors, Howells continues to insist on the truth-and reality-potential of his performances:

> My time with the audience-participant was committed to talking openly and honestly about the suffering of my depression. (Heddon and Howells 2011: 3)

I became really imbued with an awareness of the opportunity for qualitative connections that this dynamic of the one-to-one could engender.
I really felt I could get to know somebody, and they could get to know
me. (Johnson 2014: 178)

Listening now to my conversations with Howells, I might describe my
earlier listening as cataphatic; that is, listening through preconceived
categories. As Andrew Dobson summarises, such listening 'verges on not
listening at all' and, ironically given Howells' commitment to dialogical practice, 'amounts to what we might call monological listening'
(2014: 67). Rather than listening to Howells, I was listening to myself and
what I already knew and thought I knew better than him.

One alternative to cataphatic listening would be an 'apophatic' practice –
'a *temporary* suspension of the listener's categories in order to make room
for the speaker's voice and to help it arrive in its "authentic" form' (Dobson
2014: 68, original emphasis). The form of this authenticity is the dialogic
development of meaning, a meaning that originates and concludes in
neither the speaker nor listener, but arises between. This listening practice
resembles Gilles Deleuze's reflection on co-authorship with Félix Guattari
and the sociability of ideas. As I have noted elsewhere, (Heddon 2012)
Deleuze recognises the potential for conversation to be 'an outline of a
becoming', a becoming that takes place between you and me, 'a sort of
active and creative line of flight' which proliferates (Deleuze and Parnet
2007: 2, 10). Listening is part of conversation, crucial to the process
of proliferation. However, in apophatic listening the dialogue remains
directed towards meaning, even if this meaning is always in the process of
'becoming'. Alongside this listening for and towards meaning, I want to
knot another vector of listening into my discussion – listening as resonance.

Johnson was in the process of reviewing the proofs for his interview
when he learnt that Howells had committed suicide. In the aftermath of
that event, he adds a new section to the interview, entitled 'In Memorium',
where he admits,

If I were at liberty to do so, I would throw out the introduction …
and rewrite it from scratch. The terms upon which I have approached
Adrian's work now seem frivolous to me. I've missed the points that
matter now. (Johnson 2014: 177)

'I've missed the points that matter now.' I don't know precisely what
points Johnson feels he missed, but his sentiment resonates. I feel it. My
'not knowing precisely' the points missed but sensing the resonance of the

sentiment is important. Listening depends literally on resonance – a to and fro across time and space, delay and reorientation a part of its materiality. In what follows, I want to listen again and better to Howells, not by foreclosing resonance through presuming or fixing meaning but by being open to meaning and rendering it mobile, as well as listening beyond or aside from meaning – both practices arising from resonance. Following Jean-Luc Nancy, resonance might also be considered from an ontological perspective. Figured as a resonant subject, the 'self' resonates to and fro too, and it is thus similarly mobile and plural, a being-with-others which is an always contingent 'becoming' rather than an essential given (Nancy 2007). Such resonance provides the gateway to the more-than-human: the human as always already more-than-human and the resonant subject as more-than-human too.

That I author this piece ostensibly on my own is one reality; when it is approached through the dialogical and resonant, another perspective is possible. My return to Adrian is not a response to a voice speaking from beyond the grave, asking to be 'understood'; rather, it is a reply to the voice that continues to circulate through its reverberations. The deliberate repetition of Adrian's words in what follows intends to both surface and perform the reverberations as they are mobilised here and now (knowing that they will reverberate differently in the relations constituted by other times and places). In their bothering, these words have called me to attention. That is their affective power. Recognising the constitutive power of listening, I like to think that I 'listen' Adrian to speech here, even if for the first time (Nancy 2007). And perhaps Howells' attentive, resonant listening was/is in its turn constitutive, bringing the more-than-human to speech too. This is the radical, ecological proposition I make for Howells' work.

Listening again

Adrian Howells created intimate and solo-performance works from 2001 onwards, many of them initially utilising his persona, 'Adrienne': 'less a drag queen than another version of me; a man wearing thick make-up and rather unglamorous, woman-next-door clothes' (Heddon and Howells 2011: 2). Performances included *Adrienne's Dirty Laundry Experience* (2003), *The Great Depression* (2004), *Adrienne's Room Service* (2005), *Salon Adrienne* (2005), *An Audience with Adrienne: A Lifetime of Servicing Others* (2006), *Her Summertime Special* (2007), *A Cosy-Rosy Christmas Comedown* (2007) and *A Night at the Opera* (2009). Whilst not all of these performances were performed for an audience of one, all of the 'Adrienne' shows could be deemed as autobiographical/confessional and more-or-less dialogic in form. Reflecting on *The Great Depression*, Howells writes the following:

> My time with the audience-participant was committed to talking openly and honestly about the suffering of my depression and confiding very private details of attempted suicide, self-loathing, pain, and despair. I hoped that this gesture of openness would encourage my guests to share their moments of darkness too, lightening them in the process. (Heddon and Howells 2011: 3)

In our co-authored article, Howells acknowledges explicitly the mutuality of the spoken and heard to this practice of dialogical exchange – 'the exchange was constantly dialogic, predominantly both an oricular (spoken) and auricular (heard) experience' (2011: 2).

From 2006 to 2009, supported by his AHRC award, Howells developed four new pieces: *Held* (2007), *The 14 Stations of the Life and History of Adrian Howells* (2007), *Foot Washing for the Sole* (2008) and *The Garden of Adrian* (2009).[6] Howells' commitment to intimate performance structures and the experiences that they potentially offer endured throughout all of these performances, but two additional aspects are worth remarking upon: the 'mask' of 'Adrienne' is dropped, and silence is used as a material. Silence is first introduced in the final section of *Held*, where Adrian invited participants to be 'spooned' on a bed with him for 30 minutes, with the option of not talking for the duration. For Howells, 'This final action unexpectedly revealed to me the potential for bodily – or non-verbal – exchange ... and *a different way of listening*' (Heddon and Howells 2011: 5, emphasis added). Howells closes our co-authored article with the following reflection:

> Rather than contributing to the deafening 'white' noise [of mass-mediatised confessional forms], an alternative performance strategy might be to carve out other spaces, *other modes of connection than the spoken exchange, other forms of the dialogic*. (2011: 12, emphasis added)

The majority of critical writing about Howells' work, and 'one-to-one' performance more generally, has focused largely on ethical concerns surfaced by intimate practices, addressing questions of risk, vulnerability, agency and responsibility, as well as identifying ways in which risks are mitigated through the performer's care and skill.[7] Mitigation is also mobilised through a somewhat tautological deployment of an ethical analytics focused on the concept of exchange; the one-to-one is ethical because it is one-to-one. According to Erini Kartsaki et al., 'one-to-one performance work … creates the conditions for a particular ethical relationship' (Kartsaki et al. 2014: 104). Emanuel Levinas' relational ontology of radical heterogeneity – the Self and the Other or being-other – is a frequent reference point in these discussions. For example, the one-to-one (the one and the other, a duality) supposedly activates an ethical response, a mutual response-ability:

> [S]pectators and performers have to respond to the question: How shall I act? The question of acting *for* the other has been explored by Levinas: … 'The other becomes my neighbour precisely through the way the face summons me, calls for me, begs for me, and in so doing recalls my responsibility, and calls me into question'. (Kartsaki et al 2014: 104)

In the face of Howells' explicit reference to the potential of the 'face-to-face' encounter in his work, invoking Levinas is both reasonable and useful. Levinas' ethics of alterity offers one way to approach and engage critically the participatory structure of the one-to-one form. However, the specific, urgent call to listening issued in Howells' later performances, and in his reflections on those, goes unheard. Interestingly, Levinas does have a relationship with listening, but it is a negative one. According to Lisbeth Lipari, Levinas' focus on the face places us in a world 'that privileges vision over audition' (Lipari 2012: 230). Yet, as Lipari goes on to note, Levinas' face commands the Other through speech. The face speaks: 'The first word of the face is the "Thou shalt not kill." It is an order' (Levinas 1985: 87–89). Whilst Levinas might recognise the power of speech – such power here residing in the voice of God – in Lipari's analysis he falls short of 'pursuing listening as a door-way to the ethical' (2012: 233). This failure, according to Lipari, arises in part because the voice threatens alterity, mingling and crossing the 'boundaries between inner and outer' (2012: 233). Where the face is exterior and preserves distance through a duality of subject/object and seeing/seen, listening 'connects and bridges', thus dissolving distance and risking the replacement of alterity with union (Lipari 2012: 233). It is precisely this bridge of listening that offers a way to connect with Howells' comments about a listening that includes but extends beyond the oral/aural.

In notes for a talk given at Central Saint Martins in 2013, called – wittily but significantly – 'Back to Nurture', Howells produces a list of 'nurturing' features. Amongst them are taking time – slowing everything down; listening – *really* listening with our ears and our bodies; paying attention; being and beingness; presence; and touch-without-touch.[8] It is entirely possible that Howells intended listening here as both metaphor for and practice of being-together, conjuring through the discourse of listening and 'attending to' an intimacy not reliant on literal closeness. I want to be open to Howells' language of being-together through listening but to open it further by bringing Jean-Luc Nancy into the exchange, proposing a different but nevertheless resonant sounding of being-together through listening.

Resonant subjects: Listening with Jean-Luc Nancy

Where Levinas' ethics depends on a relationship of one *and* the other, a radical alterity, Jean-Luc Nancy proposes instead a social ontology – being-singular-plural. We are, each of us, singular plural beings. Being-singular-plural renders one *with* the other, the hyphens a mark of both union and division (Nancy 2000: 37). Nancy arrives at this construction and understanding of 'being' by recognising that the 'I' can never be immediately present to itself, because it is constituted through being-exposed to others – 'correlation, combination, contact, distance, relation' (2000: 97); there must always be another – one, thing – to whom one is disposed and exposed, in order to say/be 'I'. To be is thus always to be with (Devisch 2013: 99). Nancy's notion of singular-plural thus challenges concepts of the separate 'individual'. As Christopher Watkins explains,

> [t]he relation that is primary for Nancy is not a relation between substances existing independently of and prior to those relations (the 'I' does not precede the 'we'), but being as relation, a being-in-common where being 'is' the *in*. (2007: 51)

Even this 'in relation' requires subtle nuance – it is not that there are two things or selves that are then related; rather, the self *is* in relation, the self is a 'self-as-relation' (Watkin 2007: 54). As Nancy writes in *Being Singular Plural*, '[b]eing with, being together and even being "united" are precisely not a matter of being "one"' (Nancy 2000: 154). The co-existence of being-singular-plural signals the openness of the subject. One's being is always an other (Devisch 2013: 91), that other including other-than-human. For Nancy, '[t]he ontology of being-with is an ontology of bodies, of every body, whether they be inanimate, animate, sentient, speaking, thinking, having weight, and so on' (Nancy 2000: 84).

'Being-*with*-one-another' implies a space between and therefore a linking across, that is, a being together separately (Nancy 2000: 53). Such a conceptualisation of being proposes a haptic ethics, one that resists both unification and appropriation. If we are always *in* touch, then we are always separate too because 'the law of touching is separation' (2000: 33, 30); in order *to* touch, there must be distance (Watkin 2007: 59). The singularity of plurality, meanwhile, is to be found in its relational specificity (Nancy 2000: 35). If I expose myself to others in order to distinguish myself from them, then each time I am different (singular), though still with others (plural). Each 'we' is contingent (Devisch 2013: 100). The 'we' conceived by Nancy comprises everything in the world: 'all existents, those past and those to come, the living and the dead, the animate, rocks, plants, nails, gods – and "humans"' (Nancy 2000: 21).

Might Nancy's 'we', a co-constitutive sharing without fusion (Devisch 2013: 106), usefully sit beside the multiplicity that marks an encounter where species are interdependent and, in Donna Haraway's terms, 'become with' (Haraway 2008: 19)?[9] These are knots I seek to tie here, entangling different philosophical threads in a spirit of openness to the play of resonances. Can Nancy's 'we', both a multiplicity and a mutuality, be presented as a version of entanglement, with ethical consequences? Christopher Watkin suggests as much:

> The ethics of mutuality is a potent solidarity, where the suffering of any one, of each one, is a suffering which I share and, concretely, for which I have responsibility. Why? Because I am not *in* relation; I *am* singular plural relation. ... Participants have nothing in common; they *are* in-common. (2007: 61, original emphasis)

It is the touch that structures Nancy's 'being-with' which presumably attracts him to listening (the same touch of listening which repels Levinas). To turn this around, listening is a model (of) 'being-with'. In *Listening*, Nancy asks, 'What does it mean for a being to be immersed entirely in listening, formed by or in listening, listening with all his being? ... What does *to be* listening, *to be* all ears, as one would say "to be in the world," mean?' (Nancy 2007: 4–5). Here, Nancy presents the subject as a resonant chamber 'that is listening or vibrates with listening to – or with the echo of – the beyond-meaning' (2007: 31). *Écouter* ('to listen'), as Nancy reminds us, is derived from *auscultare* – 'to lend an ear' – which means to listen attentively.[10] For Nancy, to listen – to stretch the ear – is listening with 'an intensification and a concern, a curiosity or an anxiety' (2007: 5). *Entendre* ('to hear') contains a doubled sense (as indeed it does in English) – to understand ('*comprendre*'). In working towards a mode of thinking that is listening, rather than interpretation, Nancy distinguishes listening from hearing: 'If "to hear" is to understand the sense ... to listen is to be straining towards a possible meaning, and consequently one that is not immediately accessible' (2007: 6). There is no meaning transcendent to its resonance – there is, rather, a coming-and-going (2007: 7). Sound, like/as meaning, is constituted through reference and referral, is never self-present. Invoking resonance, a touching that unites and divides, sets up a referral too to the space or interval of the being-with of the singular-plural.

> One can say, then, at least, that meaning and sound share the space of a referral, in which at the same time they refer to each other, and that, in a very general way, this space can be defined as the space of a *self*, a subject. (2007: 8)

The subject of listening is conceived as nothing to which one can be present, 'but precisely the resonance of a return [*renvoi*]' (2007: 12). In listening, one is simultaneously outside and inside – touching/ being touched through sonority, referring presence to 'something other than itself' (2007: 25). The sonorous is never self-present, but is always rebounding (2007: 15). The reverberation of resonance which opens and closes a listening self (dis)orientates its being in the world (Janus 2011: 191). The listening subject – 'constituted as (a) listening' (Gitten 2010: 116) – feels itself listening, but this 'self' that is felt always escapes since it 'resounds elsewhere as it does in itself, in a world and in the other' (Nancy 2007: 9). Distinct from 'visible or tactile presence', sonorous presence is mobile, its vibration an effect of 'the come-and-go between the source and the ear, through the open space' (2007: 16); 'it is precisely from one to the other that it 'sounds''' (2007: 16). This listening as referral as sounding resonates with Howells' insistence on the possibility of different '*modes of connection than the spoken exchange, other forms of the dialogic*' (2007: 12, emphasis added).

In many of Howells' performances, touch is a key component: hands are held; feet, hands, and arms are washed; mouths are fed; bodies are spooned. Instructed by Haraway, I recognise this touch of Howells, which unavoidably touches me, as one which has ramifications in its shaping of accountability, caring for and being affected by (Haraway 2008: 36). Such touch informs world making. For Howells, however, touch is also offered explicitly as a way of listening. As noted above, *Held* was the first performance in which Howells introduced silence as a feature of his work. Let me listen again to what he wrote about that experience:

> This final action unexpectedly revealed to me the potential for bodily – or non-verbal – exchange … and *a different way of listening*. (Heddon and Howells 2013: 5, emphasis added)

To this point, Howells' practice had been filled with talking, with verbal exchanges. *Held* marks a move away from the spoken, but not from exchange. Whereas silence was introduced in the last section of *Held*, *The Garden of Adrian* is predominantly silent – or, at least, non-verbal – signalling a further move from the oral and towards the aural. Here are Howells' closing words from our article again:

> Rather than contributing to the deafening 'white' noise [of mass-mediatised confessional forms], an alternative performance strategy might be to *carve out other spaces, other modes of connection than the spoken exchange, other forms of the dialogic.* In a noisy culture like mine, silence rings out loudly, *offering another place to "be" or to become.* (Heddon and Howells 2013: 12, emphasis added)

One mapping of the trajectory of Howells' work would trace the shift from an audience predominantly listening to his verbal speech, to participants' and Howells' listening to each other, to Howells' predominantly listening to the participant's verbal speech, to both listening to each other but non-verbally. But what if Howells was offering a space to *become listening*, to be a listening being, through a resonant touching? Here we hear Nancy again: 'What does *to be* listening, *to be* all ears, as one would say "to be in the world," mean?' (2007: 4–5). For Nancy, the subject who is listening is a resonant subject, *without* 'an intentional line of sight', one in which spacing allows for echoing which leaves the subject of listening – the subject listened to – always still to come. Listening, then, is not intentionality towards meaning, nor is listening deployed from or to a stable subject, but rather listening is a 'straining' towards sense or an exposure to sense, an attending (2007: 27). But sense refers also to the sensory – 'touch, taste, smell and sight' – and this sense resonates too, as well as having resonance in Howells' work as we are invited to touch, taste, smell, see and hear – to sense resonantly and sense *as* resonance (Janus 2011: 183). Nancy's listening subject is a resonant subject, thus extending beyond the human subject, an observation made also by Adrienne Janus:

> As a place of resonance, and a resonance that penetrates, fuses, goes toward and comes back from other places of resonance, the *listening subject may be human, animal, or thing.* (2011: 194)

In *The Garden of Adrian*

Having set up the terms of Nancy's resonant subject, let me turn my being-ear more fully towards *The Garden of Adrian*. *The Garden* was the final performance work arising from Howells' AHRC fellowship.

Performed in June 2009 as part of a symposium also organised by Howells (*I Confess*), the piece was sited in the theatre space of Gilmorehill Halls, home to theatre studies at the University of Glasgow. The theatre is a renovated church, with some original features intact, including a stained glass window bearing the inscription 'he that soweth/to the Spirit shall of/the Spirit reap life/everlasting'. Howells chose to leave the curtains of this window open so that the stained glass was visible. The representation of sowing seeds and gathering abundant harvests struck me as ironic in the contemporary context of reaping environmental catastrophe. The mise en scène of the show, designed by colleague Minty Donald, was minimalist, with seven defined zones or stations connected to each other through a wooden boardwalk. A small conifer marked each zone. The first station was a wooden garden shed, reached by taking a lift. When the doors of the lift opened, I was deposited directly into the shed, inside which was a garden chair, a pair of flip flops, a flask of tea and a box of shortbread. A radio playing inside the shed tuned into different frequencies automatically, broadcasting choral singing, bird song, static, piano and conversation. Sitting on the garden chair, I removed my shoes and socks and put on the flip flops. I sat. I waited. I listened. After some time – what felt like a long time – I heard Adrian call my name, 'Dee', and when I opened the shed door, he welcomed me to the garden of Adrian, inviting me to descend the stairs and join him. I transitioned from a godlike view to a grassroots perspective. After hugging me warmly, Adrian informed me that in this piece he was interested in exploring a silent relationship.

For the next 45 minutes or so, Adrian held my hand and guided me to each station in turn. In the second station, sitting side by side on the board walk, bare feet planted into the soil, we looked at a white freesia, also planted in the soil and encased under a bell jar. After some time, Adrian lifted the jar, and we continued to sit silently and look at the freesia – though not, in fact, in silence. A soundtrack, instrumental, with bird song overlaid, filled the space (this accompanied the entire performance). In the next zone, my bare feet settled onto rough tree bark, we sat on a wishbone-shaped bench. I closed my eyes while Adrian fed me strawberries from his fingers. In the fourth zone, the sensation underfoot was of stones of different sizes, shapes and textures. I sat on a large, rough-hewn rock, with Adrian's head laid in my lap. We sat like this for five minutes. In the fifth station, my feet this time on smooth, small pebbles, Adrian washed my hands and forearms with clean, warm water from a stone bird bath. Each hand, arm, finger was dried carefully with a white towel. In the sixth zone, the underfoot texture was grass, each blade seemingly detectable by the soles of my feet. Adrian spread a tartan blanket over the grass and we lay together, spooned into each other, Adrian's arm around me and our breath rising and falling in synchronicity. After about five minutes, Adrian led me to a line of conifers, behind which was a long table, set with seedling pots. He hugged me again and told me to follow the instructions laid out on the table: I was instructed to choose a seedling and transplant it into a separate container, write my name on a plastic label, put the label in the empty seed pot and take the transplanted seedling home with me. I did as instructed and planted the seedling in the window box of my kitchen.

Jennifer Doyle, describing Howells' practice as 'open, kind, and intimate', claims it as a form of 'deep listening' (Doyle 2014: 27). Her use of this term may be borrowed from the well-known artist of 'Deep Listening', Pauline Oliveros. Like Nancy, Oliveros distinguishes between hearing and listening: 'To hear is the physical means that enables perception. To listen is to give attention to what is perceived both acoustically and psychologically. ... *Deep* has to do with complexity and boundaries, or edges beyond ordinary or habitual understanding' (Oliveros 2005: xxii–xxiii). To be a deep listener is surely to be a resonant subject sensing beyond meaning. I want to extend Doyle's insight, by suggesting that Howells' deep listening also cultivated the resonant subject and the capacity for an entangled listening.[11]

According to Lipari, listening, as a co-constitutive act of communication, animates what is listened to: listening persons into speech (2012: 239–240). Whilst Lipari's oppressed subjects here are human, her transitive use of the verb 'to listen' can be applied to the more-than-human – they too are listened into speech. This offers one approach to the challenge of political history's tying of politics to speech, epitomised in Aristotle's *The Politics*:

> the real difference between man and other animals is that humans alone have perception of good and evil, right and wrong, just and unjust. And it is the sharing of a common view in these matters that makes a Household or a city. (Cited in Dobson 2010: 753)

As Dobson notes, if speech is central to a conception of the *polis*/politics, then the consequence is that politics itself is made discriminatory at the outset, since only human beings have the capacity for speech (2010: 753). One effect of politics' definition as the 'deployment of "reasoned speech"' is the subsequent focus on 'the struggle for the right and capacity to speak' (2010: 753).[12] Another consequence, though, is that this focus on speaking neglects almost entirely the necessity of listening (2010: 760). What is the point of developing speech if no one hears it? Responding to this deficit, Dobson promotes '*dialogic* democracy', where speaking and listening are regarded as of equal importance (2014: 34). Dobson's overall project seeks to improve listening through changing the conditions in which listening takes place (or is given place) and by cultivating listening as a virtue or 'a mode of being' (2014: 78–79). I am sympathetic to Dobson's cause. However, Lipari offers a way to consider listening itself as constituting speech. As Don Ihde writes, 'listening is listening to', whether that 'to' is 'the voices of language, of instruments, of the earth' (Ihde 2007: 23). From this perspective, nonhuman vitality is discerned through the cultivation of listening because listening must *presume* resonance and therefore, returning to Nancy, a resonating subject. This surely resonates with Jane Bennett's critical positioning of matter as vibrant and agential, with 'trajectories, propensities, or tendencies of their own' (Bennett 2010: viii). The political stakes in Bennett's repositioning of matter are high. In her view, our habit of seeing matter as simply 'dead' or inanimate contributes to 'human hubris and our earth-destroying fantasies of conquest and consumption' (2010: ix). 'Vibrant' presupposes vibration and oscillation. Bennett introduces the vibrant matter of her study by depicting an urban scene which at first hearing seems a predominantly visual description. However, listening again, I notice that she advises that everyday things exhibited their thing-power by *issuing a call* (2010: 4). Bennett admits to being '*struck*', which led to a realisation 'that the capacity of these bodies was not restricted to a passive "intractability" but also included the ability to make things happen, to produce effects' (2010: 5, original emphasis). I hear Bennett's '*struck*' as the sonorous '*attack*' of sound that Nancy describes, which, whilst penetrating through the ears, 'propagates throughout the entire body some of its effects' (Nancy 2007: 14). Bennett, to be so struck, must be *listening*, or deploying an 'aural eye – an eye that listens', hearing through the eyes (Lipari 2012: 234). If listening is always to listen to resonance, it is to encounter the entanglement of resonance's collision and impact. As Lipari notes, sound is an embodied affect – one that ripples 'through skin, muscle, bone, and synapse' (2012: 234). We hear through bodies as well as ears, with sound's 'engulfing multi-dimensionality' blurring distinctions between inside/outside, public/private, subject/object (Bull and Back 2003: 5). I am *struck* by Stephen Connor's phrase, which says that 'there is no sound that is not collateral': the condition of sound, he writes, is an *interface* (Connor 2003: 72).

Listening environments

Howells' approach to developing new performances was to engage in an extensive period of research, with research materials, ideas and discussions noted in process-journals. Part of the research for *The Garden of Adrian* entailed visiting a number of garden sites around the UK, including the Lost Gardens of Heligan, the Eden Project, Kew Gardens and Ian Hamilton Finlay's Little Sparta. In his journal, Howells refers also to the publication, *Derek Jarman's Garden*, noting the

> IDEA of a *garden* with non-living items – i.e. the flints, shingle, drift wood, corks, etc – & stones and pebbles.
>
> Jarman's encouragement to allow wildness/randomness etc in a garden
>
> How he has relationships with butterflies, lizards, moths etc and describes these.
>
> How he is in a total RELATIONSHIP with his garden – he *understands* it.[13]

Other notes from Howells' journal include mention of the sensorial experience of visiting gardens – touching earth and grass by hand or foot and the effect of the background sound of a waterfall on focus and attention. Whilst noting that neither Eden nor Heligan was particularly inspiring, Howells admits that as environments they prompted specific conversations, thereby recognising nonhuman subjects as agential. The journal reveals, then, a developing interest in and exploration of the status of 'nature' and the relations between humans and the natural world, as well as recognition that gardens are wholly aesthetic sites. (*The Garden*, with its precisely laid out zones and walkways, never hides its status as a deeply artful construction.) This shift into a concern with ecology has to this point not been addressed in any of the critical writing around Howells work.

Informing Howells' journal reflections is John Newling's essay, 'From My Garden: Being Human in the Anthropocene Era' (2008), in which Newling attempts a phenomenological hermeneutical understanding of his experience of gardening. Howells' recording of some of Newling's propositions signals again his opening out from the one-to-one-human to the more-than-human.

> Is Station 7 [the final station on the journey] like Heidegger's 'clearing'?
> 'The clearing is the place where entities that are independent of human

purpose and human existence, seem to reveal themselves and fuse with human nature (Newling)'.[14]

'The clearing is any space that encourages the speculation and questioning that can connect us to the other entities that define our human-ness (Newling).'

'My desire then is to understand and connect to the natural laws and also to speculate on the consciousness of the other species. I wish to cross the border from being simply contiguous to these other entities to feeling a greater sense of connectedness (Newling).'

Returning and listening yet again to Howells' reflection on his later work, the aim for *The Garden* seems to have been to create just such a clearing:

Rather than contributing to the deafening 'white' noise [of mass-mediatised confessional forms], an alternative performance strategy might be *to carve out other spaces*, other *modes of connection* than the spoken exchange, other forms of the dialogic. In a noisy culture like mine, silence rings out loudly, *offering another place to "be" or to become*. (Heddon and Howells 2011: 12, emphasis added)

Whilst the work is not literally silent, it seems that Howells intended to create a listening environment, one which offered (cleared) space to attend. Howells' instructions for bringing us 'back to nurture' recognise that there is little space or time available in most of our lives to cultivate attention; the pun in his workshop title, 'Back to Nurture', suggests quite explicitly that without the preparation of attending, no 'return' to 'nature' is possible. Howells' cultivation of listening seems, then, to address a need identified by Bennett for 'a cultivated, patient, sensory attentiveness to nonhuman forces operating outside and inside the human body' (Bennett 2010: xiv). Bruno Latour's proposition comes into earshot here too. Drawing on the work of Vinciane Despret, he states that to 'have a body is *to learn to be affected*, meaning "effectuated", moved, put into motion by other entities, humans or non-humans' (Latour 2004: 205). Latour wants to describe a body that is neither essence nor substance but is, rather, *'an interface, ... a dynamic trajectory by which we learn to register and become sensitive to what the world is made of'* (2004: 206). Listening – or the body/being as ear – is the site of such an interface. In explaining what 'learning to be affected' means, Latour uses the example of 'noses' being trained for the perfume industry. Through training with an odour kit, one becomes a nose, or rather, one acquires a nose through practice. As Latour puts it, 'body parts are progressively acquired at the same time as "world counter-parts" are being registered in new ways' (2004: 207). The acquiring of a nose allows one to inhabit an odoriferous world. Prompted by Latour, I imagine that Howells' work assists in the acquiring of and becoming an 'ear'. Sitting with Adrian's head on my lap, my body a listening – resonating – interface, I hear my breath, his breath, the recorded composition, the electricity of the stage lights, the traffic noises outside, including emergency sirens, my saliva being swal-lowed…Becoming an ear affords sensitivity to the world's noises. Such listening is beyond significatory or indexical sounds.

Howells' cultivation of listening is bound up with his creation of a clearing. Gemma Corradi Fiumara suggests 'listening silence' as an attempt to 'give space to the inexpressible' (2004: 99). For Fiumara silence is a 'state of listening' (Fiumara 1990: 101), a dialogical and 'relational space' which 'can be used to restore the expressive potential of *objects and persons*' (1990: 95, 107, emphasis added).[15] Silence is the 'empty space' or 'distance' *that allows objects to speak* (1990: 102). Like Lipari, Fiumara believes that something can 'speak' if it is listened to (1990: 72), with periods of silence serving to dissolve the theories, interpretations and explanations which form around the subject and blunt its potential eloquence (1990: 107):

> [W]e leap into the saddle of an explicatory discourse in order to seize the object and say to it: 'Shut up, I've caught you, now it's my turn to talk'. … [A]t the very moment in which we 'arm' ourselves with a cognitive model we are, paradoxically, justified in losing interest in the object. We no longer consider it as enigmatic since it is our turn to speak to it – the object no longer has much to say to us. (1990: 106)

We are back with the trees in the Forest of Dean. Fiumura's expectations of a 'listening experience' are uncannily in tune with Howells' aims: 'A listen-ing experience could actually come across like a storm and overwhelm us – silently – distancing us from the constant din of the discourses that saturate our culture' (1990: 122). This other-than-the-discursive resonates with Jean-Luc Nancy's meditation on listening too. Nancy draws our atten-tion to 'silence', offering it as 'an arrangement of resonance', a resonance which listens and resounds (although for Nancy there is no separate object to consider) (2007: 21).

Entangled listening

Fiumara evocatively asks, is listening the 'vital, eco-logical rationality of times to come?' (Fiumara 1990: 9). If it is, then both her and Dobson's acknowledgement that the act or practice of listening in Western culture is undervalued is worrying.[16] Both are clear about the potential of a listening attitude. In Fiumara's terms, 'A person who simply listens is ... connected once again to a network of vivid, moving and complex dynamics' (1990: 61). Such dynamics, I would suggest, are not only moving and complex but also multiple and entangled. Listening in its entangled form is a dialogical listening which stretches a radical openness towards interconnections, 'listening with'. An entangled listening, then, does not countenance compartmentalized contemplation or the emergence of subject/object. Rather, this plurality generates and appreciates multiplicity and, in this multiplicity, *noise*. Adrienne Janus, in her exegesis of Nancy's philosophy of listening, notes the 'relative absence of noise in Nancy's embodied resonance'. The resonating body is paradoxically silent. She wonders whether Nancy reduces noise in order to be able to think, asking, 'is there no way that noise could be productive to thinking?' My own question flips this formulation, extending the plural of Nancy's listening, resonant being: does listening afford a means to sense, think and be noisily, messily – bodily – entangled? And does such entanglement bring the more-than-human into the scene as a participant? As Catherine Laws writes, listening offers a 'messy reality': 'the collision of the sensual impact of sound with the perceptual impulse to order and make sense, the conjunction of personal listening history with the sound encountered in the moment, the muddle of subjectivity and objectivity' (Laws 2010: 2). Following Nancy, as a 'listening being' the noises being listened to include the resonances of all the other senses too – these are similarly messy not only in their resonating, intersubjective multiplicities but also in their entanglement with each other.

It is impossible, in summarising the 'content' of *The Garden*, to communicate its complexity as a listening, resonant experience, one which through this frame of listening renders the more-than-human as co-participant in the event. In the resonance of listening, we go to-and-fro-being-with; 'we' are more-than-human; simply, 'human' is always 'more-than'. Each station, described above, offered itself as an environmental microcosm, a congregation of co-constitutive materials – water, stones and hands; wood, fruit and mouth; soil, plant and glass; grass, fabric and breath; lights, sound and air (mine, Adrian's, the trees'). If

The Garden extended the venture in *Held* into an exploration of 'a different way of listening', what sort of listening was this? My recollection of my experience of *The Garden* is a dynamic network of *resonant sensing*: freesia-colour-scent-shape-material-memory-aesthetic (beauty)-fragility-silence-sadness-soil-softness-colour-skin-particles…Though on the page this looks like a linear accumulation, it was experienced as a densely entangled simultaneity, intermingling and sparking off the resonances of the material, political, corporeal, autobiographical, performative, discursive, aesthetic, human and more-than-human, and, definitely, the theatrical-technological. Reading through feedback left by other human participants, the 'noise' rendered present by *The Garden's* space of attentive listening seems equally tangible:

> [N]ervous, intrigued, relaxed, happy, surprized and open…I have felt all of these things. How much we miss from making too much noise, how much we gain from paying attention (audience participant).

> No need for words. Each experience invoked a different thought or feeling (audience participant).

> I remember the creaking of the wooden slats as we walked over them hand in hand. I remember the warmth of your body as it rested on my lap, your breathing and the smooth hardness of the rock underneath me. I remember looking at individual blades of green grass as if it was a forest (audience participant).

Interestingly, one comment seems counter to my argument:

> You achieved that sense of time standing still, an amalgamation of all the sound being unentangled so each strand can be followed.[17]

However, this reflection serves to reveal the everyday entanglements of which we are typically and insufficiently aware. The attentive listening cultivated by Howells brings such entanglement into earshot and, for this participant at least, afforded the space and time to identify the knots of interconnections.

The Garden seems explicitly not about meaning making but about being – the nurturing of a resonant being. 'My' listening-being is cultivated through the staging of a listening event in a sonorous environment, setting up resonances dependent on resounding separations and connections. Some of these resonances bounce between times, with many participants testifying in their feedback to echoes from the personal past. The piece itself is built on resonance, its timbre being that of Howells' earlier performances – the hand washing echoes the foot washing in *Foot Washing for the Sole*, spooning on the grass echoes spooning on the bed in *Held*, the seven stations of the garden echo the 14 stations of *14 Stations*. My memories of those earlier works are entangled with my experience of *The Garden*. Similarly, my reflection on *The Garden*, here and now, is undoubtedly entangled with the noisy, demanding, dissonant silence of that which is yet to come – Adrian's suicide. This too is a resonant subject.

The multiple, resonant subjects listened to in *The Garden* are agents in and of a complex and dynamic conversation, setting me to think and feel certain things. The look, shape, smell of the freesia calls me. I stretch towards it, open to our resounding; neither of us, in this *encounter*, is fixed, settled or essential but is always relational, an echo-location (Carter 2004: 45). *This* resonating-with – a singular-plural – might be Adrian's proposition in his appeal to authentic conversation. Another sense of *entendre* is 'intend', to listen – *'tendre l'oreille'* – 'literally, to stretch the ear' (Nancy 2007: 5). Though I want to listen again to Adrian, to stretch my ear towards him, my intention is not to propose or settle his intention or his self-presence through a return to the *logos*. That would be a return to a singular identity, a singular agency. What I hear in trying to listen better, to listen dialogically, attentively and with curiosity, is an echo which is always a displacement, inevitably but generatively and creatively hearing and expressing things beyond the intended – his and my own – continuing a dialogue with the resonances that resound between and which acknowledge the participation – the 'speech' – of a multitude of other being-singular-plurals in that betweenness, that 'we'. There is never a 'one' to which 'one' can be 'one'. In these times of environmental crises, 'one-to-one' is never enough.

Adrian takes my hand and leads me to the large rock in the fourth station. I settle myself into its shape – the only possible position to take – my shape forged by the rock's shape (forged by its materiality, which is forged by the operations of deep time in combination with the more recent operations of quarry machines), offering a combined shape for Adrian to shape himself around, our combination setting off other participating resonances for me, multiple beings brought to 'speech', including theories of feminist caring, ecological inter- and intra-actions, discourses of ethics and politics, feelings of loss and tastes of grief, hardness of stone and softness of flesh, scent of grass and freesias, tastes of tea and strawberries, soil, bark, birdsong, and the mobility and plurality of the seemingly set … A temporary ensemble, 'I' am entangled (in) listening.

Endnotes

1. 'The cultivation of entangled listening' is a companion essay to 'Con-versing: listening, speaking, turning', in *More-Than-Human Participatory Research*, eds. Michelle Bastian et al (London: Routledge, forthcoming).). Both essays are prompted by my experiences of attempting to co-produce knowledge with nonhuman subjects, and thus both essays offer a description of the motivating scene (though 'Con-versing' offers a longer account). Both essays also feature in collections dedicated to exploring the practice of participation. For further information about the more-than-human project, see http://www.morethanhumanresearch.com/

2. See http://www.ahrc.ac.uk/Funding-Opportunities/Research-funding/Connected-Communities/Pages/Connected-Communities.aspx [Accessed 15 January 2015].

3. Michelle Bastian, http://www.morethanhumanresearch.com/ [Accessed 7 January 2015].

4. http://www.morethanhumanresearch.com/conversations-with-plants.html [Accessed 8 January 2015].

5. For a short video of this workshop, see https://www.youtube.com/watch?v=SGKh836eVm8#t=61 [Accessed 8 January 2015].

6. Separate from his fellowship, in 2008 Howells also created *Won't Somebody Dance with Me?* (2008).

7. See Helen Iball, 'Towards an Ethics of Intimate Audience', *Performing Ethos: An International Journal of Ethics in Theatre & Performance*, 3:1 (2014), pp. 41–57.

8. Document from Adrian Howells' archive (uncatalogued), Scottish Theatre Archive.

9. Haraway equates subjectification with acquiring a face (p. 25). My focus here on listening prompts me to err towards aligning becoming a subject with having a voice – listening subjects into being. In both perspectives, response and respect are foundational.

10. One exercise Adrian did with clients at TouchBase, a day centre for disabled people, was use stethoscopes to listen to each other's hearts simultaneously.

11. There is a resonance here too with the notion of deep time – an approach to time that also serves to unsettle an anthropocentric perspective.

12. Dobson summarises the ideas of Bruno Latour and Jane Bennett as two approaches which allow 'mute' objects to speak as political subjects. Nancy's is another approach.

13. From Howells' journal. All misspellings are from the originals. Howells' documents are located in the Scottish Theatre Archive, but at the time of writing, they have not yet been catalogued.

14. All citations were taken from Howells' journal.

15. Of course, some silences are intended to block communication.

16. It is worth remembering that there is nothing essentially 'good' about the act of listening. As Michael Gallagher reminds us, listening, as much as sound, enacts power, and it can therefore be deployed in different contexts with different outcomes – for example, surveillance, interrogation and regulation of behaviour. 'Listening, Meaning and Power', in *On Listening*, eds, Angus Carlyle and Cathy Lane (Axminster, Uniform Books, 2013), 41–44, p. 43.

17. All comments taken from the feedback logbook for *The Garden of Adrian*, Scottish Theatre Archive.

3   Renegotiating Immersive Participation in Analogue's *Re-enactments*

Liam Jarvis

In Andy Warhol's ghost-written autobiography, he documents vicariously his dissociated experience of the world following an assassination attempt by Valerie Solanas in 1968: 'Before I was shot, I always thought that I was more half-there than all-there – I always suspected that I was watching TV instead of living life. ... Right when I was being shot and ever since, I knew that I was watching television' (Warhol 2010: 91). This quotation usefully typifies a Warholian lens on the world, much as the artist's aesthetics provided a stage-space to emphasise copies without originals and life as an endlessly reproducible image. The analogy between Warhol's post-traumatic experience and 'watching television' suggests the way in which dissociation can induce a mediatised and detached sense of both one's body and one's immediate environment. Beyond this anecdotal account, Suzette Boon, Kathy Steele and Onno van der Hart examine dissociative conditions through the lens of clinical psychology, stating that dissociation interferes with both one's ability to integrate experiences into a 'unified whole' and one's capacity 'to be present' (Boon, Kathy, and van der Hart 2011: 4–7). Theatre critics and other commentators have identified an ontological desire that undergirds participation in immersive theatre as the desire to 'experience more fully' (Trueman 2015), but research in trauma studies has illuminated that one's capacity to either participate or become 'immersed' cannot be assumed. Certain modes of being in the world elicit a distinct sense of non-participation and a lack of immersion inside one's lived experiences, let alone inside a participatory work of art: the verb 'participate' means to 'be involved' or to 'take part',[1] while in contrast 'dissociation' means 'the state of being disconnected' or in its psychiatric derivation, the 'separation of normally related mental processes, resulting in one group functioning independently from the rest'.[2] As I will expound, to dissociate problematises one's capacity to be 'present' and can prompt disunities of self, such as experiencing one's surroundings as 'unreal'

Figure 3.1   A re-enactor points a gun at the audience.
Photography by Richard Davenport.

Figure 3.2   A publicity image for *Re-enactments*.
Photography by Alex Markham.

(commonly termed as 'derealisation') or feeling as though one's mind is no longer situated within one's body (termed as 'depersonalisation'). In the context of immersive theatre-making, how might an artist reconcile the paradoxical ontological promise that theatre audiences might be able to feel a fictionalised other's dissociation 'more fully'?

In this chapter, I will critically read *Re-enactments* (2012–14), a multi-stranded headphone performance that I created with my company Analogue and Sound Designer Tom Wilson for up to eight theatre-going audience members to participate in at a time. I will situate the work among parallel examples of theatre practice that deploy headphones to atomise audience groups and locate them within a 'cinematic space', thinking through the implications of this mode of spectatorship and the framing of spectators as 're-enactors'. I will then consider the modes of playing and watching elicited through the work's participatory architecture, examining how the half-in/half-out of *Re-enactments*' participation provides a means of reflecting on the interrelationship between theatre and trauma – the live restaging of a post-traumatic character's memories becoming an allegorical artistic form-as-symptom. It will then be important to examine known and unknown participation, procedures for opting out and whether participation is acted or perceived. Finally, I will draw on the closing event of *Re-enactments*, in which the audience participate in a 'fake-hold up' to illustrate how the mechanics of immersive participation are put to the test. I will argue that the work invites critical reflection from inside the act of re-enacting on biddable and wilful blindness to participate, confronting its own theatrical limitations in the process.

In my research as a practitioner, I have become engaged with a subset of *soi-disant* immersive performance practices that attempt to mobilise the promise that audiences might illusorily 'enter' not only a designated environment, or more problematically a dramatic universe,[3] but also a first-person reconstruction of the experience of another via immersive technologies (e.g. virtual reality head-mounted displays) that induce body transfer illusions. The latter refers to experiments in body ownership in which participants are able to experience the sensation of 'owning' a body other than one's own. The induction of body transfer illusions in performance has evolved from open-source neuroscientific research in embodiment from scientists such as Henrik Ehrsson at the Karolinska Institute. There have been numerous experiments conducted in this field that use body illusions to investigate how one comes to experience their body as their 'own'; for example, VR has been used to investigate the feeling of whole body ownership in Valeria I. Petkova and H. Henrik Ehrsson's paper 'If I Were You: Perceptual Illusion of Body Swapping' (2008). Ehrsson's whole-body illusions use virtual reality in laboratory contexts to permit a subject to experience the sensation of feeling with another's body through the manipulation of three-way interactions between vision, touch and proprioception. Evidence that these illusion-inducing techniques are being incorporated into immersive art practices can be found in

BeAnotherLab's qualitative role-playing system *The Machine to Be Another* in which interaction protocols from neuroscience afford participants the physical sensation of feeling with the simulated body of another.[4] But what about a performance in which there is no experience of another to be accessed? In *Re-enactments*, the narrator is a construction, and his dissociative state is correspondingly fictionalised. This fact highlights that the work's concern cannot be strictly about faithfully reconstructing an 'authentic' lived experience or bridging epistemic divides between the body that knows an experience and the body that cannot know without occupying its unique point of view. *Re-enactments* was instead conceived of as a critical interrogation of received ideas about immersive participation as a strategy towards a 'fuller' spectatorial experience as an audience-character. Furthermore, it sought to problematise a radical and unrealisable promise that undergirds certain conceptions of 'immersive' performance via which the spectator might 'be' the other body. *Re-enactments* is not a performance that attempts to offer 'ownership' over a fictional other's dissociation; it is rather a participatory structure that draws on research in post-traumatic dissociation to place audiences within a continually deferred reality using the headphone form as an analogue for the narrator's fragmented and dissociative mode of being in the world. The interest was to stage a productive tension between the immersed audience's participation in staging a character's actions in the immersive artwork and the fact that the character's anomalous perception of their dramatic world leaves them unable to feel as though they are participating inside their own lived experiences.

Analogue's *Re-enactments*

The research and development process for *Re-enactments* occurred in a variety of different contexts. Initially, the work was created as part of an artist-in-residence programme called *Art in Progress* at the scientific institute, Hanse-Wissenschaftskolleg (HWK) in Delmenhorst, Germany, in 2012, which culminated in a work-in-progress performance at the Upstairs Gallery (Oldenburg).[5] Following this period of research, an early iteration of the project was tested by audiences as part of the Oxford Samuel Beckett Theatre Trust Award's (OSBTTA) *The Finalists* festival in October 2012 (under the working title *Everything Must Leave Some Kind of Mark*). It was subsequently commissioned by Shoreditch Town Hall, with an initial run of the finished work in October 2013 and a further run of performances in January/February 2014. *Re-enactments* took place in the basement of the Town Hall (The Ditch), a warren of interconnecting subterranean rooms beneath architect Caesar Augustus Long's imposing civic building. The work generates an ephemeral collaboration among combinations of either strangers who have never met, groups who know each other or admixtures of individual attendees and sub-groups of participants who have pre-established relationships with one another. In advance of the performance, each audience member receives a set of headphones plugged into an Apple iPod Touch device,[6] which is pre-loaded with the StageCaller app.[7] This software connects the audience's smart devices to a MIDI (Musical Instrument Digital Interface) network, enabling Analogue to trigger audio content using cuing software (QLab 3). Four pre-designed audio tracks (A, B, C and D) are synchronously activated, generating different pathways through the script and the space; track A is a group pathway, via which commands are distributed to a collective audience of up to five people. In contrast, tracks B, C and D are localised to individual participants who take on specialised roles within the re-enactments. B is cast as the 'narrator' in various reconstructions, while A, C and D play peripheral characters from the narrator's memory. Through the impromptu enacting of received commands, a live role-play unfolds in which the participants stage reconstructions on film sets, piecing together the life of the disembodied narrating voice and fictionalised trauma survivor after an accident that has left him feeling desperately detached from the world around him. The framing conceit of the narrative is that the narrator (voiced by actor Dan Ford) has enlisted the audience as 're-enactors' to vicariously restage events from his past so that he might enter a simulacrum of his memories and feel 'real' again. Thus, there is a duality to immersive participation in *Re-enactments* since not only does it concern the audience's mode of engagement through its theatrical form, but it is also conceptualised as the narrator's dramatic objective.

The prerecorded voice guides the headphone-wearing audience through the cavernous basement to the set of a dressing room, where they learn that they will take responsibility for performing re-enactments of the narrator's life. The re-enactors are then invited to close their eyes and listen to the sounds of the character's accident (the 'inciting incident' of the plot), while one of the re-enactors follows diverging instructions to exit the dressing room unnoticed by the others, entering the film set of a hospital where the rest of the audience re-encounter them as the 'narrator' awakening from his coma. Individual instructions prompt another re-enactor to sit at the narrator's bedside, performing the role of an unremembered, visiting relative while another re-enactor takes on the part of a carpenter sanding shelves in his ward (who is later employed by the

45

narrator to construct the film sets upon which the re-enactments take place). As they witness this 'spectator-as-narrator' undertake a process of rehabilitation, the re-enactors learn that he had developed a fascination with actors on his television screen whose thought and action seemed more authentic than his own 'second-hand' movements. A scene from the narrator's television screen that intertextually references Stanley Kubrick's *The Shining* is re-presented by re-enactors who are instructed to enter the film set of a bar; this bar scene is relayed via a live video broadcast to the other observing re-enactors on the set of the hospital, signalling the crossing over of live re-enactors into mediatised representation. The authenticity that the narrator perceives in the enacting of this filmic scene leads to further proliferating re-enactments that fail to get the narrator any closer to the 'more fully' experience of his life pre-trauma that he is attempting to retrieve. The failure of the simulacrum as a vehicle through which he might feel real again spirals towards the possibility of violence in the narrative, as in the theatrical circumstance of the performance a re-enactor follows a command to point a gun at the rest of the audience. It is the possibility that the fake gun and, by association, theatrical artifice might cross over into the order of the 'real' that becomes a potential site where a character who attempts to counteract the feeling of being fictional might enter the order of the 'real' (a logic that is, of course, never realisable). The restaging of memories becomes a methodological framework to aid a fictionalised narrator in feeling like he is participating in the world. *Re-enactments* intertextually references Tom McCarthy's cult novel *Remainder* (2005) and Charlie Kauffman's film *Synecdoche, New York* (2008), with which the performance shares a particular commonality – these adjacent texts portray protagonists that deploy re-enactments, in part as a therapeutic methodology to work through their respective conditions, only for these performances to become manifestations of their suffering (hence, they represent artistic 'form-as-symptom'). The significant development in *Re-enactments* as a structure to be performed by a live audience (as opposed to these examples of literature and film) is the sense that audiences might be directly implicated from inside the re-enactments – becoming complicit with an unreliable narrator and experiencing the attendant risks of their own participation.

I should acknowledge that while the word 'immersive' is an imprecise term that has been ascribed to a heterogeneity of participatory theatre forms, through this examination of *Re-enactments* I am pursuing Josephine Machon's notion that the immersive event must establish a unique '"in-its-own-world"-ness' (Machon 2013: 207). The 'world' that she is describing goes beyond the 'world of the play' which operates only at the dramatic level. In contrast, Machon suggests that the world of immersive practices encompasses the imaginative realm as well as the theatrical situation of the audience-participant who is 'haptically incorporated' into the experience (2013: 207). The immersed audience in *Re-enactments* is a peculiar simultaneity of selves; situated as re-enactors both in the 'here' of the theatrical situation and the 'there' of the narrator's dramatic space. It is the incongruity of the audience's bodily presence 'inside' the elsewhere phenomena of the narrator's drama (to which access is never truly possible) that intersects with my interest in dissociative conditions via which the world is experienced as an unreality. In light of my focus on a case study that incorporates headphones and portable media devices, adjacent conceptualisations of 'immersion' in the parallel field of media theory become even more relevant. In Oliver Grau's *Virtual Art: From Illusion to Immersion* (2003), he argues that immersion 'arises when artwork and technologically advanced apparatus, message and medium, are perceived to merge inseparably' (Grau 2003: 339). This contention follows various other commentators in this field who have similarly argued that immersion in the technological paradigm elides with a progress-seeking strain of discourse around media which increasingly permits an immersant to be 'surrounded', to 'enter the image' or, in the case of virtual reality, to 'enter information'. These discourses around mediatised immersion are entrenched in an ontological preoccupation with liminality, or more precisely, crossing over the threshold and entering the simulacrum. At the level of narrative, this technological preoccupation parallels the narrator's approach in the story of *Re-enactments* in staging headphone reconstructions as a strategy to counteract the perceptual effects of his post-traumatic experience and 'enter' his memories. The feeling of mediatised distance initiated by the narrator's altered consciousness precipitates the narrator's operationalising of a transformative concept of 'immersion' to shift his impassive observation of events (as if 'watching television') to a directly felt participation 'inside' of them.

Scoping adjacent practices: Headphone performance as a 'camera-less film'

Before demonstrating further connections between post-traumatic dissociation and the artistic form of *Re-enactments*, I will first situate the work among parallel participatory headphone performances that position the audience *as* the work. Of particular relevance to this analysis is a tradition of performances that integrate portable media players to distribute task-based commands, mediate participant interactions, and more precisely, conceptualise audience members as performers in a live camera-less film. For example, the 'locative cinema' of Blast Theory's *A Machine To See With* (2010–12), which casts its audience as the lead in a heist movie and dispenses instructions via mobile phones and automated call-centre technology (Asterisk™) to navigate a city as 'a cinematic space'. The company pushes this notion further by designating the participating body itself as another kind of cinematic space – the participant's eyes becoming 'the screens themselves'.[8] Correspondingly, Circumstance's 'subtlemobs' make use of the audience's personal playback devices, a public site and a specified time to initiate 'invisible flashmobs'. These works are performed by knowing participants who follow instructions distributed by headphones (having downloaded an mp3 audio file in advance) and an unknowing cast of 'hundreds of strangers' that become the extras of an unfolding spectacle. Similar to Blast Theory's aforementioned notion of audience-as-movie-actor, this company describes the experience of a subtlemob as 'like walking through a film'.[9]

While none of these practitioners claim to engage with research in post-traumatic dissociation directly, the recurrent leitmotif of the 'world-as-if-cinema' that the aforementioned works produce through their respective modes of spectatorship are concordant with the perceptual effects described in Warhol's anecdote cited at the start of this chapter. Allusions towards performance in which one's eyes become either the 'screen' or a roaming camera, introduce a peculiarity in relation to spectatorial proximity that shares some correspondence with the gaze of a dissociated subject – the audience member simultaneously takes on both performing *and* spectating roles; put differently, they enter a feedback loop in which they are both the object of their gaze and audience to themselves in their own act of performance. This simultaneous involvement/detachment has correspondences with the knowledge that one might feel only 'half-there' through the lens of dissociated experience. The audience are situated in between the duality of being present both here and now, and a removed observer of their actions in the subjunctive premise of a cinematic narrative layered over real-world locations. They are framed as half instrument of reception (e.g. a 'screen') and half performer, half participating and half observing, or in the case of *Re-enactments* 'half here' (as a re-enactor in Analogue's performance) and 'half there' (as a 're-enactor' in the narrator's drama). But what does it mean to conceptualise an audience member as a 're-enactor', and what further elisions exist between *Re-enactments'* theatrical form and post-traumatic dissociation?

Conceptualising the audience: 'Re-enactors' and 'received actors'

The noun 're-enactors' requires examination to clarify precisely what kind of spectator the performance designates. The hyphenated verb 're-enact' means to 'act out (a past event)' – 're-' originating from the Latin *again, back* which prefixes the verb 'enact', meaning to 'act out (a role or play) on stage'.[10] In relation to historical re-enactments, Rebecca Schneider contends that 'participants fight to "keep the past *alive*". ... The effort is to provoke an in time experience bearing some relation to "living"' (Schneider 2011: 37). And yet, any enactment or bodying of history in the lived present might be recognised as a matter of 'againness' through the 'manipulation of give-way signs of theatricality' (Schneider 2011: 32). Participation in a re-enactment in this sense is an attempted retrieval of, and immersion within, the past that resists the tell-tale signifiers of one's contribution in the present to an ongoing cycle of 'againness'. While most theatre might be understood as a form of 're-enactment' to some extent (if not a restaging of historical events, then a restaging of a dramatic structure intended to be enacted multiply), inevitably not all theatre places the same participatory demands on its audience. In *Re-enactments*, the audience perform the narrator's story to, and for each other, without the involvement of any live pre-rehearsed actors. The work is an example of total participation to the extent that without the audience's complicity, it exists only as a structure without content. Thus, it engenders a form of interactivity that especially emphasises the spectator's indispensability to the performance.

Re-enactments is situated on the continuum of what Umberto Eco defined as *The Open Work* (1962), indicating an open-ended composition within which there are varying degrees of autonomy as to how the participant chooses to play their role (Eco 1989). The work is not, however, predicated on 'emancipating' its audience, nor does it represent the kind of openness associated with a 'sandbox', 'free-roaming' or 'open world' experience.[11] The 'what' of the distributed tasks is tightly delineated, but the 'how', or modus operandi, by which they are executed is 'open' to each re-enactor's interpretation. Claire Bishop argues that 'every reception of a work of art is both an interpretation and a performance of it, because in every reception the work takes on a fresh perspective for itself' (Bishop 2006: 22). Consistent with this idea, each re-enactor's participation in *Re-enactments* is a performance of their interpretive act rendered visible to others. And yet the unknowability of each other's audio instructions draws attention to what is concealed as much as what is interpreted and performed. Therefore, the immersive promise of access, of being 'in on it', is deliberately problematised – the re-enactors are inside a performance coordinated by Analogue (who frame it as an event orchestrated by the story's post-traumatised narrator), but outside of information at crucial junctures because of the way in which invisible commands are transmitted. In this respect, the audience are invited to critique the performance's constructed inequities of information – a point that I will return to regarding a key event in the work's dénouement in which the audience stage a 'fake holdup'.

The implied requirement of 'enacting', meaning to 'act out' a role, applies to *Re-enactments* insofar as the staging of fictionalised events necessitates acting of a kind – I would contend that acting in this context is task oriented (disseminated via audio instruction), transactional (occurring between the participants) and requires a voluntary, or substitutionary, 'standing in' for the different characters within the story (e.g. the narrator is 're-enactor B-*as*-narrator'). I use the term 'standing in' since the participants are never met with the request to mimetically represent characters and are cognisant of the doubleness of a role and its incumbent re-enactor. This distance between the re-enactor and the other for whom they 'stand in' corresponds with the fictionalised narrator's sense of detachment from his own lived experience and post-traumatic alienation from characters that populate his story.

The requirement to perform in *Re-enactments* raises a further issue in terms of audience demographic. Crucially, this participatory structure could not be created with the assumption that a confident, theatre-literate or gaming savvy audience would attend, which might be the assumption of a self-styled 'interactive' work taking place in an area of East London that is famed as the home of the 'hipster', the pop-up cafe and the tech start-up. The ease and ability with which different audience groups might play along is facilitated by assigning simple tasks that do not necessitate any acting competency. I would identify that 're-enacting' in this context is akin to what Michael Kirby referred to in *A Formalist Theatre* (1987) on his continuum between 'non-acting' and 'acting' as 'received acting' (Kirby 1987: 6). Hans-Thies Lehmann cites Kirby's term in his formulation of the *postdramatic* actor, who is no longer the performer of a role but one who offers his/her 'presence on stage for contemplation' (Lehmann 2006: 135). Kirby's notion of received acting occurs 'when the context of signs being added from outside increases without the performers themselves producing them … e.g. in a bar scene some men are playing cards in a corner; they do nothing else but are perceived as actors and seem to be acting' (Lehmann 2006: 135). In *Re-enactments*, participants 'receive' each other as 'actors' via the simple coupling of audio description and the fulfilment of an undertaking (e.g. a re-enactor is prompted to wear a velvet jacket and pour some drinks, becoming the 'bartender' to the other re-enactors in the bar scene). So what does the audience's participation *do* by restaging a fictionalised narrator's mission to reclaim a pre-traumatic sense of reality?

Re-enactments: Mediatised form as allegory for post-traumatic experience

It is my contention that *Re-enactments'* form operates as a metaphor to help think through what participation and presence might mean from inside the act of participating. The Positive Outcomes for Dissociative Survivors (PODS) website suggests that 'dissociative disorders' can refer to both 'an experience — when we feel that we are drifting off into a fog, or we switch to another part of our personality — or to the fundamental state and structure of our mind'.[12] Therefore, to dissociate can refer either to something that we *do* or something that we *are*. In *Re-enactments*, the theatrical form became an allegory for its constructed character's dissociative experience through the re-enactors' *doing*, while at the level of narrative, the narrator's altered consciousness has transformed who he *is*. Thus, the re-enactors' *doing* is a product of a pre-scripted narrator that is attempting to overcome an unwanted change of bodily state, only to unintentionally reproduce his sense of unreality through an allegorically dissociative theatrical form. Headphone performance understood as a 'camera-less film' produces a 'half-out' experience precisely by positioning the individual as their own spectator.

The narrating self in *Re-enactments'* story is atomised post-trauma – mind and body are no longer unified, and simple physical actions require being exhaustively thought through before being able to perform them. Analogously, the collective body of the participating audience becomes atomised as re-enacting bodies are seemingly apprehended by interlocking sets of instructions. The illusion is of participation in the narrator's shared but altered consciousness, and the fragmentation of the participating group produces a dramaturgy of partialness that disturbs consensus reality by instating a 'need-to-know' reality. This raises a tension in regard to whom participation in the work is for, since it operates to render visible the story to the re-enactors through their actions, but it ultimately serves the desire of a fictional character at the dramatic level towards immersion inside 'memories' (that are, in themselves, fictionalised by Analogue).

Regardless of the fidelity of the immersive environment within which participants are surrounded, audiences are never unaware of immersive performance's devices or contrivances. *Re-enactments* exploits this paradox by deliberately situating participants inside and outside of different scenarios simultaneously. For example, the illusion for re-enactor B via their headphones is of hearing *with* the narrator's ears. However, through the binaural sound design, his voice when issuing commands for action is always located outside of the participant. This dispersion of the narrating self corresponds with traumatic disintegrations of personal experience, resulting in the 'separating of observing ego and experiencing ego' (van der Kolk, van der Hart and Marmar 1996: 303–327), through which one views one's own experiences 'as if' from the outside (e.g. as if 'television') – both participating *and* not participating simultaneously.

Beyond these disunities of the narrating self, *Re-enactments* produces a mode of spectatorship that is multi-perspectival. A kind of metaphorical 'body-hopping' occurs in which the re-enactors occupy neither a fixed position nor a single identity that can be owned throughout the performance. Participants are fluidly transitioned between different performing roles and performed 'audiences' in the story that bear witness to the narrator, spectating 'hospital staff', onlooking 'family members' or by-standing 're-enactors'. These shifts provide an allegory for the attributes of depersonalisation via which one comes to experience oneself *as other* through the separation of egos. It is the impossibility of occupying or fully knowing the narrator's experience, since one cannot be 'immersed' through the lens of a dissociated subject, that provides a space to stage a productive agitation to the immersive promise of 'experiencing more fully'. The interest in problematising this ontology derives from wanting to critique adjacent practices that have exploited the form as a means through which audiences might re-experience extreme events of trauma (e.g. the 'physical and psychological insanity' of the gas chambers at Auschwitz–Birkenau in Badac Theatre's *The Factory*) by way of a theatrical representation.[13] The resultant of this troubling logic is to simply position audiences as passive enactors of historic acts of suffering, replicating inequities of power to which any act of resistance ultimately brings the audience only closer to the mechanics of representation. The resistance of a spectator-character to the commands of an actor-Nazi soldier can only possibly expose the limitations of a theatrical simulation to be the thing that it simulates. In contrast, *Re-enactments* uses immersive reconstruction precisely to restage it as a site of inevitable failure to 'know', contain or access the narrator's unresolved post-traumatic experiences.

In *Trauma-Tragedy: Symptoms of Contemporary Performance* (2012), Patrick Duggan identifies an insightful corollary between trauma and performance, illuminating that recent trauma theory has suggested a 'performative bent in traumatic suffering', which is relevant to the notion of artistic form as an allegory for post-traumatic symptom (2012: 4). Duggan cites Dominic LaCapra's *Writing History, Writing Trauma* (2001) as influential to his thinking and draws out two performative elements in relation to the experience of trauma; first, 'trauma might be seen to perform itself, as it were, within a collapsing of time; in a sense the inability to 'exist in the present' is a traumatic performative disruption/disturbance of time' (2012: 4). And second, the 'survivor-sufferer might be seen to perform the symptoms of their suffering' (2012: 5). Duggan extends on this latter idea in reference to Roger Luckhurst's *The Trauma Question* (2008), in which he contends that individuals, collectives and nations can become trapped in 'cycles of uncomprehending repetition' until such time as that repetition becomes a process of 'healthy analytic ... "working through"' (2012: 9). Both of these performative elements are crucial to the experience of trauma-induced dissociation and are central to the concerns of the narrator in *Re-enactments* who implements immersive role-playing to counteract his inability to feel 'present'. But these acts become an infinite regress of 'working through' without resolution. A productive tension is staged in the performance between the content of the narrative and its mode of presentation; the participation of the audience in *Re-enactments* cannot satisfy the narrator's desire to feel 'real', since the retrieved events are always already twice behaved, as per the definition of a 're-enactment' to 'act out (*a past event*)'. Vicarious participation, film lighting and preset marks for the re-enactors to 'hit' (indicating the positions of characters on the film sets) are all 'give-way signs' exposing artifice in the present and incomplete immersion in the past. Schneider notes that the discrete act of re-enacting is 'never temporally singular nor straightforward but double, triple, or done "a million times before"' (Schneider 2011: 32–33). The multiply revisited event of the 're'-enactment, which aligns with the aforementioned notion of Warholian reproducibility and copies without originals, becomes itself an obstruction to the narrator's desire for authentic lived experience. Furthermore, his desire to 'exist in the present' cannot be fulfilled by immersive reconstruction, as there is a tension between immersivity's promise of *presence*, of 'being there', and the fact that the 'there' that the narrator wishes to be is always other than where he resides – namely, immersion inside his memories and, by association, inside the inaccessible elsewhere of his untraumatised body *prior* to his accident. In *Re-enactments'* narrative, it is the attempt to reconcile an inner conflict between dissociative experience and the desire for bodily immersion which drives the central plot.

There is a tension between form and content that occurs through a metatheatrical doubleness in *Re-enactments*. As I have noted, the immersive re-enactment is deployed simultaneously in the dramatic 'world of the play' and in the theatrical mode. In the dramatic mode, or what Keir Elam defines as the 'there and then' of drama (1980: 98), it is mobilised by the narrator to re-associate mind, body and environment. Corresponding with this, in the 'here and now' of the theatrical mode, the re-enactors are located inside the same immersive participatory form as a means of exploring the mechanics of unrehearsed participation in an act of performance. The 'dramatic world' of *Re-enactments*, termed by Elam as 'hypothetical "as if" constructs … recognised by the audience as counterfactual' (1980: 90), has deliberate congruencies with its theatrical form. Participation is framed as indispensable at both the theatrical and dramatic levels because the narrator is corporeally manifested only through the performing re-enactors' bodies. Beyond generating an '"in-its-own-world"-ness', the work hints at the possibility that a fictional narrator's world might infect the audience's reality.

The narrator of *Re-enactments* conceptualises immersive participation as a strategy via which his desire to 'experience more fully' might be fulfilled. It is this ontological promise entrenched in the immersive form that motivates its application in the fiction, operating under the logic of intensification. A *hyperreality* is staged within which the narrator deliberately aims to blur the distinctions between simulated and real events. These reincarnated moments were intended to parallel Umberto Eco's notion of 'authentic fakes' in *Travels In Hyperreality* (1987), as he radically conceives of his participants as a '"sign" that will then be forgotten as such: the sign aims to be the thing, to abolish the distinction of the reference' (Eco 1987: 6–7). The narrator immerses himself within historical reconstructions as a strategy to feel 'all there' and this 'unreality' substitutes real presence. Correspondingly, in the theatrical circumstance of the performance, the actor who voices the narrator's words is displaced from any direct contact with his audience. The actor's script is a model or a 'score', orchestrating the re-enactor's live actions, but he is only ever a prerecorded document of the past, a trace – only ever 'half there'. Consequently, the participating audience are also the interface in between the work's displaced actor and the physical environment from which his character's body is dissociated (and in theatre practices, all 'characters' necessitate the actor to become bodied).

The allegorical synergy between theatrical form and dissociation in *Re-enactments* that I have demonstrated in this section prompts a bigger question in regard to the core theme of this book: is participation acted or perceived? The narrator's dissociative mode of being in the world provides a means of thinking through whether one's 'doing' is necessarily enough to perceive that one is participating in either the world or a piece of art. The show confronts the audience with the idea that its very mode of participation cannot function to compensate for what the narrator has lost. Its thesis is that participation is not meaningful in and of itself. At the dramatic level, immersive participation is framed as a site of inevitable failure because it cannot mobilise its promise that either the narrator might feel 'more fully' or the audience might reduce their proximity to the narrator's post-traumatic lived experience (which is always already fictionalised). I will further unpack the notion of acted and perceived participation by examining unknown participation, the problem of opting out in the work of total participation and taking part in 'fake holdups'.

Unknowing participation

Re-enactments is a useful case study to think through the requirement of whether 'participation' need always be a conscious act in performance: must all participants consent for participation to occur? And if not, what does this do to notions of participation? Beyond the involvement of those having subscribed to take part, other modes of association with *Re-enactments* are neither conscious nor consenting. Having established Kirby's criterion that a received actor is constituted when signs are 'added from outside', it is conceivable in moments when a work overlaps with exterior public spaces that those inhabiting these environments can unknowingly accumulate layers of signification. When different groups of re-enactors emerged from Shoreditch Town Hall's basement at the end of the performance onto Rivington Place, the street was often frequented by workers on cigarette breaks, delivery men, cyclists, lost tourists and so on. During this final scene, the narrator primes the re-enactors with the idea that whenever they walk down a street like this one wearing headphones, and the thought comes to mind that it might 'all be a film ... take off your headphones. And if your soundtrack is still playing, perhaps this *is* your film after all'.[14] Upon removing the headphones, the non-diegetic soundtrack/narration continues through unseen speakers positioned in the street, creating the illusion of the voice's migration from the headphones into the spaces beyond the performance. Concurrently, pedestrians on Rivington Place are framed as extras of a spectacle that constitutes the narrator's ever extending *theatrum mundi*. This moment stages the 'as if' of the pedestrians' conscious participation, minus the conscious action of their 'taking part'. The invitation is to view these unknowing received actors on Rivington Place as if part of the proceedings and through the lens of the derealised subject, invoking a *Truman Show*-esque paranoia that those frequenting the street might also be 'in on the act'. The participation of others becomes a question of what is perceived. In turn, *Re-enactments* activates its audience only for the narrator to problematise the notion that their action alone is enough to fully participate in his world; his dissociated experience raises the question, if one is actively involved but shares in his feeling of detachment, is one still participating? The value of participatory form as dissociative allegory is that it provides a space to think more deeply about the importance of participation as not only a question of being active but as something that must be meaningfully felt.

Opting out

While *Re-enactments'* audio tracks present audience members with varying levels of active engagement, there exists no position from which to 'step back' from the work. The invitation in our marketing copy for the performance as an 'actor-less ... interactive audio performance' is to participate in the delivery of the 'scripts' (scripts for action rather than for dialogue) and consequently share in the responsibility for the performance. The absence of dialogue removes a potentially inhibiting responsibility for the re-enactors to give voice to unrehearsed characters, instead superimposing prerecorded dialogue over their actions. However, the requirement to 're-enact' creates a problem in maintaining an important underlying principle that audience participation in the performance should be wilful and voluntary throughout. During the R&D performances, I observed different re-enactors opting out of performing particular commands. Over repeat performances it became apparent that this occurred most frequently when re-enactor B's instructions differed from those of the other participants for the first time, prompting them to stand 'centre stage' on the set of the dressing room. Through informal post-show discussions, different participating 're-enactor B's' ascribed their choice to opt out of this command to different reasons (e.g. anxiety around getting it 'right', not having developed the confidence to be led by the instructions rather than the behaviour of their fellow audience members, etc.). Each participant's trust in the conventions of the piece is not assumed, and observation of repeated performances evidenced development in a group's confidence over *Re-enactments'* duration as its particular interaction protocols became more familiar to unrehearsed audiences. However, a choice for one re-enactor to not perform an action results in something missing from the other re-enactor's sequence of events. For this reason the audience are monitored by Analogue's production manager (Helen Mugridge), and whenever a command would be disregarded, she would deputise for reluctant participants, filling in the action. To this extent, non-participation for the audience is always possible, but their stepping back becomes a 'cue' for a company member to complete an unfulfilled interaction. In this way, provisions are made for non-participation in the work of total participation, but the appearance of opting out of an instruction is largely rendered imperceptible. What we negotiate in these moments is our inevitable dependency on the audience to maintain the fiction (by performing tasks) with a sensitivity to the fact that our instructions are not known in advance, and correspondingly 'total' participation cannot be unconditional; every action is an agreement, and spaces for inaction must similarly be built into the work (conceiving of 'inaction' as a choice that is similarly active).

Staging participation in 'fake holdups'

There is an inherent contradiction within *Re-enactments*: the narrator and Analogue's personnel must necessarily represent very different kinds of custodians to their respective re-enactor's experiences. Within the fiction, the 're-enactors' are dispensable agents. The narrator assumes no ethical responsibility for the lives of others. Instead, his participating re-enactors are exploited to perform increasingly violent re-enactments in his pursuit of feeling 'real', to the point that the reality status of the events that they are instructed to simulate become increasingly unclear. In the theatrical situation, to superimpose our re-enacting audience as the narrator's 're-enactors' is a layering choice that must be delicately navigated, since we have a responsibility that the narrator does not to protect the welfare of our participants. The work must negotiate a common paradox within the immersive work of providing a safe environment, but one in which the associated risks of becoming implicated in precarious circumstances might be felt. The 'fake holdup' in which re-enactors participate at the end of *Re-enactments* is a useful test site to illustrate and expose the limits of immersive participation. The holdup in *Re-enactments* might usefully be related to two antecedent articulations of the 'fake holdup'; the first was published in Jean Baudrillard's philosophical treatise *Simulacra and Simulations* (1981), interrogating the relationship between reality and symbols. The second occurs in Tom McCarthy's novel *Remainder*. I will briefly consider these different manifestations of the fake holdup before progressing to consider the issues that the theatre-maker must addresses when positioning participants 'inside' such an experience.

Baudrillard provocatively invited his readers to stage a 'fake holdup' in demonstration of his point that the simulated and the real cannot be easily delineated. He argues that a real holdup 'only upsets the order of things, the right of property', whereas the simulated holdup 'interferes with the very principle of reality. ... Simulation is infinitely more dangerous, however, since it always suggests, over and above its object, that *law and order themselves might really be nothing more than a simulation*' (1994: 38). He suggests that this imitation of a crime is objectively indifferent to the real act; thus, to the established order, a fake holdup is always received within 'the order of the real' (1994: 38–39). Baudrillard's example might be understood more precisely as a *fake real holdup*, or put another way, the artificial appearance of a robbery using fake weapons in a real bank. In this example, the person participating in the 'crime' is cognisant that their act is a parody, while the bank staff and passers-by participate as if it is real.

The holdup that takes place in McCarthy's *Remainder* is a complex variation of Baudrillard's since it transitions from a re-enactment of a heist on the set of a bank constructed in a warehouse to one staged in a real bank that has a different reality status for all of the participants involved. When he decides to 'transfer the re-enactment of the bank heist to the actual bank', all subsequent re-enactments shift status to 'pre-enactments', or rehearsals towards an anticipated future event (McCarthy 2010: 242). In his co-ordination of this holdup, the narrator instructs his 'facilitator', Nazrul Ram Vyas, to neither get the bank's permission nor inform his hired re-enactors or the bank's staff of the planned 'transfer'. All the participating re-enactors are stratified into different 'NTK (Need To Know) categories', and within each category 'how much they need to know, and when they need to know it' are determined (2010: 246). Thus, there is a dangerous inequity of knowledge between what the participants believe they have consented to and what is actually taking place. The rationale for transferring the simulated heist to an actual bank is that the novel's protagonist wants 'to cut out the detour that sweeps us around what's fundamental to events, preventing us from touching their core: the detour that makes us all second-hand and second-rate' (2010: 244). The dissociated narrator identifies the seamless merging of simulated robbery with reality as a strategy to feel real again, to 'live inside the core' (2010: 245). The inevitable outcome is tragedy, as one of the re-enactors pulls the trigger of what he believes to be a fake gun, shooting another re-enactor and killing him. The contamination of reality and artifice is exposed in a horrifying moment of *anagnorisis*, as a re-enactor exclaims, 'Oh my God. ... It's *real*' (2010: 269–270). In this *stratified holdup*, the crime is staged by participating agents situated within different spheres of knowing. Fake guns are substituted for real ones, and the re-enactors become aware of their true mode of participation only when a 'fake gun' produces a lethal wound.

Unlike both Baudrillard's *fake real holdup* and McCarthy's *stratified holdup*, the example in *Re-enactments* might be termed as a *real fake holdup* in the sense that its audience is never unaware that they are participating in a performance. However, the 'command/response' mode of interaction similarly stratifies the participating re-enactors into different orders of knowing. Epistemically, the audience are cognisant that the performance disseminates different fragments of information to assemble a picture of the work; there is no possibility of experiencing *Re-Enactments* as a 'unified whole'. The technical apparatus of the performance is an intervention that introduces paradoxical effects; personal media is used to coordinate the audience's actions while continually keeping them separate from one another. While any theatre work cannot ethically stage the lethal inequities of knowledge between *Remainder*'s narrator and his participating re-enactors, the work prompts the audience to critically interrogate the information disseminated to other audience members. The re-enactor who points the gun at the audience hears that while it's a 'toy', the other re-enactors are being told that 'the gun is real', prompting the gun-wielding re-enactor to question whether their causal responses are the result of continued instruction or off-script improvisation. Simultaneously, the hijacked audience members hear that the re-enactor holding the gun seems 'unaware that it's real'. Had an audience believed that the re-enactor posed a genuine threat, resistance would have been the inevitable result. The most that this deception can do is play upon the doubt and uncertainty in between its constructed strata of knowledge – to stir the audience to question the reliability of the truths presented by a dissociated narrator and analyse the status of their own participation, critiquing the work and their mode of participation from within the act of participating.

Conclusion

Re-enactments is an example of an immersive participatory work that is not simply a question of mobilising the desire to be 'inside' another's experience, since the other in question is both fictional and unable to access their own sense of lived experience as a consequence of trauma. The allegory of artistic form-as-dissociative-symptom in *Re-enactments* can be identified through the audience as both performer/spectator of their actions, the atomisation of the audience as a collective body and its multi-perspectival mode of spectatorship. The significance of the re-enactment as a metaphor is that it provides a way of thinking about notions of participation as something that is acted, but also something that must be perceived. It is the narrator's perception that he is not participating in the world at the dramatic level that provides a trigger for proliferating acts of immersive participation in the theatrical circumstance of *Re-enactments*. Non-participation in this context might be understood as a re-enactor's wilful disregard of an instruction in performance, but equally it is intrinsic to the dissociative state of the fictionalised narrator who is acting out his experiences while simultaneously being a detached observer of them. Non-participation can be something that we *do* (or an active choice of what *not to do*), but furthermore, it can also be a state through which one's doing is not enough in itself to feel that we are participating. The narrator is a hyperrealist that seeks to actuate an immersive ontology that might relocate him inside his memories and ultimately his pre-traumatised body. Consequently, the related agenda of transferring ever greater degrees of what the narrator perceives to be 'reality' into the re-enactments draws critical attention to the limits of theatrical representation. In the article 'The Theatre of Reality…and Avoiding the Stage's Kiss of Death' (2014), Tim Crouch addresses the danger that exists in an artist's attempt to 'annex the real' as a way for audiences to access experiences that might be 'more authentic, more honest, more deeply felt or perceived' (2014). Corresponding with this danger, it is the narrator's desire to feel 'real' that produces an extreme solipsism in which his 're-enactors' in the dramatic mode are exploited in service of another's need to resolve their anomalous perception of the world. Meanwhile, in the theatrical mode, Analogue must negotiate the formulation of a participatory structure in which audiences can take part in the 'as if' of their being at risk. The audience are placed inside an unreliable 'need-to-know' reality, and they are increasingly left outside of information as the reconstructions hint towards their potential for violence, instating inequities of information among different strata of participation. When a re-enactor points a 'gun' at the rest of the audience, they are prompted to critically question these inequities and are brought to the theatrical limits of the mechanics of the production itself.

Endnotes

1. 'Participate'. *OxfordDictionaries.com* <http://www.oxforddictionaries.com/definition/english/participate> [accessed 13 January 2015].

2. 'Dissociation'. *OxfordDictionaries.com* <http://www.oxforddictionaries.com/definition/english/dissociation> [accessed 12 January 2015].

3. The promise that audiences might 'enter' a dramatic universe in relation to immersive theatre practice is critically interrogated elsewhere in Gareth White's article 'On Immersive Theatre' in *Theatre Research International*, 37 (3), p. 221–235.

4. 'BeAnotherLab', *The Machine to Be Another* <http://www.themachinetobeanother.org/?page_id=820> [accessed 29 June 2015].

5. 'Art in Progress'. *Hanse-Wissenschaftskolleg Institute for Advanced Study (HWK)* <http://www.h-w-k.de/en/arts-and-humanities/art-in-progress.html> [accessed 13 November 2014].

6. iPod Touch® is a trademark of Apple Inc.

7. StageCaller was developed as a software solution for generating live sound effects on stage (e.g. a phone ringing). On the StageCaller website, the makers note that this technology avoids the necessity in contemporary sound design for 'practicals all over the stage, or faking it from nearby sources', replacing antecedent technologies such as TeleQ™. 'StageCaller: Home'. <www.stagecaller.com> [accessed 12 December 2014].

8. Blast Theory acknowledge that the notion of the participant's eyes as 'screens' is a reference to Chris Hedges' *Empire of Illusion: The End of Literacy and the Triumph of Spectacle* (2009) in which he says 'we try to see ourselves moving through our life as a camera would see us, mindful of how we hold ourselves, how we dress, what we say. We invent movies that play in our heads'. 'A Machine To See With'. *Blast Theory* <http://www.blasttheory.co.uk/projects/a-machine-to-see-with/> [accessed 1 April 2015].

9. 'As If It Were The Last Time'. *Circumstance* <http://wearecircumstance.com/project/as-if-it-were-the-last-time/> [accessed 3 April 2015].

10. 'Re-enact'. *OxfordDictionaries.com* <http://www.oxforddictionaries.com/definition/english/re-enact> [accessed 12 January 2015].

11. 'Open world' is a term commonly used to describe a type of video game in which a player can roam through a virtual world with a certain amount of freedom in choosing 'how or when to approach objectives'. 'Open World', *Wikipedia* <http://en.wikipedia.org/wiki/Open_world> [accessed 17 January 2015].

12. 'What is Dissociation?'. *PODS (Positive Outcomes for Dissociative Survivors)* <www.pods-online.org.uk/whatisdissociation.html> [accessed 27 October 2014].

13. *The Factory*. Directed by Steve Lambert. Pleasance Courtyard, Edinburgh, 1–24 August 2008.

14. *Re-enactments*. Written by Liam Jarvis (with contributions from Hannah Barker). Devised by Analogue. Sound Design by Tom Wilson. Voiceovers by Morag Cross, Dan Ford & Brian Martin. Produced by Ric Watts. Shoreditch Town Hall, London. 9–12 October 2013.

4   Mute Stages

Performing Silent Lives

Anna Harpin

Discussing the dread reaction of the Governess to her charges' manic play in Anne Brontë's *Agnes Grey*, Sally Shuttleworth illuminates the longstanding 'popular need to overcome the daunting alterity of childhood by bringing it under the control of adult classifications' (2010: 18). Shuttleworth continues to note, in her exploration of Victorian literary and scientific discourses of childhood, that children have oft been perceived as a 'threateningly unknowable species of humanity' and considers how far childhood has been understood as a 'natural' state of unreason (2010: 19). In pursuing the question whether a child can be mad, Shuttleworth exposes adults' desire to wrest unruly alterity back into familiar form. She elucidates how far wider social discourses, such as those around race, gender, and selfhood, are refracted through the figure of the child (2010: 4). The wilful child is also the subject of this chapter. In general, I consider the extent to which childhood might be understood conceptually as a place apart that refuses to fully participate in adult consensus reality. More specifically, I will investigate how 'disturbed' children amplify questions about social participation and political structures of communication. I wish to linger over the relationship between difference and defiance, and consider how nonconformity is read, understood and classified. In order to examine these concerns, I will explore the lives and cultural representations of elective mutes, June and Jennifer Gibbons, also known as *The Silent Twins*.[1] This chapter, then, aims to assess how childhood alterity, as figured in theatre and performance, may help us to understand the nature and limits of adult normalcy off stage. In so doing, it is hoped that I will uncover some new reflections on the meaning and value of social participation and perhaps more importantly non-participation. Can rethinking the value of the participation/non-participation binary broaden horizons of thought with respect to ways of being? Indeed, is the term non-participation itself unhelpful, insofar as it necessarily sustains pre-established terms of participation? And to what extent can social non-participation actually be a peculiarly strident way of joining in by reimagining the terms of participation? In short, these pages aim to revaluate the nature and value of opting out.

Raise your hand if you want to speak

Tim Crouch's 2003 play *My Arm* is a tale of a young boy who puts his arm in the air and never puts it back down again. It is, as the play script describes, the 'story of an empty gesture' that becomes overburdened with meaning. In the course of the performance everyone from family members to doctors to psychologists to peers to artists try to make varied sense of the obstinate action with the tools at their disposal (medicine, bullying, paint, and so on). They attempt to narrate its wilful pointlessness into legible form. Yet the play is precisely framed by its exquisite lack of referent:

> Don't think that this gesture is about belief. It isn't for a moment about belief, or conviction or integrity. I'd like to be able to tell you that this all sprung out of some sort of social protest. That I was incensed by the stories from Cambodia. Or even that it was an heroic gesture in the face of an abusing father, or separating parents, or – I think it was none of these. If anything it was formed out of the *absence* of belief. I think at some point I was struck by the realisation that I had nothing to think about. I was thought-less. I couldn't cause thought. I was not the effect of thought. (Crouch 2003: 14, emphasis original)

Moreover, the peculiar gesture is set amid a cluster of eccentric childhood behaviours:

> I was put in a group of similarly aged adolescents with similarly idiosyncratic manifestations. There were twins girls, Helen and Alison, who had refused to open their eyes since they were nine.
>
> *Presents photo provided from the audience.*
>
> Andy Beglin, who wouldn't open his fists.
>
> *Presents another photo.*
>
> A girl called Barbara Matthews, who had had the contents of her stomach removed regularly since the age of five because she kept eating batteries.
>
> *Presents another photo.*

Myrna Kendall, who refused to wash or cut her nails or clean her teeth, ever.

Photo.

There was an even fatter kid than me who had big issues with his own excrement, so we all kept our distance. And there was Kevin Proctor, who was perfectly sensible but who would never wear any clothes if he could help it. (Crouch 2003: 24–25)

Contrarily, the opening to Sara Ahmed's *Willful Subjects* retells a Grimm tale of a disobedient little girl who dies but whose arm protrudes noisily and repetitively from her grave until it is struck into submission by her mother with a rod of iron: 'and then at last the child had rest beneath the ground' (Grimm, qtd in Ahmed). Unlike Crouch's arm, Ahmed's is apparently so full of meaning that it rattles with the energy of the undead. The arm accuses. However, what both arms essentially ask us to consider is the cultural legibility and value of alterity and resistance. The arms request our attention (even witness) but contest our attempts to control them. They are defiant and strange. And, moreover, they appear to address us, soundlessly.

My Arm, as with all of Crouch's work, is concerned with the nature and limits of theatricality and representation: it explores the relationship between action and meaning. However, like Ahmed's figuring of the wilful child, this play also illuminates a number of ideas that are at the heart of this chapter: questions of reality, participation, and alterity. Firstly, it returns our attention to the precarity of reality insofar as it narrates the multiple and shifting manners in which the arm is *made to mean*. The gesture is intolerable, owing to its steadfast departure from normative behaviours and common horizons of meaning. Similarly, the Brothers Grimm's arm operates as a malleable and paradoxical metaphor: a dead arm that thrusts, for a time, with wild life. It defies its position and thereby unseats its audiences. In both cases, we are invited to ask: what do you mean? Secondly, both arms, in different ways, shine light on our collective intolerance of signs and gestures of, and towards, nothingness (one might even include suicidal actions here). Indeed, the ambiguous spirit of the Grimm's arm must be beaten into its proper place; neither seen, nor heard. Thirdly, both demand that we think about nonconformity as, in some ways, a performative action. This in turn invites us to reflect upon how and why one might represent a non-conformist gesture in manners that remain true to the original action. Finally, both stories pay attention to a tendency in authorities that 'manage' childhood to pathologise or condemn non-normative childhood behaviours. Disciplinary strategies in psychiatry (and related disciplines) and education prescribe what is and what is not acceptable, whether through diagnosis or regulations and punishments. This need to make sense of difference, to explain away those children who won't play along (or won't play *properly*), has profound consequences for how we collectively conceive of acceptable selves and acceptable realities. This is not to imply homogeneity of social attitudes; rather, it is to underline the normative values that are at play in structural responses to alternative experiences and ways of being. I propose, here, that the manners in which we apprehend and attend to unusual behaviours tacitly demonstrate the values ascribed to personhood and a viable (and valuable) life. This is not offered in an 'anything goes' spirit that implies we should simply ignore difference entirely, or that children do not need support; rather, I am specifically questioning, in the case of the twins, the structures of listening and the limits of our collective capacity to productively hear (and read) silence. These defiant arms, then, offer us a valuable departure point for our exploration of the lives and cultural legacies of June and Jennifer Gibbons insofar as they ask us to consider the meaning, purpose and representation of acts of non-participation and alterity. Moreover, they ask us to examine the social and structural conditions of communication. These arms, like June and Jennifer, are far from silent. Their inaudible defiance helps us to think about what happens when we press mute and opt out.

'Words seemed too much'[2]

Before turning to the twins' onstage representation, it is important to survey their biography. June Alison Gibbons and Jennifer Lorraine Gibbons were born as monozygotic twins on 11 April 1963 to Gloria and Aubrey Gibbons, who had immigrated to the UK from Barbados in 1960.[3] The girls lived around the UK during their childhood in Yorkshire and Devon and then finally settled in Haverford West, Wales. Their father worked on Royal Air Force bases, and so the family moved with his career. There were three other children in their family: Greta (older), David (older) and Rosie (younger). The twins' early infancy passed without notable difficulty or upset. By the age of three, the sisters would play happily together, but their language was restricted to a handful of unclear words and phrases. As June and Jennifer joined school, their underdeveloped language skills became more audible and they were sent for weekly speech therapy to little avail. Marjorie Wallace's biography of June and Jennifer, *The Silent Twins*, offers a detailed account of the two girls' childhood development.[4] What is apparent from the biography – which was written based on their diaries and interviews with the twins, the family and key figures in their histories – is that their silence became steadily more entrenched and mutually reinforced. Gloria, however, remains steadfast in her sense that the 'twinnies' are just shy. The twins certainly have a mild speech impediment, but they do have the physical capacity to talk. As the twins progressed through their school years, they were not only subject to playground racist bullying but accused by exasperated teachers and educational support workers of 'dumb insolence' (Wallace 2008: 16). It is striking how their silence is understood by many as aggressive, even violent. Indeed, one teacher went so far as to imply supernatural malevolence:

> They were always apart from everyone else, trying to be invisible, yet they attracted attention in a way I disliked. I've had 6,000 children go through my hands in thirty years and I've encountered only four I felt were evil. ... The fourth was Jennifer. ... The bad one would not have been so bad had she not been able to draw strength from her twin, and the other one would have been normal. (John, qtd in Wallace 2008: 17)

In practice, then, their silence is experienced as anything but passive: they are assertively present.

The educational authorities sought to physically separate the twins as a strategy to demolish the perceived over-intensity of their psychological relationship. Moreover, their tongues were operated on 'despite uncertainty among medical consultants as to whether lingual mobility was an issue in their mutism' (Couser 2009: 69). Here one can begin to witness the abrasive responses to their socially intolerable silence. We return thus to the threatening unknowability of childhood that Shuttleworth identifies. The authorities' fierce reactions to June and Jennifer are marked by a clear need to make these girls 'normal' and thus bring them back within the comprehensible regime of consensus reality. Their shared refusal to participate in verbal dialogue appears to deafen those with duties of care towards June and Jennifer and prompts a series of interventions aimed to force them back to voice. The point here is not that no one should have intervened or made efforts to help the twins speak (their voluminous diaries testify to their profound desire to talk); rather, it is to reflect, as we move through this history and latterly the cultural works about the girls, as to whether what needed to be altered was the structures of both speaking and listening. The repeated attempts to invite the girls to speak via varied technologies of social participation (medical, creative, educative, and so on) failed to set up conditions that might enable such participation and instead perpetuated the terms of exclusion. Indeed, as Sara Ahmed writes in her discussion of Derrida's *On Hospitality*, '[w]hen participation depends on an invitation, then participation becomes a condition or comes with conditions' (Ahmed 2014: 53). How might we, as a society, have afforded a more expansive field of communication and participation to enable June and Jennifer to move differently and independently through (and with) silence and voice? Could we have participated differently in their mute reality, rather than wrenching them back to the dominant system of speech? How might we have made participation unconditional?

The next significant development in the twins' lives was their transfer out of mainstream education at the age of 14 to Eastgate Centre for Special Education, where they worked extensively with their teacher Cathy Arthur. The work ranged from crafts to excursions to psychological testing to therapy to the secret observation of the girls playing together. Experiments with separation were also conducted by staff with wretched results for the twins' personal well-being and health.[5] After school was over, June and Jennifer signed on the dole and retreated more completely into the private realm of their bedroom and disappeared into a fantasy world of dolls, creative writing and play. Both kept diaries and together recorded plays, cookery programmes, mini-dramas and so forth. They engaged in correspondence courses, including one entitled 'The Art of Conversation'. Drawing heavily on Americanised teen schlock, they created fictive worlds of peculiar romance and melodrama. However, the rhetoric and behaviours of their fictional imaginations washed into reality as June and Jennifer became involved with a small family of (American) boys who introduced them to drugs, alcohol, arson, and sex. And despite the boys' open antipathy and physical violence towards both girls, the twins described their encounters with romantic zeal:

> The thought of leaving you sends shudders of fear and sadness through me. Even though we are enemies, you are the boy who broke my virginity. Carl Christopher Kennedy, I sucked your penis and you entered me. I thank you for hurting me when you did. My happiness will only come when I get to touch you once more…you will stay in my heart forever. (June, qtd in Wallace 2014: 112)

For a while, it appears that the drugs, booze and fire functioned as ways of loosening the stranglehold of silence that each twin had locked the other in: 'I don't crave for it [alcohol]; I just use it to help me be more social' (June, qtd in Wallace 2014: 125). Moreover, analysing her dreams of fire Jennifer writes '*Fire:* desire for escape' (Jennifer, qtd in Wallace 2014: 83). After the boys left to return to North America that summer, June and Jennifer conducted a five-week-long miniature spree of petty crime and eventually were caught and charged with arson. These transgressive antisocial actions were read simply as criminal rather than a crooked attempt at social dialogue. Could the authorities have listened to these paradoxical acts of social participation differently? Indeed, far from being straightforward gestures of antisocial disobedience, it is perhaps valuable to conceive of these actions as precisely attempts to 'join in'. Vitally, I am not proposing a simplistic 'cry for help' narrative; rather, I wish to underscore how far the meaning of the twins' behaviour is shot through with normative adult readings (criminality, pathology, insolence). Aberrant behaviour here is a protruding arm to be beaten back beneath the surface as opposed to being held and helped to stand back up. If participation is not simply an action but also demands recognition as such, if it is dialogic in this way, one wonders how far the manners in which the twins' behaviours were read were as significant as what they did. Moreover, what is (in)audible within such social discourses (legal, medical, educational)? To put it another way, to what extent were June and Jennifer opted out?

The final stage of the twins' shared story begins in Pucklechurch Remand Centre and ends at Broadmoor Hospital. On 10 November 1981 June and Jennifer, now 18, were remanded in custody for burglary, arson and theft – they had stolen, among other minor items, a 'carton of Play-Doh', a 'half-eaten packet of polo mints' and a 'quantity of keys' (Wallace 2014: 201, 137, 202). During their stay at Pucklechurch, the girls' 'non-participation' was, once again, intolerable: '[they] caused havoc, not by any overt misbehaviour but by their increasing resistance to the regime' (Wallace 2014: 151). Yet simultaneously their longing to join in raged in their writing. June's diary describes it: 'watching life go by, wanting desperately to participate and not being able to, this everlasting feeling of being cut off' (June qtd in Wallace 2010: 156). The governor of the Remand Centre, however, assured the twins that their obstinacy, ultimately, would not triumph over societal norms: 'It [society] will win in the end. If you want to live in this world, then you must accept its conventions' (Governor, qtd in Wallace 2014: 192). Here we encounter the moral strain that snakes through the authorities' responses to the twins' behaviour. Their silence is read as a choice. And on the one hand, it is: they can, theoretically, speak. On the other, however, verbal participation is entirely impossible in the world they experienced. Thus, June and Jennifer come to be suspended between adult narratives of being either simply bloody-minded or pathologically different, between being bad or mad. The twins remained here for months, awaiting trial and psychiatric assessment. In the end, they were assessed by only one psychiatrist, who determined that they were both psychopaths who needed to be detained indefinitely at Broadmoor Hospital – a hospital of the highest level of security possible in the UK forensic psychiatric system. June and Jennifer would spend the next 12 years in Broadmoor. As Wallace observes, 'it was difficult to ignore the irony of locking a girl whose main offence against society was being mute and withdrawn into a silent cell' (Wallace 2014: 192).[6] During this time, both June and Jennifer were subject to a wide variety of treatments and latterly diagnosed as schizophrenic.[7] Despite the prosecution's having used their diaries as proof to help with their conviction, their psychiatrist, Dr Le Couteur, never read a single word of their writing.[8] The nurses had said that their diaries were 'fantasies and obscenities', and so Le Couteur reasoned, '[i]f they want to talk to me, I'll listen. But I'm not going to waste time' (Le Couteur, qtd in Wallace 2014: 252). There was some overall progress in their communication skills at Broadmoor but one wonders about the cost given that the twins were subject to a heavy pharmacological regime and still faced signifi-cant psychological challenges when they were deemed ready to leave the hospital (quite apart from the life-long legacies of spending their entire twenties at Broadmoor). Shortly before discharge, June wrote: 'I am taking thirteen tablets every day which to me is unnecessary, but to the doctors vital. They have left me here so long a part of me has died. Yes, we have both suffered' (June, qtd in Wallace 2014: 263). After 12 years in Broadmoor, on Tuesday, 9 March 1993, the twins were transferred to a medium secure unit. Jennifer died that same day from a rare, but rarely fatal, inflammation of the heart called myocarditis.[9] June spent a further year as the Caswell Clinic and was finally released in 1994. Speaking at the time of her discharge, June was asked how she felt about everything that had happened. She replied, 'one big mess'. She concluded by saying that she was still a twin: 'I was born a twin and I will die a twin' (June, qtd in Lichtenstein 1994: np). June currently lives independently and without any psychiatric treatment in West Wales.

'Vulnerable as flowers in hell'[10]

June and Jennifer's unusual shared story has captured the imagination of many. Twins, and particularly identical twins, often arouse social and artistic curiosity. Indeed, Juliana De Nooy's study *Twins in Contemporary*

Literature and Culture notes the mythological and metaphorical qualities of twin tales:

> It is not by chance that these studies of literary doubles are predominantly psychoanalytical: the topic of twins and doubles appear made to order for a psychoanalytic reading, with its easy links to the mirror stage, narcissism, the uncanny, separation anxiety, sibling rivalry, the false self, projection of the unconscious, and exteriorisation of inner conflict. (De Nooy 2005: 2)

She continues and highlights how twins are also frequently put at the service of myriad notions of difference: 'any figure of the Other (another ethnicity, gender, class, sexuality) and any duality, and to explore nature/nurture debates in any field' (De Nooy 2005: 4). I would suggest that one might add questions about the performativity of identity to De Nooy's list. Identical twins disturb the habitual traffic between self and other. Moreover, they appear to unsettle the notion of autonomy that lies at the heart of contemporary discourses of selfhood. The visual double exposure that twins present also serves to relocate ideas of 'nature' front and centre. It is perhaps unsurprising then that June and Jennifer's tale of pathological sameness has found repeated theatrical form. However, it is the contention of this chapter that, while multiple artists have sought to creatively communicate their story (with varied merit), none has managed to overcome the tendency to fill their silence with noise. Whether through song, voice-over or narrative, the cultural works about the twins have tended to colour in their blanks with explanatory hues. This not only serves to replicate the dichotomy of silence/voice that shaped their historic 'treatments' but, moreover, over-determines their story in ways that erases the complexity of the challenge that silence poses to the meaning and the terms of participation and social value. At root, these works tend to re-silence the twins by tidying away their mess:

> I am immune from sanity or insanity
> I am an empty present box: all
> unwrapped for someone else's disposal.
> I am thrown away egg-shell,
> With no life inside me, for I am
> not touchable, but a slave to nothingness.
> I feel nothing, I have nothing, for I am
> transparent to life; I am a silver
> streamer on a balloon; a balloon
> which will fly away without any

oxygen insider. I feel nothing,
for I am nothing, but I can
see the world from up here.[11]

To date there have been a number of artworks created about the twins. There are two TV works: *The Silent Twins* (1986), a docudrama directed by Jon Amiel based on Wallace's biography, and a BBC documentary directed by Olivia Lichtenstein entitled *Silent Twin: Without My Shadow* (1994). The band *Manic Street Preachers* released a song on their 1999 album *This Is My Truth Tell Me Yours* called 'Tsunami'. Luke Haines also named a track 'Discomania' (inspired by Jennifer's novel) on his 2001 album, *The Oliver Twist Manifesto*. Two operas have been composed about June and Jennifer: a French rock opera *Jumelles* (1992); and a British opera *The Silent Twins* (2007).[12] Finally, a number of plays have been written, including Seth Bockley and Devon De Mayo's *The Twins Would Like to Say* (2010), and Linda Brogan and Polly Teale's *Speechless* (2010).[13] It is this latter play that will form the focus of the discussion. Brogan and Teale's play offers a sympathetic and faithful account of a period in June and Jennifer's lives and attempts to communicate the stultifying racial pressures exerted upon these two young women. It offers creative responses to the challenge of staging mute lives through movement and voice-over. However, there are a number of problems that remain unsolved at the play's close, with respect to the very act of telling this tale, and moreover, telling it theatrically. The remainder of this chapter will turn then to discuss the following questions. First, what happens when you press a story of silence into a text-led form? Second, how far do the theatrical strategies that Brogan and Teale use to ventriloquize the twins' history replicate the failures of listening that marked the twins' lives? Third, how can a form such as theatre, which amplifies dynamics of social participation in its very structure, accommodate the complexity of June and Jennifer's steadfast refusal to join in? Or, to put it another way, what pressure does the social form of theatre exert upon their apparently antisocial story? Finally, how are we the audience invited to participate in their story as spectators? How does my creative participation in their story as an audience member amplify or mute their tale? In short, what and how does silence mean in *Speechless?*

Shadow play

Speechless premiered at the Traverse Theatre during the 2010 Edinburgh Fringe Festival. Inspired by Wallace's biography, the play was written by Linda Brogan and Polly Teale with the theatre company Shared

Experience.[14] The piece explores the period in June and Jennifer's life from Eastgate Centre to their arrival in Broadmoor. The play was very well received by critics and won a Fringe First Award. Lyn Gardner found that '[t]he power of *Speechless* is that it gives these young women a voice' (Gardner 2010). Michael Coveney described it as 'a story of stunning and stark oddness…brilliant, bleak, but redemptive' (Coveney 2010). Gina Allum, echoing Gardner, noted that a real strength of the production lies in the clarity of the twins' voices: 'The play skirts the issue of the twins' private idiom, their dialect of two, and we understand them perfectly (when they are alone) as articulate girls, with writerly aspirations' (Allum 2010). What the reviewers value is that the play affords generosity towards June and Jennifer and that it attempts to make their silence sing. The empathetic approach of the dramatists to the girls' story allows us to better understand their heretofore private world. Rather than exoticising their history through spectacular gestures of unknowability and enfreakment, the play (for many) made their oddity somewhat more legible and quotidian. This is a significant decision if one reflects on Petra Kuppers' observation that 'mad' bodies on stage are all too often frantically Other, thereby leaving an audience to 'read for symptoms of inner states' (2003: 134). Indeed, if stage madness is all too often Day-Glo bright in its portraits of alternative mental experiences, the decision to cast a warm light around June and Jennifer's ordinariness is a marked political choice.

Speechless appears to disrupt the diagnostic gaze in this way. In this portrait of the twins, if one peels back the outward veil of silence, an audience hears familiar strains of sisterly strife, top of the pops, crinkle-cut chips and teen romance set amid a fraught social context of racial inequality. There is much value and political purpose in the playwrights' decisions to 'give voice' to June and Jennifer in order that their tale be heard. However, in the pursuit of conferring ordinary dignity and personhood upon the twins, the play relies on a causal dramaturgical structure and overwrought narrative of racial and gender politics that actually serves to paper over their silence (to say nothing of the vexed issue of normalisation and 'passing'). I am not suggesting here that I know the *real* reason June and Jennifer stopped speaking and that the play has simply 'got it wrong'; rather, I am drawing attention to the fact that the very gesture of giving voice may, paradoxically, silence. Moreover, I am asking if the pursuit of 'why' they do not talk is necessarily bonded to a reification of fixed modes of communication and a tacit need to make them talk. Indeed, perhaps, nested within the desire to crack the enigma of their silence lies a need to sustain the silence/voice binary, instead of expanding our structures and manners of listening properly to others. I am also not here romanticising their silence as a countercultural gesture of deliberate nonconformity that ought to be celebrated – the twins, according to their writings, generally loathed their mute state. And certainly, their story is race-marked, gender-marked and, importantly, class-marked (an often overlooked aspect of their biography). However, I am interested in examining further how far *Speechless* restages established modes of listening and seeks to make *them* understandable to *us* as opposed to asking us to retune our ears. Indeed, as Dee Heddon argues elsewhere in this book, it is urgent that we radically expand the notion and practices of listening carefully to others.

You are Jennifer. You are me.[15]

Muteness poses a particular theatrical conundrum. How does a playwright tell a silent story on stage? Or more specifically, how does one tell this silent story on stage without re-cocooning June and Jennifer in a muffled, strange fog? This is a conundrum that is further complicated by the representation of childhood. There is a doubled act of ventriloquism at play here insofar as adult bodies are giving voice to silent children. One partial answer to these issues of representation appears to emerge through the archive. As Wallace writes, '[w]hat I discovered was that June and Jennifer, physically rigid, did all their dancing in words' (Wallace 2008: 279). Couser similarly argues that the twins used their writing as a means of splitting from the tyranny of sameness that dogged their day-to-day lives. If the twins were persistently treated as a single unit, 'the diaries exert the will of autonomy and individuation in furious, prolific manners. They write their separateness'(Couser 2009: 81). Given that the twins captured their lives in prose, it appears logical that their diaries ought to animate the stage. They appear to offer a transparent means of articulating private lives. *Speechless* makes extensive use of verbatim voice-over from June and Jennifer's diaries, frequently acting as scene-ends:

> **JUNE** *I blame the daffodils. Who wants to hear summery sounds? Not me. I hate summer. The same old outings, happy people going on long-planned holidays. Children sucking ice cream, pregnant women wearing blousey dresses. Why can't it be winter the whole year round? Do we really need summer?*
>
> *Lights change.* (June, qtd in Brogan and Teale 2010: 17, emphasis original)

The voice-overs serve a double function here as both authentication and explanation. One can perceive here the promise of authenticity that

Janelle Reinelt identified in relation to documentary theatre practices more generally.[16] The framing of the play as a true story renders any 'real' words burly in their authority, but also the diary entries' location at the conclusion of scene positions them to retroactively comment on what has passed in a quasi-omniscient manner. However, the argument that the dramatists are simply 'telling it like it was' immediately flounders if one accepts that in fact there is a double (if not triple) intervention here.[17] As Cathy Caruth intimates, any incursion into the archive necessitates mediation: 'The encounter with the archive is thus an act of interpretation that appears like a return, but it is also an event that partially represses, as it passes on, the inscriptions it encounters; that passes on not only an impression but also, somewhat differently, its repression' (Caruth 2013: 78). Not only are Brogan and Teale delving into the archive, but they are also engaged in an act of representation that is scored with decisions and omissions, that is scored with repression. Thus, while the diary entries appear to offer a theatrical strategy to unzip the 'real' tale for an audience, one ought to caution against the consequences of positioning us as spectators, in this manner. The opening line of the play assures unparalleled access to truth: *First of all, let's get things straight: nobody knows us really. All these things you say about us are wrong* (June, qtd in Brogan and Teale 2010: 3, original emphasis). One may want to read this moment of voice-over as precisely framing the instability of the narrator, but the voice-over format amplifies its authority as emanating from within the authentic origin of the tale. The question here is how far the strategy of voice-over privileges an audience to *understand* June and Jennifer's story (in contradistinction to most people in their lives) without ever challenging us to think differently about voice, silence, listening or how we respond to difference. Indeed, we are never invited to experience the fullness of their silence, because it is always retranslated back to us in our own tongue. June and Jennifer's life history was marked by an enduring and systemic failure of listening. *Speechless*, I suggest, through its use of voice-over and allowing us inside the belly of the twins' muteness, prevents a more nuanced encounter with radical non-participation. As an audience member, I am permitted to perceive other's failures of understanding while being reassured that, to a degree, *I* understand via listening to the truth-telling diary. However, the play poses no challenge whatsoever to me with respect to how I might listen and participate in alternative ways of being and communicating. In this way, the piece inevitably replicates consensus reality and established horizons of dialogue and experience. Alterity in *Speechless* is explained to me and for me, rather than examining the structures and conditions of inclusion and exclusion and asking if they are humane. In this way, the play sustains the very terms of social participation that excluded June and Jennifer in the first place.

The second scene of the play is a violent but profoundly moving scene of movement. We witness the twins stalk, tussle, embrace and suffocate one another in silence. The scene is described as having 'the quality of a nightmare although it is in fact happening' (Brogan and Teale 2010: 4). The desperate choreography allows one to perceive the intensity and complexity of the struggle without recourse to narrative. This scene is immediately followed by one in which we hear a psychiatrist ask a series of unhelpful and reductive questions in ways that are redolent of the psychiatric dialogue in Sarah Kane's *4.48 Psychosis*. Instead of Kane's 'Did it relieve the tension?' we hear Brogan and Teale's 'Why did you stop talking to us?' (Kane 2001: 216; Brogan and Teale 2010: 6). Kane and Brogan and Teale offer useful critiques of the marked limits of psychiatric assessment. In both plays what is claimed as dialogue is in fact a monologic set of questions aimed to produce a set of responses that can be measured according to pre-existing norms and assumptions. The psychiatric encounter in *Speechless* also serves a simply expository function. However, the play's dramaturgy complicates the clarity of the interrogation that is mounted regarding the inadequacy of our collective response to nonconformity. The psychiatrist's question – 'Why did you stop talking to us?' – is immediately followed by this:

The sound of children's voices shouting at a deafening pitch.

JUNE *and* JENNIFER *stand facing one another, with one arm cradled above their heads, like wounded birds trying to protect themselves…*

Amidst the shouting are racist taunts and references to the TWINS' *strange speech. They are told to 'Go back to the jungle' and 'learn to speak English'. We hear the words 'wog', 'sambo', 'nignog'.* (Brogan and Teale 2010: 7)

There is a causal structure at play here that is reductive. The dramaturgical logic is that racism was the root cause of their mutism. There can be no doubt that the racist bullying that the twins experienced had a very significant impact on their shared decision to remain silent. However, to render it *the* determining factor once again explains away the complexity of the story and bypasses the fundamental challenge to social meaning-making that is posed by their silence.

The framing of their mute lives as a consequence of racial inequality is embedded not only in the dramaturgy but also in the somewhat heavy-handed contextual framing of the piece as set against the Brixton riots and Lady Di's wedding, and the preface by Yasmin Alibhai Brown:

> For a minority disillusionment [with the hopes of Windrush immigration] led to anger which was either internalised – leading to mental chaos – or externalised, acted out in crimes and acts of destruction. In the Gibbons family, you witness the range from denial to destruction. The father, mother and children incarnate different reactions, as characters do on stage in the great tragedies. ... Theirs, arguably, is a potted black history of those times. ... Their personal tragedy flashes blinding light on the political and social landscape of the time and of post-war immigration. (Brown, qtd in Brogan and Teale 2010)

Alibhai Brown is careful to note that this is a dual tale of private grief and public politics and suggests that one needs 'bifocal vision' to understand the twins' story (Brown, qtd in Brogan and Teale 2010). Alibhai Brown's framing of the twins as paradigmatic or emblematic in ways also underscores De Nooy's earlier concern regarding the tendency to culturally read twins as metaphor. However, the point is absolutely not to diminish the unquestionably vital role of racism for this tale of desperate social isolation; rather, I am suggesting that by placing this so front and centre, alongside the explanatory mechanisms noted above, one casts the twins in a neat, digestible form without agency or nuance. The logic of both the play and its framing argues *this is why* in some unhelpful manners.

One sees this explanatory structure echoed again at the play's conclusion. The twin's arson is dramaturgically framed as a direct consequence of Kennedy's influence: his burning of their diaries forms a visual precursor of their final act of fire: '*They toss them* [Barbie's outfits] *onto the pyre as* JUNE *throws vodka onto the flames*' (Brogan and Teale 2010: 61). Again there is some truth to this, but once again it positions the twins as passive victims in their own all too easily explainable tale. Furthermore, by changing the location of the twins' actual arson to their secondary school, Brogan and Teale amplify the causal narrative through a motif of (erroneous) revenge: 'We've burned down Sir Thomas Picton Secondary Modern' (2010: 61).[18] The dramaturgy and extra-theatrical framing thus serve to subtitle the twins' silence with a clear message: racist and sexual violence caused their mutism and crimes. And perhaps it did. Or perhaps it was just their shyness, or their schizophrenia, or their psychopathy or Jennifer's supernatural forces. However, focusing on why they 'did it' absolves us of the question of why we as a society could not hold their experiences more safely or humanely. We become, in this way, the mother from Grimm's tale, hammering an arm we cannot or will not grasp until it is back out of sight.

The final explanatory note that the play strikes is around the question of trauma – a familiar figure in mute stories. As Sara R. Horowitz writes in relation to Holocaust fiction, '[i]n survivor writing the trope of muteness functions as an index of trauma, which both compels and disables testimony' (Horowitz 1997: 30). The bullying, the socio-political landscape and Kennedy's raping of the twins are understood through a prism of trauma that translates their silences into a register of unsayability.[19] For example, the celebratory hoots of Gloria Gibbons at Lady Di's wedding dress pearls is carefully juxtaposed with the bleak sexual violence of Kennedy's abuse of the twins in order to underscore the tragic and unwitnessed affliction of June and Jennifer's situation. Again, the twins, like the Grimm's arm, tacitly call out to be witnessed, but their voices are buried alive:

> GLORIA Here she come! Here she come! Out onto the balcony of Buckingham Palace! Oh my goodness.
>
> …
>
> *While* GLORIA *speaks*, KENNEDY *climbs on top of* JENNIFER *and shags her.*
>
> JUNE *watches, paralysed with rage and jealousy.*
>
> KENNEDY *cums and climbs off.*
>
> *The* TWINS fight. (Brogan and Teale 2010: 58)

However, here again the play abolishes silence. Horowitz discusses how far mutism invites us to think about what has been omitted and censored. *Speechless* fills the silence with causal noise and narrative. The secret verbiage is made to disclose their story amid a landscape of violent social dispossession. However, not only were June and Jennifer not heard because they did not speak; they were not heard because we did not find a way to listen to or to sit kindly with their silence. In her discussion of Ariel Dorfmann's *Death and the Maiden* and with respect to listening to pain, Caruth argues that '*in the performance of the very act of listening*' we pass on 'the evidence of an event that can no longer be reduced to the simple referent of any language' (2013: 71, original emphasis). Caruth, here, underscores both how far listening exceeds language and also is not a singular action or experience. It is the contention of this chapter, then, that the collapsing of their silence into voice and narrative explanation in *Speechless* fails to engage with the fundamental challenge that silence poses to language. Silence brings into question language's very capacity for meaning-making. Silence marks a radical rejection of established codes of social value and understanding insofar as it troubles the fundaments of our sense-making capacities. Indeed, it brings into doubt – marked by death as it is – the essential value of acts of social participation. June and Jennifer's radical non-participation, therefore, corrodes the stability and values of the strategies and structures of ordinary communication and normalcy. Non-participation is intolerable in part because it exposes the absurdity of joining in. Non-participation, like suicide, can be felt as an affront because it tacitly asks: what on earth are we doing? And why on earth are we doing it? Again this is not to 'read' the twins' gesture of silence as a deliberate act of political resistance or suicidal ideation; rather, it is simply to attempt to redirect the traffic from examining why they did not speak and towards why we could not listen. In short, I propose that in making the silent twins speak, *Speechless* risks further deadening our capacity to empathetically embrace non-normative experience.

What are you trying to say?

In one of the early scenes of the play, one hears the following exchange:

GLORIA	See them there.
	Standing amongst all the other children in the
	class. Eleven, twelve, thirteen, them always the
	only coloured children in the picture. [...]
	Me look at the photographs.
	Each year it getting worse.
	Them favour ghost while the other children thrive.
HEADMISTRESS	I'm sorry, Mrs Gibbons, but I'm not sure what
	you're trying to say. (Brogan and Teale 2010: 9)

The play here, and elsewhere, is keenly alive to the numerous involuntary acts of non-participation that shape the girls' lives. The twins do not simply opt out; they are opted out. Their multiple social exclusions on the grounds of race, gender, silence, age, class and to a certain extent twinhood are made luminous in the play. Moreover, from an audience's privileged theatrical vantage point, audience members are able to lean into the muteness and thereby hear its melancholic refrains of ordinary voices lost in extraordinary silence. *Speechless* also captures the claustrophobia of their quicksand intimacy through its inventive staging that confines the actors in closeted spaces that collapse into one another. However, the compression and adaptation of Wallace's biography creates a set of theatrical impressions and repressions that I suggest are detrimental to the telling of this tale. It is the central argument of this chapter that *Speechless*, in its desire to give voice and understand the silence, re-mutes June and Jennifer. Its causal dramaturgy, deployment of voice-over, positioning of its audience and deliberate foregrounding of pertinent social politics cumulatively fill in all the blanks and thereby explain away the void. In so doing, the play places no demands on its audience to examine how far the manners in which they are being asked to listen might replicate the strategies of listening and communication that led to June and Jennifer's tumbling through 12 years in Broadmoor. In these ways, *Speechless* reaffirms the values of normative social participation and forgets to consider the radical value and meaning of opting out.

The purpose of these pages is to not to exonerate June and Jennifer; nor is it to glorify or romanticise their silence. I am concerned instead to examine representations of their lives in order to ask how we as a society listen and thereby consider what structures and conditions audibility. The chapter argues that their silence challenges us to examine the embedded values and hierarchies of participation. Indeed, rather than understanding them as simply not participating, I propose that we need to re-evaluate the political terms of social participation. June and Jennifer's profound vocal non-participation was, in many ways, a personal catastrophe for each of them. However, rather than burrowing further into the dominant individualised psychological examination of *why* they did not talk to most people, the challenge is to think about *how* we might create expanded models of communication that can embrace alterity. The catastrophic consequences sprang forth not only because they were silent but because they were silenced. Theatre's capacity to curve one's perceptions around hard edges marks its political capacity. To translate silence back into voice and difference into sameness thus re-establishes a constraining grid-system of orthodox thinking. In this way, audiences fail to look around corners or hear the noise in silence. By sustaining the dominant structures of listening and understanding, *Speechless* missed an opportunity to allow an audience to participate in a reimagining of perceptual and political realities. Indeed, by leaving an audience bonded to an ordinary contract of listening, we mute the possibility of alternative dialogues. This chapter suggests that it is only by hearing 'non-participation' on its own terms that we can begin to interrogate the political conditions and values of opting in.

Endnotes

1. This is the title of the main biography of the twins, written by Marjorie Wallace and based on the twins' diaries and Wallace's time with them during visits to Broadmoor. See Marjorie Wallace, *The Silent Twins*, rev'd edn (London: Vintage, 2008). *The Silent Twins* is also the title of an opera by Errollyn Wallen with libretto from April De Angelis as well as the title of a BBC docudrama first aired on 19 January 1986, both of which were inspired by Wallace's biography.
2. June Gibbons, quoted in Wallace, *The Silent Twins*, p. 25.
3. Interestingly, Gloria did not think that the twins were identical until they reached their twenties.
4. I am drawing heavily from Wallace's work here the key source of information about their early life.
5. There is a much more detailed story to be told about June and Jennifer's biography, but this is beyond the scope of this chapter. See Wallace's biography for a fuller account. I also recognise here that I am tending to collapse the two individuals into one by referring to 'the twins' as though their experiences were interchangeable, which of course they were not. For a good discussion of each twin's separateness, as well as the ethics of Wallace's biographical approach, see Couser.
6. The twins were, of course, not kept in solitary throughout their time at Broadmoor. I take Wallace's point here to refer to the broader regime of detention and social isolation.
7. Wallace and others have questioned this diagnosis. See p. 262.
8. Le Couteur was the RMO [Resident Medical Officer] for the female wing at Broadmoor.
9. Jennifer had, in the weeks leading up to her death, told June and Marjorie that she knew she was going to die.
10. June, describing herself and Jennifer, in Wallace, p. 225.
11. June, from one of her 'September Poems' in Wallace, p. 251.
12. The latter featured a libretto written by April De Angelis and was first performed at The Almeida.
13. There are other unpublished plays that appear to be inspired by the twins' tales, such as Vanessa Walter's *Double Take*. The twins are also represented in a number of other works including a self-published collection of ghoulish photography that renders the twins freaks: Al W. Blue II, *Book of Strange Medical Oddities and Post Mortem Photography* (Create Space Publishing, 2014).
14. Interestingly, in 2005 Teale wrote *Brontë* about the Brontë sisters – another piece about sisters writing their passionate literature in stark isolation.
15. Linda Brogan and Polly Teale, 'Jelly Babies', *Speechless* (London: Nick Hern Books, 2010), p. 26.
16. See Janelle Reinelt, 'The Promise of Documentary' in Alyson Forsythe and Chris Megson (eds), *Get Real: Documentary Theatre Past and Present* (Basingstoke: Palgrave, 2009), pp. 6–23.

17. I say triple here as Brogan and Teale are reliant on an already mediated intervention insofar as they rely so heavily on Wallace's biography. I too, therefore, must acknowledge that this chapter is similarly culpable of the mechanisms of impression and repressions that Caruth signals.

18. The twins did set fire to a number of schools, colleges and civic buildings. However, as far as I am aware, they did not set fire to their own secondary school.

19. While some may argue that the twins consent to Kennedy's sexual demands, I would contend that the twins are coerced into sex in ways that complicate notions of consent.

5   Participation, Recognition and Political Space

Colette Conroy

It's cold and I am wearing a bin bag. It is early morning on the last Saturday in October. It is raining and there is a stiff breeze. We are in North Wales, just outside the Snowdonia slate mining town of Llanberis. Five hundred adults are dressed in shorts or running tights. Cold flesh and goose bumps. Rummaging in waist packs, drinking sports drinks. There is a strong smell of Deep Heat and the sound of nervous chatter and laughter. There is a man with a megaphone engaging in banter with somebody, but I can only hear his amplified part of the conversation. Small groups of people are gathering in running club groups, their coloured vests identify the club and the place of origin. The road has been closed, the army cadets are stationed around the route at drink stations. There is even a crowd – friends, spouses, children, injured club mates, baleful dogs on leads. In a moment the gun will fire and there will be a cheer and the marathon will start.

For the next four hours or so, I will be running around the highest mountain in Wales in company with the driving rain and the crowd of runners. I will be towards the back, sometimes chatting with other runners, sometimes simply absorbed in the gentle forward momentum, or watching the water stream down gullies in the mountains. After 17 miles, my legs will hurt. I will get irrationally grumpy, and I will remember that of all things in the world, I hate running marathons the most. The last two miles will be one single intense and happy moment when I let my legs descend the mountain on their own. I'll hear the Tannoy in the village down below. I will unhook my brain and enjoy the relationship between the run and the finish line, tiredness and delight, flow and adrenaline. The intensity of this pleasure draws me back again and again.

The process of discussing the marathon through the frame of performance studies is fairly commonplace. For me, the process of thinking in public about marathon running draws me closer to understanding some of the difficulties of making participatory artwork. Marathon running also stretches my mind towards the notion that participation is bound up in notions of politics and the political, and even that these abstract and contested notions may touch upon the problems of embodiment and individualism and the ways in which the individual life may be thought about in political terms, in amongst all these abstractions.

As part of my critical method, I consider my example modes of participation through the frame of disability performance analysis. This is not always explicit: it forms the silent core of the way I think. My readings of physical alterity come from long-standing engagements with disability cultural studies. I hope that my reasons for using disability cultural perspectives come to make sense as the chapter proceeds, but it might help if you bear in mind that I see disability cultural practices as exemplary rather than exceptional, as a way to think about bodies and embodiment. It might even make sense to wish that we could *disable* theatre and performance studies, the better to understand notions of subjectivity and alterity in performance by interrupting *(disabling?)* the undoubtedly ideological notions of bodies and the body, selves and the self. I even wonder whether it is helpful to think of disability as a sort of disavowed core of theatre and performance studies and as a way of making explicit the dynamics of politics and aesthetics in participatory theatre. (Disability is a black hole of specificity: it packs a huge theoretical punch, but we may not use it to talk about other aspects of our subject area in case its specificity sticks. I would like to help to shift this.) Finally, I am deliberately choosing to ignore the distinction between art and not-art. Helped hugely by the freedom that performance studies offers to look at events as performance, I am looking through the same frame at participatory sport and participatory art, in search of the pleasures and conceptual problems of both.

Agonistics

In Chantal Mouffe's 2013 book, *Agonistics: Thinking the World Politically*, she sees the ineradicable dimension of 'the political' as an intrinsic aspect of society (2013). The political is the area where antagonism is enacted. Politics is an ensemble of practices and discourses that seek to establish a certain order for human coexistence (2013: 2). Politics is also concerned exclusively with collective identities and is the realm where a social group seeks dominance or hegemony through agonism (struggles between adversaries) or antagonism (struggles between enemies). Mouffe's work asks about the uses and functions of social institutions as potential spaces where agonism can emerge. The emergence of a common cause is crucial for politics. Political identity is oppositional and relational. The evolution of consensus or unanimity is problematic for Mouffe: The constitution of 'we' involves the demarcation of 'they' (2013: 5).

Mouffe follows Antonio Gramsci in arguing for the centrality of cultural and artistic practices in the formation and diffusion of 'common sense' (and its role in relation to making and maintaining hegemony) (2013: 89). She sees a connection between cultural practices and the political in a way that points towards the dialectical structuring of consciousness and the role of imagination in the foundation of the notion of selfhood:

> Critical arts foster practices through which specific forms of individualities are constructed. To construct oppositional identities, it is not enough to simply foster a process of deidentification. (2013: 93)

Mouffe points towards the political possibilities of pleasurable interactions, to crowds that appear together through choice and in the pursuit of pleasure. She specifically offers the argument that large-scale events that create public interaction (not unanimity, not consensus) give a valuable model for the 'self-organization of the Multitude' (2013: 99).

The structural and conventional elements of the marathon rely on the chosen adoption of the values of amateur athletics – ideas about competition and mass participation, about sporting behaviour and convivial relations between runners. For Mouffe, institutions are an important terrain of struggle (2013: 94), which is not to say that running clubs and organisations are inherently radical or political, but to emphasise that the engagement of individuals in these structures has a value to the establishment of agonistic space.

Running is a discourse, subject to discussion, training, self-awareness. It can exist only through practice. It has an elaborated culture of organisation and competition which makes a basic physical activity into a complex event with multiple social meanings. Cultural running or running cultures give meaning and intensify the pleasures of the activity. It provides the occasion for interaction, cooperation and competition. It would be a mistake to argue that running is a radical cultural form though, any more than I could say the same about theatre or performance. If politics is a space created for the enactment of antagonism, then perhaps the act of stopping the traffic for the London marathon can be seen as (partially and ambiguously) political. Or the New Orleans marathon, run as an assertion of hope for the city's regeneration after Hurricane Katrina. These are organisational claims for space, and in the case of big city marathons, this space is bought from the city, with the runners' fees and sponsorship deals buying five or six hours of non-prime time on the city's roads on a Sunday morning.

On an individual level, we would usually assume that running in a marathon is not political, except for those occasions when somebody qualifies unexpectedly or is the first person from a specific group to run the race, or whatever. Perhaps there must be a performance of alterity if it is to appear as political, and that creates a specific regime of political articulation. Kathrine Switzer's participation in the 1967 Boston Marathon is one example of an obviously political act of marathon participation, made explicit to subsequent generations of runners through the photographs of the attempts made to push Switzer off the course, as well as the support and the solidarity of the male runners who surrounded her and so enabled her to finish her marathon despite the race officials' attempts to physically stop her.[1] The running of a race counters the claim that you cannot run. It does so publicly; it claims space and duration. But it might go no further. The 2013 Boston Marathon opened up the realisation that marathons were targets for terrorist attacks; the presence of vulnerable and disorientated bodies in shorts and vests at the scene of the bombing underlined the 'softness' of the target. The 2014 Boston Marathon was a commemoration of the bombing, but it also realigned the confusion and panic of the previous year with an overt performance of defiance: the often explicit message was that marathon running is part of 'our way of life', and that runners run as a manifestation of the value and tenacity of Western liberalism. The race cannot be seen necessarily as a place of speech or articulation. One might see it as a place of mere appearance that can offer the 'beating of number' in the form of a crowd. Its politics reach the limits of its articulacy when the participating bodies are counted and assigned a type according to whatever representational schema is used. At this point, perspective becomes all-important, and it is necessary to start asking questions about the given or adopted perspective or perspectives through which we think, even about something as familiar as assembling to run a marathon.

What I am interested in chasing down for this chapter is the deeper levels on which we might look at running as a way of understanding the politics of participation. I'm concerned with the ways that individual and collective acts are made comprehensible to and by the individual. I'm also following Mouffe in attempting to find and resist the powerful narratives of unanimity and identity that arise on and through our bodies, despite our repeated best efforts.

When talking about running, people who do not run are often startled by how very slow my running is. They also worry about what I do with myself for over four hours (nearer five, if I'm honest) as I run slowly around a marathon course. What is the interest? The winner of the race will have nearly finished by the time I get to the half way point. It's not that I am not as good as a good runner; it's that I am having a completely different experience. What is the engagement? What is the purpose? Am I competing? Do I seriously think I will ever win? And if I cannot run as fast as Paula Radcliffe (and I can't – not even for ten seconds), what's the point? I would like to extend this analysis into a consideration of the pleasures and the politics of participation. What is the point of running without ever being competitive? If the pleasures of running are not related to competition, then why specifically run marathon races? Why not just go for an unpressurised run somewhere scenic? In this conversation, where I own up to the extreme slowness of my running, there is a struggle for a frame of interpretation. At some point, all the things we both know and experience come into contact with all the things we know about running, and there is a struggle to assimilate my slow and wholly talentless running body into this version of the world.

Onlookers and spectators

In performing this analysis and in putting my body at the centre of it, I am offering myself as a text for a very specific form of reading or misreading. I don't know of any other way to get at this problem. Marathon running creates a methodological problem when trying to write about it as performance. *There is no live spectator on the outside of the race.* There may be crowds and onlookers, but there is nobody with an overall vision of what is happening. There is, however, a culture of reception which finely discriminates between the different parts of the spectacle. In durational terms, the live onlookers will be able to appraise the race based on where they are standing – at which mile, for example. The meaning of what they see will be framed (or determined) by their knowledge of what time it is – that is, how long it has been since the starting gun. The process of watching the fatigue of mile 21 follow a wave from the fastest to the slowest is emotionally moving. The narrative structure of the race determines the most appealing perspective for the onlooker. Do you stand at the finish line? Or the top of a hill? Where will your loved one be looking for encouragement? The place to watch the marathon as an event is from the inside or on TV (but the TV construction of races is another essay altogether).

At the point that I start to develop this analysis, aspects of my body are presented as texts for reading to those outside the event. Since I cannot control the context of this reading, the event itself – and my body within this event – is likely to be seen in multiple ways. This is most acutely evident at times when I have been verbally abused or spat at as I ran. I can speculate (based on the utterances) that my gendered appearance or my stockiness, my skin or hair colouring, my disability or my age may each and variously provoke responses of fear or hatred. My younger brother also runs marathons but is much faster than I am. He has never received any form of abuse while running. Since I have seldom received derogatory comments while walking, I have to suppose that for a (not thin? disabled?) woman, the act of running in public space is still regarded by some as transgressive or threatening. I cannot really know this, only speculate based on my own reading of the appearance of my body in public space. This speculation about how we are perceived is part of a process of empathising with the onlooker, imagining then interiorising their perceptions.

A more detailed account of this convoluted, interiorised reading process in a recreational runner comes from the novelist Haruki Murakami. In his autobiographical work *What I Talk About When I Talk About Running*, he uses the bodies of young running women to muse upon thoughts about time and to speculate about the way that young women might look at him, a slower runner in his 50s:

> As I'm leisurely jogging along the Charles River, girls who look to be new Harvard freshmen keep on passing me. Most of these girls are small, slim, have on maroon Harvard-logo outfits, blond hair in a ponytail, and brand-new iPods, and they run like the wind. You can definitely feel a sort of aggressive challenge emanating from them. They seem to be used to passing people, and probably not used to being passed. They all look so bright, so healthy, attractive, and serious, brimming with self-confidence. With their long strides and strong, sharp kicks, it's easy to see that they're typical mid-distance runners, unsuited for long-distance running. They're more mentally cut out for brief runs at high speed.

> Compared to them I'm pretty used to losing. … Not to brag, but these girls probably don't know as much as I do about pain. And, quite naturally, there might not be a need for them to know it. These random thoughts come to me as I watch their proud ponytails swinging back and forth, their aggressive strides. Keeping to my own leisurely pace, I continue my run down along the Charles.

> Still, it's wonderful to watch these pretty girls run. As I do, I'm struck by an obvious thought: One generation takes over from the next. This is how things are handed over in this world, so I don't feel so bad if

they pass me. These girls have their own pace, their own sense of time. And I have my own pace, my own sense of time. The two are completely different, but that's the way it should be. (Murakami 2009: 93–94)

The reading of a series of socio-political dynamics from the body of another person and the extrapolation of this reading into a meaningful social relationship is, of course, crucial to the development of political space and political relationships, and so running permits me a way of thinking about problems of participation as political problems. Part of Murakami's experience of the social space of running comes from his anticipation of how he is regarded by the onlooker/fellow runner. His interpretation of 'these girls' anticipates their perception of him. His reading emerges from his own fatigue and a wish to assert superior powers of endurance. He insulates himself against the injurious effects of being 'passed' and dismissed as an older, slower man by creating a garbled dynamic of looking and knowing, recognising and misrecognising. His reading successfully builds for him superior endurance and the pleasures of watching 'pretty girls'.

The idea that an individual's reading of others is actually a reading of himself as perceived by another, and that this is a crucial part of the development of a sense of self, is not unfamiliar. It is described and elaborated both in psychoanalytic theory (the whole palaver about the introjection or notions of melancholia in Freud, perhaps) and in philosophy. To choose one example from many, Etienne Balibar sees individual consciousness as a dialectical entity:

Each responsible individual or person imagines a consciousness analogous to his own in the minds of others, in other words, consciousness is already the form of a virtual relation to others at the same time that it is actually the form of the relation to oneself. (Balibar 2013: 64)

The first principle of participation emerges for me: the pleasures and sensations of participation involve a speculative and imagined or imaginary relationship with others. At this point the onlooker or spectator has a form of power that fluctuates hugely, that is imprecise and possibly not knowable, but which is part of the embodied experience of the individual consciousness. The sensory world of running is founded on a consciousness that is relational and political. It has its origins both 'elsewhere' and in my own consciousness. The embodied experiences of running involve a dialectic between self and other, even when I am running alone or in a situation without onlookers. However, there is no possibility that the same cathartic experiences could be achieved in a training run. The formal structure of the event and the presence of the crowd give me the experience for which I train and prepare. Running a marathon is a dialogue with an onlooker, a process of profoundly experiencing my own consciousness as an imaginary relationship to others and to myself. The presence of onlookers (including myself) is crucial to this experience.

This is not restricted to participatory events. The consideration of the onlooker and their embodied experiences of the performance is crucial to this imagined dialectical relationship. I'd like to consider a theatre example. The queer performer Peggy Shaw created a work called *RUFF*, based on her experience of having a stroke. Shaw talks about the stroke as a way of clearing space, of focusing on the new and the newly important. In a post-show discussion, Shaw and director-collaborator Lois Weaver talked about their habitual DIY (do-it-yourself) approach, the idea of 'getting what you need' on the stage and of establishing the conditions for the watching of the work through close engagement with the audience and its culture (Shaw 2014). While the stroke has affected aspects of Shaw's memory, the whole performance is designed to make the form of the performance accessible to the performer through screens to navigate the text and the use of mnemonic prompts.

In the performance, Shaw speaks about the act of making the performance as a form of therapy or rehabilitation for her, as a way of getting well, and returning her body to what it liked to do. She also wanted to make a funny show about strokes. She doesn't like to merely talk about the stroke, because 'people have preconceived ideas' – performing her own show, under her own control enables her to develop a frame that demands that the audience laugh.

Shaw brings a bottle of water onto the stage and hands it to an audience member. She explains that she has a cough – a result of the stroke – and that she may need the water to be passed to her. 'It doesn't help my cough' she explains to the audience, 'but it might make you feel better'. Shaw empathises with the audience by imagining them empathising with her cough. The solution is an ineffective cure for the cough but an effective cure for the isolation of empathy. Unpacking this complex behaviour is a crucial part of the work of performance. This should not imply that Shaw thinks that the whole audience thinks as one. There is a strong possibility that the response to a cough is widely held, that most audience members will feel similar wishes to offer water or to soothe the cough. However, Shaw introduces this idea in advance of the exchange happening, and so the problem and its solution are offered together in a witty way that does not overburden the audience relationship with heavy-handed reading, but which cites what we know about empathy. We *may* feel this empathy and so gain the humour of Shaw's counter-empathic response.

Murakami and Shaw each offer an analysis of onlooker responses as a motivation for their participation and also as a dialectic that is articulated in performance. The disparity between the participant and the onlooker is explored, reversed and synthesised in a deft and pleasurable way by each of them. Carried by the figure of the newly disabled veteran performer or by the enduring older runner, the dynamics of identity are experienced as simultaneously claimed by the subject and attributed by the onlooker. These opposing dynamics are resolved and revealed to be crucial to the individual's performance. In these examples, and perhaps as a general principle of participation, the imaginary onlooker is part of the performance of the participating self.

The unmaking and remaking of empathy

If the relationship between participant and onlooker matters to this experience, I can also see that the participant could be injured by the dialogue. Or perhaps the participant may be already injured and performing an identity through the anticipation and incorporation of theorised or abstracted onlooker responses. As participant I contribute to this dialogue by imagining that the onlooker sees me in various injurious ways. The cultural value of bodies and identities exists as a working dynamic that takes more than assertiveness and willpower to alter. The dynamic and dialogic framing of bodies, perception and social value is an issue for individuals on all sorts of levels.

Access to public space and to political space requires the ability to appear and to claim certain sorts of meaning. Awareness that we are being 'seen as' pitiable or weak or unintelligent is a lesson we learn repeatedly through encounters with onlookers, and which takes multiple powerful experiences to learn to overcome. Strategies to interrupt the coherent appearances of injurious perceptions can't be reduced to manifestos because it is imagined as well as real, private and owned as well as public and disavowed. The fissure between my sense of self and my sense of social value is crucial.

The value of Peggy Shaw's performance work to her long-standing audience involves recognition of the specific requirements she has to make the form of live performance accessible. My impression from audience responses was that most of the audience knew Shaw through her previous performance work, and so the understanding of the performance and the mnemonic accessibility was regarded as a development of her lifetime's work. The audience signalled their recognition of Shaw as a performer in their response to her stage entrance: I'm not sure Elvis would have received a louder or more articulate response. The performance can't be seen so much as an aesthetic object, but more of an ongoing durational dialogue using performance and its capacity to adapt to the body's needs. I can't verify the audience's prior encounters with Shaw, unfortunately. However, this question opens up the question of how the performance may be framed as a single art object and, indeed, how useful such framing may be at the complex point where performer and audience meet. This question becomes crucial when one starts to think about performance quality and participatory work.

For Murakami, vulnerability to the perception of the 'pretty girls' is revealed to be an invention of his own, and the injurious effects are undone, ultimately, by his freedom to look at them in return, and to experience pleasure. Whereas Shaw and her audience recognise each other in the encounter, Murakami's sense of self relies on a misrecognition of the 'pretty girls'. He sorts out his own feelings of inadequacy by arguing for his own strength and scopophilia. Ultimately, he is not at all vulnerable in this context.

The differing interpellative moments in Murakami and Shaw help me to understand that there is something here beyond the spectator experience, which points to a form of interpersonal exchange that isn't about reading a body. The process of engaging in reading or misreading the participant body is deeply personal and also highly political. If Mouffe is right to point towards cultural institutions and to the ways we deal with difference, common cause and disagreement, then it may be helpful to find a way of analysing this process of reading. The participant can be characterised as a person having an experience. However, they are presumably surrounded by other participants, and so the notion of participation is relational and interpersonal. There also exists a wider structural level at which the frame for participation is chosen, negotiated and set up. Whereas my everyday running is organised around road safety, free access to farmland and rights of way, levels of lighting or dark, my ability to read a map and my notions of personal safety or risk, the marathon takes place when all of these structures have already been negotiated. My running body and its needs are anticipated. The meaning of the event has been articulated through a series of adverts, road closures and other events. There's even a reward and memento for my own indulgence in the race. It's all about me, me, me…

I am spectator and participant of the event. The subject and object of the experience is me. The experience of the self as durational, changing, in pain are all aspects of the experience. My immersion in landscape gets deeper the longer I run. The precise nature of my contact with the ground, the moments in the air and the abrasive texture of the wind and the rain are part of the experience, quite as much as the progress of the landscape through time. To return to Balibar for the moment, we can think of consciousness, or consciousness of the self, as relational and also as a temporal entity that relates memories and experiences forward and back in time, relating thoughts to a self, which serves as the focus of a wide range of experiences, past and present. He writes:

> Consciousness is an operator that will always relate any thought to an ego that can think it and that reciprocally inscribes the subject among other thoughts (determining that there is, among other things, a thought of myself). We are tempted to say: the 'I' or ego, this self that thinks, walks, sees, etc., is also 'objectively inscribed (that is, as an *idea*) in the world of thought. It is not *external* to it. (Balibar 2013: 23)

Balibar points out the process of relating thoughts to an ego while allowing us to see these thoughts as fragmentary and relational. The 'I' is made up (in part) of the way that you see me, or the way I imagine that you see me, amongst many other fragments that form the 'thought of myself'. My experiences of running in the past, present and future are brought together in an activity that forms consciousness. What are the implications of extrapolating this to a mass participation event? How do these experiences become relational? How might we think of them as political?

Recognition

Interpersonal political subjectivity might be thought about in terms that relate the individual to a deep attachment to cultural intelligibility. The political theory of recognition bridges the gap between participation, affect and processes of inscribing cultural intelligibility. It also retains a degree of individual autonomy in this cultural inscription and emphasises the contribution of individual processes of reading, response and cultural validation to processes of cultural participation.

The notion of recognition[2] outlines the needs and responsibilities of the individual, without which nobody can thrive. It is a three-part structure of love, esteem and respect – that which we 'cannot not want' (Butler and Athanasiou 2013). In brief, love is the process of recognising the individual's simultaneous difference from and dependence on another. It involves infantile experiences of parenting but also experiences of friendship and romantic love. Love is an empathetic dynamic, not based on notions of rights or individuality, but upon notions of dependency and contact. The capacity and the right to be loved seem to be the basis of empathetic engagements. The foundation of my capacity to relate to others is founded on feelings that I myself have. There is a problem of normalising notions of love. As in psychoanalysis, recent cultural experiences of shapes and forms of infantile development, friendship and romantic love are founded on specific cultural forms. Readings of the patterns that underlie these forms may offer a normative and beguilingly context-free version of a culturally specific phenomenon. My deep and attached feelings for others are crucial to fully understanding the worth of them as individuals, and of course, this may seem to be a normative basis for my attachment.

Respect and esteem rely strongly on institutional structures and upon the individual's understanding of these structures. Respect has a classically liberal form. It is the acknowledgement of the potential that the other has to pursue her or his own objectives and goals. Educational contexts and conversations about ambitions are places where this might be experienced. Freedom of choice and equality of opportunity are discourses that relate to respect for the individual. Esteem is the process of earning the approval of society through socially esteemed activities or contributions. The individual cannot thrive without the right to participate in socially esteemed activities, whether this is work in a particular job, participation in politics, art or culture.

The sport of slow marathon running is built around respect and esteem. The process of setting my own goals, sharing a temporal and spatial event with others, irrespective of our different levels of achievement underlines the extent to which the individual's goal and her or his ability to set that goal is understood and culturally enabled. The social esteem of slow marathon running has a broader biopolitical set of meanings, often structured into fundraising activities, wearing fancy dress and collecting sponsorship, but also connecting to discourses of mental health and physical activity.

Misrecognition

I ran a terrible marathon in Connemara one year – a course I had run many times before. I was well trained and felt fine, but at about 20 miles I came across a tiny lamb that had been separated from its mother when the flock of sheep stampeded. In my energy-deprived state, I blearily tried to reunite lamb with ewe, presenting to other runners the spectacle of a tired woman in shorts holding a sheep. I tried for some time to pass the responsibility on to marshals and other bystanders, but nobody would take the sheep off me. When I eventually got running again half an hour later, I had seized up completely and had to pretty much walk and stagger the last six miles. I wasn't last, but the commentator had, it seemed, gone off to the toilet and handed his microphone to a bystander. I managed an animated shuffle as I approached the finish line and the stand-in commentator mournfully intoned 'Erm, this is one of the *slower* runners…Erm…Stephanie…' Apart from the name, the misrecognition was not a misrecognition of me or my running – the commentator was exactly right about being a slower runner. What she had done was fail to offer the structure of support and approbation that the ethos and the conventions of the event guarantee. Supposing that the job of the commentator was to explain to the spectators at the finish line, she had said the only thing that seemed to be sayable. The runner coming in after five hours and twelve minutes is a *slow* runner. The commentator's job is, of course, to structure the experience of finishing, to offer a sound backdrop to the moment of crossing the finish line, ending the event, arriving at the end of a difficult journey. The commentator briefly brings together the runner's happiness and relief with the empathetic knowledge that the people clustered around the finish gantry recognise and enjoy.

However, the overbearing reading, the spectatorial perspective, frequently offers to the participant an experience of hurt as well as hilarity. Recognition is an interpersonal regime of political articulation. It helps with analysing and evaluating what happens when political performance occurs, especially in contexts where the individual anticipates or experiences disparagement. Misrecognition is a complex process that involves the imaginary consciousness of others and their imagined perceptions of the self. The structures of recognition are necessarily inclusive, demanding that there is no division between internal and external perspective. Creating participatory theatre would seem to be an oxymoron if you follow this argument, and the frequent concerns about quality and standards seem to offer a tension between the overbearing notion of spectatorship and the recognition of the right of the participants to appear on stage and to receive space and attention to create their own artwork.

Often at the boundaries of the professional and the participatory, disability arts is a site of struggle with multiple layers of misrecognition. It also offers a glimpse of some limits of intention. Imagine that it is 1982 and the UK. A disabled performer walks or wheels onto the stage. It is political – as Richard Tomlinson said at the time, '[s]ociety expects its disabled people to act crippled' (Tomlinson 1982).The disabled performer claims a space and embodies a struggle for the power over and ownership of this space. Or, it is 2015 and perhaps a disabled performer walks or wheels onto the stage.

So what? It's not 1982 anymore, the act of claiming the space has been repeated and cited, and there are whole tranches of theatre programming and arts subsidy to reflect social respect and esteem for disabled performers. Perhaps the space already belongs to the disabled performer. Certainly, the impact of mere presence is no longer political but is just part of the cultural performance of diversity. It might be that other transgressions must be performed and the performer has to do a trapeze act in order to make any kind of comparable impression.

This *impression* previously might have been called politics, but now retrospectively it may appear to be artistic novelty. The same body has different meanings in different contexts, and in both the aesthetic effect is predicated on a transgression of supposed or anticipated expectations about the performer's body and presumed abilities. The problem in this formulation is in the assertion that the space 'already belongs' to the disabled performer in 2015. Despite the fact that the funding structures exist to support *some* disabled performers, the potential meanings of the 'mere' appearance shift decisively, depending on the theorised dynamics of perception and expectation that exist in the complex series of exchanges that constitute spectatorship.

Aesthetics and equality

As with marathon running, the processes of opening techniques of arts practices to mass and non-specialised participation can be seen as a way of fostering the neoliberal exploitation of creativity and cooperation or as a point of resistance, a way of developing spaces of social agonism.

It seems to make a difference how we talk about participation. Of course, I'm not always sure what others experience when they engage with art, and this uncertainty makes it difficult to extend the discussion of participation into a way of characterising aesthetic responses as political or contributing to the political in a direct way. One of the reasons for using an extended study of marathon running to understand the pleasures of participation is a distaste for sociocratic analyses or speculations about others' responses, across differences, to the same experiences. So I can speak on a personal level. My tastes and interests lie in an impulse to examine the structures of the world and our habits of perception. I see this activity as both life enhancing (and *as* life if we see it as the pursuit of understanding) and political.

For Peggy Shaw, returning as a different performer after a disabling illness, it matters that the shifts she makes in her actions and the structures of her performance are understood as formal shifts, that they are sewn into a life narrative. This connection between performance and biography should be extended into participatory theatre work. Jacques Rancière and Chantal Mouffe have both considered the aesthetic dimension of the political. Mouffe says that 'the political ... concerns the symbolic ordering of social relations, and this is where its aesthetic dimension resides' (Mouffe 2013: 91). Rancière emphasises the extent to which *equality* must be assumed, must be the starting point of every form of political or cultural exchange. The specific *form* of the exchange is crucial if this presumed equality is to have any meaning beyond platitude. I find it difficult to locate specifics about what this equality looks or sounds like in Rancière's writing. The analysis offered by recognition helps partially. Opening space for the theatre work of young people or disabled artists may offer respect for their ambitions to make work, and it may offer the ability for them to earn esteem by making cultural or artistic works. However, without the deep engagement or empathy that is both structural and directly individual, without the component of love, with its disinterest and its presumed universality, equality is a goal and not a practice. The quality of reciprocal engagement, or love, may be thought about as aesthetic.

For a detailed account of the ways in which the form of reciprocal engagement may be made to shift or to cohere, I find Jan Mukařovský helpfully specific, offering me help in puzzling through the implications of Rancière's calls for equality. It may seem strange to return to work written in structuralist semiotics in the early twentieth century, but at the moment I cannot find a more precise way of thinking about the ways that aesthetic norms might shift. Acting as a bridge between the 'radical presumed equality' of Rancière and the ways that we might actually start to create cultural articulations of selves and bodies that are frequently misrecognised (and seeing misrecognition as important to the understandings we have of our selves), Mukařovský considers the aesthetic function to be, among other things, a way of isolating and analysing the 'maximal focus on a given object'. He continues:

> Wherever in social intercourse it becomes necessary to emphasize any act, subject or person, to focus on it, to free it from undesirable associations, the aesthetic function emerges as an accompanying factor. (Mukařovský 1979: 21)

Mukařovský explains the tension between aesthetic and cultural convention and the process of shifting and transgressing these conventions. He claims that there is an aesthetic norm, that we 'know it when we see it'. He is writing in the early twentieth century. The ability to 'feel' bad acting, to hear badly played music is both wholly intrinsic and wholly social. We feel deeply because we have learned styles and forms, and have learned through them. What I find helpful in this formulation is the idea that whole cultures operate as inherently conservative receptive entities, and there is a porous boundary between the artistic and the more general cultural articulation of the aesthetic norm and its transgressions. To participate in culture is to own and use the standards of the norm, despite the possibilities of analysing and understanding that come from the aesthetic function. Mukařovský writes about a world in which talent and privilege ration access to the arts and in which artworks gradually shift the aesthetic horizon of the masses through their incursion in the non-artistic aesthetic every day. The ways in which we separate art and life are both political and aesthetic. To participate in the arts within the aesthetic regime of theatre is to join in, to participate in cultural norms or standards. Dissonant participation may have institutional validation, in which case the dissonance is avant-garde, or else it is 'bad'. The power to shift these norms lies beyond participation and the ability to see alternative ways to distribute 'the sensible' is, in Mouffe's terms, counter-hegemonic. Running as a slow runner and performing a script with impaired memory can both be done; both can be part of rich elaborations of culture which require a reassessment of the context of the performance and perhaps a shifting of the frame through which it is watched.

I tend to start by thinking that the structures and habits of perception and cognition that make up sociality and the experience of the self are both the grounds and the event of theatre and art. Since I write from the perspective of disability and also from a profound ambivalence about gender, the modes and the matter of the cultural world have always seemed already strange to me. For example, the centrality of impaired bodies in the theatrical works of Samuel Beckett and Tennessee Williams feel like a pleasurable truth about the ways we can disable and queer the perceptible fabric of the world, to deform hegemony to the point where other bodies and subject positions may appear, otherwise. I'm profoundly suspicious of forms which contrive to add structures of veracity or documentary truth to the artwork. The strategy of 'giving voice to' or 'bearing witness to' seems to me to be a form of political and aesthetic stasis, a way of ordering the world so we think we know what truth feels like. For example, plays based on testimony order individual experiences within a hegemonic structure – the revelation, the denouement, the climax of the action are all used to give a simulacrum of veracity to real events. Its form offers a claim of truth. The sense that an account is transcribed *from the real* is conveyed in its style. The result is that attention is turned away from the context and causes, away from the political spaces of the circumstances shown and away from the structures and forms experienced by the givers of testimony. Instead we focus on the structures of the reported-on event, with its restricted dramatis personae and its simplified modes of analysis, glued naively into the present tense. The account includes the 'voice' of a participant in an event. However, the voice is placed into a form which commentates. For me, there is the formal equivalent of a commentator intoning mournfully about the veracity and authenticity of the representation. The dynamics of representation frame others' experiences in a form for which we are already prepared and in which we already have our place.

In the context of the participatory artwork there is a need to identify and articulate the nature of the participation. If we make some works that are deserving of audiences and others which simply affirm participation, there is absolutely no possibility of equality. In this situation, participatory artwork would be a performance of inclusion (on the basis of respect and esteem), but it would lack the power to make a difference to the political claims for equality. The standards of judgement turn out to be not just inadequate, but quite wrong. What is a good performance or a good race? The quality of the interactions, the immersion of all in the event, the connection with life narratives, the stickiness of empathy.

Much of this lies in the status of the onlooker. Let's deal first with the question of diversity and representation. It might be said that we all need access to agonistic space in order to learn how to unpack the 'obviousness' of the hegemonic world. It might also be said that we all need access to a space of representation to counter the expectation of who may and may not appear in public space.

It seems to me that this second proposition has two problems. First, it supposes that there is a pre-existing space, and second, it assumes that there is some form of institutional responsibility for the facilitation of access to this space. Mouffe sees agonistic space as aesthetic space. She says that 'works of art allow us through imagination and the emotions they evoke, to participate in new experiences and to establish forms of relationships that are different from the ones we are used to' (Mouffe 2013: 97).

Sociocracy

The argument about access to space relies on a sociological concept of diversity. If diversity is a way of looking at the world in a culturally redistributive way, as a way of establishing equal access to cultural (and therefore political) space, we may think of it as a product of what Rancière criticises in Pierre Bourdieu, calling it sociocracy (2004: 165–202). For Rancière, sociology is anti-philosophical and anti-democratic. In his reading of sociology, culture is seen as the product of its context and also as a deterministic expression of the identity of a specific group. Difference is therefore both determined (by the group's identity) and deterministic (as it forms the group's identity). The argument that *giving* representational space to unrepresented groups will establish equality is seen as false by Rancière and also by Mouffe. For Rancière and Mouffe, cultural activity is agonistic. Its value lies in its ability to shift the 'common sense' shape of the world, in a way indicated by Mukařovský. The grounds for inequality do not lie in a social ignorance of specific identity categories but upon maldistribution of resources and misrecognition of political subjects. The establishment of Mouffe's 'new forms of relationship' require the shifting of forms of encounter, and not the application of cultural privilege, space or resource to a pre-existing paradigm of reception. Substituting onlookers for spectators in running helps to expand the context of the performance, to discriminate between the structures and conventions of running and also the social value of the experiential.

Conclusion

As E. P. Thompson repeats several times in his introduction to *The Making of the English Working Class*, class is not a 'thing'. It is a relation (1991). So is disability. So (more obviously) is athletic ability. So, I would argue, is the self. If we regard the goal of Mouffe's analysis to be the active negotiation of relationships in a way that disrupts hegemony, we can start to see that the dialectical model of identity formation is aesthetic and reliant on a relationship between participants and onlookers. The renegotiation of the value of the activity needs to take place more broadly than at the level of the individual's experience, simply because the individual's experience does not stop at any kind of boundaries of subjectivity. Running a marathon involves a process of encountering and sometimes arguing with the self: Keep running/Why/Because you like running/I don't like running/You do/I don't/It doesn't matter. Just keep running/I might walk for a little bit/ No. Keep running. Just to that gate there/OK.

When you think about the history of suspicion of the multitude, as Rancière prompts us to do, when you think of crowds as the 'pure beating of number' you are stepping outside the space of the race. Mass is only part of the experience of the crowd. It may be thrilling, energising or deafening. I have found myself at different times surrounded by a sea of problematic pink femininity or engaged in story-swapping with other endurance athletes. But the stories lie in the relational aspects of the race – the contact with the landscape, the weather, other people. The stories and the process of encouraging and competing. The extent to which an idea can motivate and unify is terrifying to many – it speaks of populism, of fascism even – and there's much more to say about this. It isn't too far a stretch to think of these ideas as embodied aesthetics, far away from 'the sociologist king' of Bourdieu's sociocracy. For Rancière, it is aesthetics and not difference that provides the grounds, the a priori conditions for political and social organisation.

Selves are relational and narrative forms. The process of telling the story is a transformative event. It is not a process of relating a static set of truths to the audience. The running self changes and transforms on the cathartic journey of 26 miles, creating an experience that is fully shared and fully individual. There is no transmission of an idea that we come to share – but there is a process of working through the story, an event that we re-encounter every time it happens. The relationship between performer and audience is also a theoretical one, insofar as the various manifestations of the relationship appear on a theoretical matrix which enables the individual to orient the notion of self, to locate it temporally, spatially and affectively.

Selves are highly theoretical entities. For example, Shaw's audience bring to the performance a relation to her former physicality, her narrative and her modes of storytelling and also her future and projected perception of self. Murakami recounts an experience of seeing and being seen, which he resolves into a dynamic that he can live with and that he can use to continue to run in public. The self is a relational entity. Sometimes it seems to be an object – for work and pleasure. The fiction of its freedom is an essential dynamic for the operation of our culture, but Mouffe suggests that we look at this as an aesthetic work in progress, perhaps seeing it as a fiction that can sustain argument, activism and art. There is a temptation when writing about performance to adopt the commentator's perspective. This stance draws us towards the figure crossing the finish line, the meanings that exist for us on the outside of the event. Prepared through cultural engagement as spectators or as audiences, it is very difficult to find a starting point to explore or to experience the complexity of participation with its dialectics and its multiple perspectives.

A pragmatic self, an experiential self, a well understood self are all abstracted and complex beyond the possibilities of our daily lives and even further removed from the possibilities of artistic and cultural practices. We abstract ideas through a judicious process of focusing and editing. These are exemplary narrative forms, and they are aesthetic forms. The commentator who welcomes in the slow runner is relating a fragment of a participatory event to a wider cultural understanding of bodies and capacities, one that is both given and performed and that is part of, but not all of, the performance of self in public space.

If spectatorial or onlooker politics are already written into the form then they may bring with them an ethical framework, devoid of the dynamics of hurt or love, and this does not permit us to develop political space. In sociocratic space, there is only the possibility of esteem, and this is a profoundly difficult and political dynamic on its own. To give me a chance to earn esteem is a process of making these dynamics explicit and formulaic. I may get applauded for 'keeping fit' (the last thing on my mind...), or Shaw might be seen as 'bravely battling her disability'. Without love and respect, there is only misrecognition. There isn't really a process of developing and negotiating these dynamics outside empathy and aesthetics. Mouffe points us towards institutions, theatre, amateur athletics, as a focus for struggle, towards the creation of structures to support the struggle to make ourselves heard and understood as part of the articulation of political identity. The value of this experience is communicated in running cultures and is shared across many media by millions of other runners, fast and slow. I engage in a culture that shares and supports this experience.

The process of working through ideas in a space, seen as an exemplar of participatory art, requires a process of emerging articulations and an understanding that recognition is work that may still need to be done. Perhaps a 'radical presumed equality' can't exist if one applies merely artistic (valuable) form to a specific way of looking at the world. As Shaw reinvents the way she performs to adapt to her changed body, she shifts the nature of her exchange with her audience. As I run through the driving Welsh rain, I am synthesising experiences, relating them to each other and addressing them to a reference point that is the self that crosses the finish line. The catharsis of this moment will not carry very much commentary at all. For the moment, what my own commentary offers is a need to shift the hierarchy of performer and onlooker, finding space for dynamics of exchange and agonism and recognising the synthesised overview for what it always was: a fragmentary element of a participatory whole, constituted in performance.

Endnotes

1. See, for example, Hugh Jones, 'History of the Marathon'. *The Expert's Guide to Marathon Training* (London: Carlton, 2003), pp. 8–17.
2. Simon Thompson's rigorous and wide-reaching book *The Political Theory of Recognition* (Polity, Cambridge, 2006) has framed and directed my introduction to this area of political theory.

SECTION II

LABOURS OF PARTICIPATION

6   Affective Labours of Cultural Participation

Helen Nicholson

In May 2015 I found myself eating a large bowl of steaming dahl at Battersea Arts Centre in London with a group of women I had not met before. The meal marked the culmination of a performance, *Like Mother, Like Daughter*, created by Complicite's Creative Learning Department in collaboration with Toronto's Why Not Theatre. The table was hosted by two of the performers, not professional actors, but 'real-life' mothers and daughters who had taken part in a three-week-long project that brought together women and girls of different faiths. In the kitchens, I was told, some of the women had been working hard to make the dahl according to one of the mums' recipes. It was delicious – wholesome and filling – and the conversation on my table turned to inherited recipes and childhood memories of food. But when the talk began to take a nostalgic turn, one of the older mothers punctured the moment by commenting briskly that she had spent far too much time cooking on this project and questioning how far it perpetuated a stereotype of women-in-the-kitchen that, as a young mother in the 1970s, she had been keen to resist.

Like Mother, Like Daughter illustrates some of the central questions about the relationship between performance, participation and politics that run through this chapter. As part of Complicite's creative learning programme and undertaken in partnership with the Women's Interfaith Network, the project was conceived as a form of community building, as a way to bring together women of different faiths to share stories and experiences. As a consequence of the workshops, they had designed an evening's programme that would, they hoped, extend this sense of community to their audiences, albeit temporarily; we were warmly welcomed with a pre-performance drink and guided round an exhibition that documented their workshop processes. We witnessed a performance and joined a meal. As a studio performance staged at Battersea Arts Centre, a venue known for its cutting-edge theatre, it was positioned and sold as part of their innovative programme to a theatre-going public with high expectations and metropolitan tastes. The event as a whole, with the conviviality of its shared meal and the 'real' dynamic of mother–daughter relationships, invoked the complexity of emotional attachments between mothers and daughters whether they were present in the room or – for the audience – absent, remembered and sometimes mourned. And although some of the participants lamented the lack of representation from a wider cross-section of society in the project as a whole, the event suggested a gentle domestic politics, an invitation for audiences to witness and celebrate both art-making and the art of living as a labour of love.

My suggestion in this chapter is that contemporary theatre-making is introducing new registers of participation that resist neat divisions of labour that were established in the twentieth century. The workshops had raised political questions about domestic labour, gender and craft; the performance invited reflection on listening and attentiveness as integral to participation, using theatre-making to create a temporary community. Neither amateur nor entirely professional, the exhibition documented workshop methodologies usually associated with applied theatre, and the event referenced community arts strategies by inviting audiences to share a meal as part of their evening out. The performance was professionally staged, but it also played with the idea of 'amateurism' in its dramaturgical structure; it was constructed around mothers and daughters reading each other questions from cards, prompting conversations that veered between the intensely personal and intimate (have you ever felt we favoured your younger siblings?) to the more ordinary affects of family life (favourite dinners, childhood bedtimes and catching the school bus). The unrehearsed spontaneity of the conversations seemed to translate the workshop practices into the theatre; the unscripted performance captured the aesthetic of care between the mothers and daughters, giving the work an unfinished quality that invoked past conversations as well as those yet to come.

This chapter is centrally concerned with performances which, in common with *Like Mother, Like Daughter*, have social or communitarian ambitions, and yet they are also produced and marketed as part of a programme of cutting-edge contemporary performance. Created by and with professional artists working with local participants who would not self-identify as theatre-makers, this approach to performance-making is boundary-breaking, marking how ontological distinctions between different forms of artistic participation – amateur, professional, voluntary and community – are being eroded and reimagined in the twenty-first century. This raises further questions about how far there are synergies and intersections between participatory forms of performance and the ways in which patterns of labour and leisure are being reshaped and reorganised in response to contemporary social conditions.

The chapter is animated and informed by debates about affective labour, a concept which, as I shall explain in the next section, is deeply enmeshed in the post-industrial economies of the twenty-first century. Rather than regarding this contemporary cultural shift in wholly negative terms, however, I am interested in the creative opportunities it generates, both artistically and socially. *Like Mother, Like Daughter* illustrates the debates and sets the parameters for discussion, and I shall return to this project briefly in the final section. I shall draw in detail on two further examples of practice because, in common with *Like Mother, Like Daughter*, they were programmed by innovative venues and reflected the creative vision of trained artists working with participants with little experience of performance-making. *Dad Dancing* was a project developed by London-based company Second Hand Dance and coproduced with Battersea Arts Centre in 2014, and *Night Walks with Teenagers* was a performative walk created by a group of young people working with the Canadian theatre company Mammalian Diving Reflex and performed in February 2015 as part of the In Between Time Festival in Bristol, UK.

None of the performances invoked in this chapter dramatise what Lauren Berlant describes as the 'exceptional event that shatters the ordinary'; on the contrary, it is the ordinariness of lives that is celebrated, albeit in extraordinary ways (2011: 14). Methodologically, I am interested in developing an approach that acknowledges my own embodied experience of the participatory event and the affective labour that I bring to it as a researcher. The geographer Derek P. McCormack describes 'experimental experience' as an 'occasion for thinking' (McCormack 2013: 22), and I hope to find ways to be attentive to my own sensory engagement and (sometimes) moments of resistance to the participatory process. It is a way of working that is, perhaps, most clearly symbolised by my dinnertime conversations at Battersea Arts Centre in May 2015, which were both hospitable and occasionally stilted, and by polishing off my bowl of dahl.

Affective labour

The term 'affective labour' is perhaps most regularly associated with the political philosophers Michael Hardt and Antonio Negri, who have offered a sustained and critical analysis of its political and economic significance to post-industrial global capitalism. In their book *Multitude: War and Democracy in the Age of Empire*, they argue that the demise of manufacturing industry has brought an increased economic reliance on 'immaterial labour', a phrase they use to describe labour that 'creates immaterial products, such as knowledge, information, communication, a relationship, or an emotional response' (Hardt and Negri 2004: 108). Of course this form of work is not in itself new – by this definition both theatre-making and home-making would serve as instances of immaterial labour, and all forms of immaterial labour depend on the materiality of bodies and brains. What the shift from industrial labour to knowledge-based economies has brought, Hardt and Negri argue, is a new emphasis on labour that produces immaterial *products*. There are two kinds of immaterial labour, they argue: one which generates ideas, symbols, texts and so on, and the other which they describe as 'affective labour'.

In Hardt and Negri's political analysis, affective labour 'produces or manipulates affects such as feelings of ease, well-being, satisfaction, excitement, or passion' (2001: 108). What affect does, by this definition, is not determined, and it is its porousness that makes it so politically potent. This distinction between emotion and affect is important; emotion can be identified, registered and captured, whereas affects are experienced less consciously on a visceral, sensed and embodied level, moving biopolitically between human and nonhuman materialities. Affect's biopower underlines affective labour's political ambiguity, generating human emotions that can be commodified – manipulated by advertisers, for example, to encourage brand loyalty or used in the experience economy to sell anything from restaurants to theme parks and heritage sites. Consequently, affective labour is highly valued in today's consumerist economies, described by Hardt as the 'very pinnacle of the hierarchy of laboring' in contemporary neoliberal societies (Hardt 1999: 90). Alternatively, however, affective labour's biopower can be used more positively to generate feeling of community and social networks, as Hardt and Negri point out:

> What affective labor produces are social networks, forms of community, biopower. Here one might recognise the instrumental action of economic production has been united with the communicative action of human of human relations; in this case, however, communication has not been impoverished, but production has been enriched to the level of human interaction. (Hardt and Negri 2000: 293)

Affective labour is, therefore, inevitably implicated in how power is produced and reproduced biopolitically across and within social networks. Affect is relational, contagious and goes viral, moving between people and their material environment, as an atmosphere, mood or structure of feeling, and often in ways that are not understood or even recognised cognitively but experienced, embodied or sensed.

This analysis of the biopolitics of affective labour not only draws attention to its embodied and corporeal practices; it also opens new ways to understand the politics of cultural participation in ways that are significant to theatre-makers. On one level, theatre is always a form of affective labour, but participatory performance further complicates this by offering the potential for multiple forms of authorship. Writing about the relationship between theatre and labour, Gabriele Klein has argued that 'the biopolitical interlocking of labour, life and art is not a specific feature of the artistic existence' (2012: 6), but she concedes that the creative economies and biopolitics of the twenty-first century have brought a new and compelling focus on their interconnectivity. This places the participatory qualities of contemporary performance at the centre of a paradox. On the one hand, affective labour can be used in theatre to exert power in ways that are uncomfortably manipulative, or on the other, participating affectively in performance can generate positive feelings of sociability and community, as it can shape, in Hardt's words, 'collective subjectivities, sociality, and society itself' (Hardt 1999: 98). However understood, this renewed interest in the biopolitical qualities of affective life has introduced forms of theatrical labour that emphasise relationality, coproduction and co-creation, a process that positions audiences as creative participants in the performance and appears to offer them agency.

In the creative industries, the contemporary emphasis on relationality and co-creation is changing established divisions of affective labour, introducing a series of newly coined hybridised terms that describe the fluid dynamic between artists, audiences and publics. The vocabulary has expanded from the 1970s when Augusto Boal's radicalised 'spect-actors' were regarded as agents of social change, a process whereby spectators joined the performance as actors to offer solutions to dramatised social issues. In the twenty-first century new terminologies signal both the proximity of theatre and performance to the commodified experience economy. 'Prosumer' is a term used across a range of creative and service industries to suggest people who both produce and consume the products they use, and the word 'artrepreneur' describes artists who adopt neoliberal models of entrepreneurship as part of their creative labour. Both terms have been carefully theorised by Jen Harvie in her book *Fair Play: Art, Performance and Neoliberalism* (2013), but it is her discussion of the relationship between creative labour and prosumerism that is particularly relevant here. Charting the ways in which prosumerism has infiltrated many different aspects of social life (from online banking to shopping practices), she describes how it creates audiences who are coerced into becoming 'flexible and precarious labourers' in what she, following Claire Bishop, describes as 'delegated art' practices:

> The art and performance that conscripts audiences to co-make it offers the pleasures of action, self-determination and discovery; it appears quite straightforwardly to empower its audiences as co-makers. But its benefits are much more compromised than they first appear. The engagements it offers are actually very limited, even illusionary. Its egalitarianism is compromised to retain authorial status for the producing company or 'real' artist. (Harvie 2013: 50)

Harvie's interest lies in the contemporary arts in cosmopolitan cities, where participatory performance is often marketed for a particular theatre-going demographic – the metropolitan élite – seeking the spectacle of an immersive artistic experience on their way home from work. The participatory practices she describes are, therefore, designed to capture (and manipulate) their attention within a short timeframe, and it would be naïve to anticipate any stronger authorship or political agency from such a brief engagement. Harvie notes that what is more disturbing are the ways in which theatre companies have come to rely on unpaid volunteers and use other forms of precarious work patterns that mirror and sometimes reproduce the iniquitous employment practices associated with global capitalism. Prosumerism is, perhaps, cultural participation at its most manipulative and most socially privileged.

One response to this exploitation of labour has been to revitalise the conventional role of the artist as social critic, and some artists have used delegated art practices to draw explicit attention to the ways in which labour relations are experienced. Harvie finds political optimism in the delegated practice of artists Phil Collins and Santiago Sierra:

> [I]t can powerfully bring to audiences attention precisely these problems with contemporary labour dynamics ... by enacting them, highlighting and embedding audiences in their antagonisms. ... Further, it can help audiences recognise their social responsibility for such labour dynamics and for social dynamics more broadly. (2013: 60)

Both Collins and Sierra involve participants in art-making activities, often in complex parts of the world. Collins' acclaimed installation *They Shoot Horses* 2004 (Tate Britain, 2006–2007), for example, involved a group of nine Palestinian young people in Israeli-occupied Ramallah who were paid to dance for a seven-hour day until they fell exhausted. Like Harvie,

I found the video installation that resulted to be moving and challenging, offering a thought-provoking commentary on globalised teenagers in a place of political crisis. But although Collins' work may have pricked the consciences of Tate visitors in affluent Chelsea, I was left wondering what happened to the dancers who failed the audition, how far the young people he employed were invited to make authorial decisions about the finished product, and whether Collins had offered a share of his exhibition profits to those who had given their day-long labour to its creation. Claire Bishop acknowledges that similar concerns have been voiced elsewhere, and it is significant that answers to these questions have not been forthcoming. Noting that contemporary performance art has a history of presenting non-professional performers as authentic representatives of specific social groups, Bishop observes that the ambition of his project was not to offer an 'exemplary instance of artistic collaboration' but to 'universalise his participants by addressing multiple genres of artistic and popular experience' (Bishop 2012: 226). Participation – even in performance's most social turn – appears to maintain divisions of labour between the visionary artist and the hired hand, adding to distinctions between professional artist, audiences, amateurs and volunteers evident in more commercially driven forms of prosumerism.

The idea of *affective* labour adds a different dynamic to this analysis of labour relations in relational art and participatory performance. In one conceptualisation, it is clear that prosumerism and related forms of cultural participation chime well with Hardt and Negri's view that affective labour can be personally and commercially exploitative. Alternatively, as Hardt persuasively argues, it is possible to construct less hierarchical configurations of value and affect. Hardt suggests that Michel Foucault's analysis of biopower as a form of top-down governmental control can be inverted, and it is possible to look at the affective labour of biopolitical production in more egalitarian ways. He argues that cooperation and care is immanent to affective labour, and this means that it has radical potential:

> Labor works directly on the affects; it produces subjectivity, it produces society, it produces life. Affective labor, in this sense, is ontological – it reveals living labor constituting a form of life and thus demonstrates again the potential of biopolitical production. (Hardt 1999: 99)

Although Hardt's analysis has been rightly nuanced by feminists to avoid perpetuating gendered social relations of care,[1] his sympathetic analysis of biopower as a socially productive and energetic force invites a positive reassessment of the value of affective labour, both within the arts and beyond.

Taking Hardt's suggestion seriously that labour 'works on the affects' not only illuminates the multiplicity of labour practices immanent in cultural participation; it also raises questions about how affect might be understood in performance. Affect theory, though much debated in applied theatre, has been largely overlooked in other analyses of the labour of contemporary performance art, and reciprocally, the biopolitics of labour have been under theorised in applied theatre. The theoretical architecture for affect in this chapter is furthered by political and geographical thinkers who, informed by Gilles Deleuze and Felix Guattari, illuminate the sociability of human networks noted by Hardt and Negri but also extend beyond it to address the affective relationality with the nonhuman world. Writing about affective spaces, McCormack suggests that affect is generative, associated with the energy of moving bodies as well as the rhythms, flows and atmospheres of time and space:

> Affect is ... conceived as a distributed and diffuse field of intensities, circulating within but also moving beyond and around bodies. At the same time, movement of bodies generates disturbances and perturbations that transform the intensity and reach of this field. In the process, bodies participate in the generation of affective spaces: spaces whose qualities and consistencies are vague but sensed, albeit barely, as a distinctive affective tonality, mood, or atmosphere. (2013: 3)

In relation to the affective labour of performance, this way of thinking has the potential to move beyond conventional notions of the artist as social critic towards and understanding that affective political agency is corporeal and felt as well as cognitive and reflexive. This redefines affective labour as a biopolitical practice that is socially productive, distributed across and between the flows of human and nonhuman activity, where social meanings are not projected onto the world but embodied, imagined and sensed.

Understanding participation in theatre involves recognising that all forms of affective labour are participatory to some event, and reciprocally, all participation in the theatre involves labour, whether or not it involves actively joining in. McCormack describes participation as an affective and immersive experience that is always relational:

> Participation takes place through the relational assemblages of bodies, materials, concepts, and affects: participation in these terms is always a co-fabrication, a co-production that involves more than the individual human participant. (2013: 188)

This approach to participation as an affective experience and relational assemblage serves to critically inform my reading of the two examples that follow, *Dad Dancing* and *Night Walks with Teenagers*. I am seeking to place cultural participation within a wider political imaginary and to find alternatives and points of resistance to commodified prosumerism. Bringing together political questions about the relationship between labour and affect in this way takes existing debates about the experience of performance into new territory.

Affective relations: Real dads dancing

I found the idea irresistible: three women, all professionally trained dancers and choreographers, performing with their dads, none of whom had any experience of dancing themselves beyond busting a few moves at family gatherings. *Dad Dancing: Reclaiming Fatherly Grooves* (to give it its full title) was a coproduction between Second Hand Dance and Battersea Arts Centre, and it was performed and choreographed by Rosie Heafford, Alexandrina Hemsley and Helena Webb, with their dads, Adrian, David and Andy. The performance I attended on 12 November 2014 was part of a three-week run at Battersea Arts Centre and represented an important staging post in an innovative project. Members of Second Hand Dance were joined on stage not only by their own dads but also by a supporting cast of local fathers (or father-figures) with their sons and daughters, all of whom had participated in workshops with the company over a period of weeks. As both a project and a performance, *Dad Dancing* provides an opportunity to reflect on the multiple layers of affective labour it involved and to attend to the very specific relationships that it celebrated and embodied.

On the night I attended the performance, the event was introduced to an assembled group of producers and funders by its Battersea Arts Centre coproducer Sophie Bradey, who was understandably keen to encourage an appropriate reading of this work. What was striking, however, was that she described the project in terms of its economies of labour, stressing that *Dad Dancing* was not amateur but a professional performance, but qualifying this a little by describing the dads as 'brave' and the local supporting cast as 'enthusiastic participants'. For the gathering of producers interested in hosting a tour, this was, of course, an entirely appropriate delineation, but as I entered the theatre, I wished that there was a different set of vocabularies to describe the ambition of work that reaches across conventional boundaries. Gabriele Klein and Bojana Kunst suggest that all 'performance practice is intertwined with the social aspect of labour' (Klein 2012: 2), and

I was interested how far the social qualities of *Dad Dancing* and the 'real' relationships on which it was conceived might unfix entrenched divisions of labour between professional and non-professional performers. I was also aware that, as I am no dance scholar, the nuances of choreography and technique would elude me. Methodologically, my intention was to cultivate what McCormick describes as 'an affirmative critique open to the possibility of being affected – or moved' (2013: 11). Or, put another way, I was neither trying to test a thesis nor trying to prove some prefigured ideas; I was there to experience the event and to attend to the feelings and sensibilities it generated. In many ways it was the experience of *Dad Dancing* that inspired this chapter, and my post-event conversations with the company emerged in response to its affective resonance.

The embarrassing dancing dad is, of course, an affectionate cultural stereotype. The idea of an untrained dancer performing alongside his daughter is an inspirational starting point, and in anticipating the performance, I was enchanted by this conceit and expecting that the familiar figure of affectionate fun would be taken seriously. Performed in the Council Chamber at Battersea Arts Centre, the cavernous atmospheric 'found' space was given a domestic atmosphere with an eclectic mix of sofas, table lamps and chairs assembled – apparently haphazardly – around the edge of a bare stage. Settling themselves on the chairs, the cast remained visible to the audience throughout, and the style of the performance resisted theatrical illusion, both in form and content. Composed of a fluid series of vignettes, duets and solo dances and interspersed with scenes with the supporting cast, the performance animated the interplay between social and contemporary dance, providing an aesthetic that echoed and sometimes referenced the workshop and devising processes. Each of the dads (Adrian, David and Andy) danced together, but it was perhaps their solos that defined the emotional and aesthetic register of the piece. There was a touching commitment to their performances as the exuberant choreography played with what Alexandrina Hemsley described as the 'textures of embarrassment' that the stereotype of dad dancing invokes. Their daughters honoured the aesthetic of social dance in their own solo performances, mirroring their fathers' patterns of movement and referencing their rhythms in response. Stories of births, deaths and falling in love accumulated into an affectionate picture of father-daughter relationships, inviting the audience to share, in Kathleen Stewart's words, the 'ordinary affects' of everyday life (Stewart 2007). The rhythms and movement of the dance affirmed the stories' resonance, giving choreographic shape to the 'real' relationships between the performers that are beyond words.

Dad Dancing drew attention to the generosity of its creative processes, illuminating both the layers of affective labour involved in making the show and in their father–daughter relationships. Gaining insights into their daughters' working lives was part of the motivation for the dads' involvement, not least because they had all expressed concerns about the precarity of freelance labour in the arts. This recognisable fatherly concern was captured on the projects' website:

> Meet three eccentric dads, each with a daughter freelancing as a dancer. 'Any of your jobs paid?' come the worried mutterings of Adrian Heafford, Andy Webb and David Hemsley. ... The idea for the project came about when Alexandrina, Helena and Rosie were studying dance. Their dads – David, Andy and Adrian – would come and dutifully support their daughters by sitting in the audience, but were befuddled by contemporary dance and ultimately, their daughters' career choices.[2]

Addressing this 'befuddlement' by persuading their 'eccentric dads' to take part in a performance brought creative challenges, particularly when the dads started to gain first-hand experience of their working methods. Helena Webb's monologue addressed this directly, noting with some affection how their dads' initial expectations were challenged at the first rehearsal:

> They had prepared themselves for eight hours of non-stop dancing. They thought that we were going to teach them pre-choreographed routines. With lifts. And they had prepared themselves further by purchasing high intensity lycra sportwear. What we actually did was a lot more discussing, devising, talking, shared lunches and eating biscuits.

The gentle humour of this monologue speaks to wider issues about the creative journey of the project. In a subsequent interview Alexandrina Hemsley explained that the dads had 'struggled with the meandering creative process', particularly when they temporarily abandoned one line of inquiry in order to pursue a 'new thread of thought' that had presented itself in the process, or when they revisited a scene or dance that the dads considered finished.[3] Reciprocally, their daughters were amused and touched by their dads' enthusiasm, arriving promptly at 9:30 for a 10:00 a.m. rehearsal already kitted out in shiny new trainers and making jokes about their daughters' inefficient 'faff time'. In conversation Rosie Heafford described their different working methods, suggesting that the dads' 'rational', task-oriented approach meant that they found it difficult to see how their nonlinear and intuitive creative processes might lead to product and, in turn, how a performance thus created would be legible to an audience. This was referenced in performance when Rosie used her daughters' prerogative to tease the dads by explaining to the audience that they had wanted its themes to be spelt out 'very clearly' in each scene and explained 'at length' in the programme. Some of the dramaturgical strategies used in performance captured the improvised quality of their workshops; placards with hand-written statements or questions were a recurring trope, and it was easy to imagine how they might have stimulated experimentation and discussion in the devising process. In one of the early scenes, for example, dads and daughters faced the audience in a line, stepping forward in response to questions such as, 'How old do you feel?', or, more intimately, 'How old were you when you first fell in love?'. Alexandrina Hemsley described the dads' contributions to the devising as a process of 'letting go of what they knew' and learning a different aesthetic and 'new ways to be'. She acknowledged that although feelings of embarrassment were 'so engrained' in them as daughters, they rarely came from the dancing, but sometimes the intimacy of the subject matter felt uncomfortable, particularly when their dads were, as Helena Webb put it, 'just really open'. Describing these various interventions affectionately as 'dadisms', however, suggests that the project in itself brought together the affective labour of art-making and the improvised creativity of relationships in family life.

One of the most moving aspects of the performance was, for me, the almost unconscious ways in which the father–daughter relationships were performed. A dad's affectionate smile or a spontaneous glance from a half-lit corner of the stage as his daughter recounted a story or relived an embarrassing moment, or in the case of the support cast, when a father sought out his young son across the stage, always noting where he was in a sea of other dancers. There was no attempt to disguise these small and intimate gestures – they were part of the affective resonance of the performance – and it was not difficult to pick out who was related to whom; there was connectivity between fathers and their children that is difficult to fabricate. Claims about authenticity are always problematic in debates about theatre, but the 'real' father–child relationships I witnessed in *Dad Dancing* on that evening in Battersea Arts Centre seemed to offer a creative alternative to two extremes: the manipulated affective labour of commodified prosumerism and the inclusive but artistically stale choreography so often associated with community dance. Rosie Heafford explained that her ambition as artistic director of Second Hand Dance was to negotiate the delicate dynamic between taking people 'as they are' within communities, but still maintaining a clear vision as an artist to shape their contributions. Part of the vision for *Dad Dancing* was to explore the 'real' stuff of family dynamics, and this meant that when the dads suggested that a surrogate or substitute might take their place, it was, understandably, strongly resisted by their daughters. In many ways the dads' suggestion was entirely reasonable; after all, in other forms of theatre roles are re-cast and understudies step in, a practice that Joseph Roach describes as 'the doomed search for originals' that indicates one of the many meanings of 'performance' – something that 'stands in for an elusive entity that it is not but that it must vainly aspire to both embody and replace' (Roach 1996: 3). In *Dad Dancing*, however, it was not another *theatrical* performance that was invoked but the everyday performativity of father–child bonds forged, improvised and performed over a lifetime. This echoes Tim Ingold and Elizabeth Hallam's analysis of creativity, where they suggest that because 'there is no script for social and cultural life', the boundaries between the social practices of everyday life and artistic creativity are blurred because all aspects of life are, in some way, improvised (Ingold and Hallam 2007: 1). The spontaneous qualities of *Dad Dancing* allowed this affective relationality to be witnessed, underlined by Adrian Heafford in a scene in which he described becoming a father in improvisational terms, as a process of 'making it up as I went along'. Beyond the self-conscious artistic practices of the performance, it was the glimpses of very specific, sensed and embodied relationships between family members that defined the aesthetic of *Dad Dancing*.

Much has been written about ways in which the creative economy is creating a culture of insecurity through freelance contracts, how social isolation increases through working from home, and how mobile labour is redefining domestic life and eroding leisure time. This project existed squarely within this context, but rather than asking audiences to reflect critically on these political circumstances, *Dad Dancing* invited participants and audiences to engage in the experience of performance, affirming that the real affective labour of the project was socially generative, an embodied relationality of care. The intimate relationships glimpsed on stage blurred distinctions between the social, the artistic and the personal, thereby eroding divisions of labour between professional dancers and non-professional performers. It was not only the dancers' professional skills that generated affect; it was also the 'real-life' relationships between performers that afforded the experience its affective register. Following Brian Massumi, this is what McCormack describes as 'relation-specific affects' that are temporal rather than spatial, foregrounding ongoing relations that extend (in this case) beyond the space of the theatre. This 'complicates the question of participation', he argues, because the experience becomes future oriented, 'responsive to the potential futures of these relations' (McCormack 2013: 34–36). My suggestion is that the relation-specificity of *Dad Dancing* also complicates the question of affective labour, drawing attention to affects' fluidity, complexity and temporality.

At the end of the performance, as the cast filled the stage with a dance that expressed the joy and generosity of the moment, the audience were invited to take to the floor. Habitually resistant to any kind of audience participation, I was disinclined to leave my seat and sat tight, preparing myself to analyse the ways in which the space was quickly shedding the disciplinary boundaries of a stage and how the movement of bodies was changing its spatial dynamics. The moment did not, however, require this kind of intellectual labour, and my attempts to resist joining the vitality of living, moving bodies were futile. On that night – as on every other on the run – the affective intensity of the atmosphere was contagious; it spread as Teresa Brennan promised it would, across and between objects, spaces and people.[4] But there were also glimpses of ghosts between the bobbing heads and the flailing arms, and I realised for the first time that I had never once danced with my dad and that now I never will.

Affective encounters: *Night Walks with Teenagers*

One of the central arguments in this chapter is that the dynamic between participation and performance illuminates the ways in which social worlds are practised and performed and how, reciprocally, creating a performance is, as Shannon Jackson has argued, socially generative (Jackson 2011). Affective labour extends this discussion, drawing attention to a political double-bind; on the one hand, affect is intrinsic to cooperative and sociable forms of labour, while on the other, it is a manipulative force that generates, in the words of Hardt and Negri, 'new and intense forms of violation or alienation' (2006: 67). By taking affective labour as a way of conceptualising different forms of performative participation, I shall explore this political paradox by investigating the connectivity between the improvised creativity of everyday life and artistic creativity in which experiences are framed and curated as performance. The examples of practice in this chapter offer critical insights into this set of debates. If *Dad Dancing* animated the affective relationships between father-figures and their daughters and sons, the affective labour of *Night Walks with Teenagers*, a performative walk devised and led by young people, was attuned to the rhythms and atmosphere of a particular place. My suggestion is that in both projects, the affective labour of participation conjoined the social with the artistic, and thus it speaks to broader debates about creativity and authorship. *Night Walks with Teenagers* provides a particular opportunity to dwell on the spatial and temporal coordinates of young people and to reflect further on how participation is always immanent to wider ecologies of human and nonhuman interaction. It is to this project that I now turn.

In February 2015 I boarded a chartered bus from Bristol's gentrified docks to take me to Knowle West, a suburb of the city that has been one of its most socially deprived areas for generations. I was on my way to participate in Mammalian Diving Reflex's project with young people, *Night Walks with Teenagers*, performed as part of Bristol's In Between Time Festival (IBT15). The festival is curated biannually and coproduced with the Arnolfini (an arts venue at the heart of Bristol's rebranded 'habourside'), and it brings a programme of cutting-edge live art and contemporary performance to this creative city. The audience for *Night Walks with Teenagers* had been instructed to gather at the Arnolfini's foyer and wait for the coach to arrive, and the conversation circled around other festival events they had attended. Opportunities had been rich, and popular events included Fujiko Nakaya's outdoor sculptural installation *Fog Bridge*, Lone Twin's durational performance *True West* and discussions with a guest artist, the Chicano activist Guillermo Gómez-Peña. Including a walk with Knowle West teenagers as part of the festival programme represented a significant cultural and spatial shift, and we were promised 'an incredible performative journey' led by local teenagers through their neighbourhood.[5] I had known Knowle West well in the 1980s at the height of the Thatcher era when I was a teacher in Bristol, and at the time it was home to a disenfranchised community of predominantly white young people. I had always enjoyed my encounters with these spirited teenagers, and I was looking forward seeing if anything had changed and to meeting the next generation.

The event was framed by the bus journey, and as I took my seat I was fully expecting something to *happen* – some kind of performative intervention conjured by the teenagers' imaginations. But nothing did. It was simply a bus ride to transport us out of the fashionable cultural quarter and into the deprived suburbs. My fellow travellers appeared to be Bristol's creative class, a term coined by the North American urban theorist Richard Florida to describe people working in the immaterial labour of post-industrial societies, who, despite different professional backgrounds, share similar tastes, liberal values and cultural preferences (Florida 2002). The creative city is an essential part of knowledge-based economies, not least because its cosmopolitan lifestyle is attractive to this demographic. This bus ride from Bristol's harbourside, with its galleries and café culture, to the social housing of South Bristol symbolised the uneven geographies associated with the creative city. This point is articulated clearly by Tim Edensor et al. in their book, *Spaces of Vernacular Creativity: Rethinking the Cultural Economy*:

> One of the most glaring inadequacies of the creative class thesis is its geographical specificity, privileging downtown cultural enclaves and quarters in large metropolitan centres as sites of creativity. The champions of creative regeneration have fetishized these urban settings while ignoring forms of creative endeavour that emerge in rural, suburban, working-class, everyday and marginal spaces (Edensor et al. 2010: 11).

Florida may describe the creative class as mobile and resourceful, but on this occasion we were not trusted to find our own way to Knowle West.

Seen in this light, *Night Walks with Teenagers* occupied an ambivalent position. On the one hand, it seemed that the audience had been bussed in for a one-off experience with Knowle West teenagers, and to me at least, this short-term encounter with young people in an underprivileged neighbourhood felt politically uncomfortable. On the other, the project was produced in partnership with Knowle West Media Centre, a highly successful arts charity that has long provided creative opportunities for local people. Still a socially deprived district, Knowle West is subject to its own regeneration programme, and it is significant that the charity chose to launch its new manifesto to coincide with *Night Walks with Teenagers*, a project that they were promoting as integral to their vision. Manifesto 2015 identifies five 'Calls for Change', all of which are concerned with 'democratising the next industrial revolution' by providing wider access to the creative economy and greater investment in skills and training for young people.[6] The manifesto, therefore, seeks to extend the creative city to the suburbs, bringing the social and economic benefits associated with creative entrepreneurship to a wider social group. The aim was not to gentrify the area and attract new 'creatives' to Knowle West but to provide resources for local people to develop their talents and find sustainable employment in the creative industries. Cultivating dispositions towards creativity in this way has clear implications for the concept of affective labour. If, as Florida argues, access to the creative class is achieved not only through patterns of labour but also through habitus, how might creative projects with young people (such as *Night Walks with Teenagers*) ensure that the tastes and cultural preferences of the metropolitan élite are not simply imposed on them? This question not only invites a reassessment of issues of authorship; it also places Hardt's affirmative suggestion that affective labour produces 'social networks, forms of community, [and] biopower' in a critical perspective.

Mammalian Diving Reflex offers a very clear response to this question. The Toronto-based company feature regularly on the international arts festival circuit, touring work such as *Haircuts by Children* and *Night Walks with Teenagers* to major metropolitan cities and working with young people who may not normally participate in festival events. Their political and artistic ambition is spelt out in their document, *The Mammalian Protocol for Collaborating with Children*, where they articulate how their principles and practices respond to *The United Nations Convention on the Rights of the Child*. The introduction to this document illustrates their values:

> Mammalian Diving Reflex's artistic projects with children attempt to be utopian moments that offer the possibility of seeing children differently and accepting their presence, energy and disruptive potential as important reminders that, perhaps, we are all taking things a little too seriously, moving a little too fast, and expecting too much of each other.[7]

The assumption that young people need to be seen 'differently' by adults has inspired a range of projects designed to challenge what they describe as 'the social norms and codes of professionalism that exclude or prove challenging to children', citing sitting in the theatre as one such restrictive practice. Their interest lies in animating public spaces and in creating encounters between adults and teenagers who would not normally meet. On that basis, transporting two coach loads of arty adults from the Arnolfini to undertake a performative walk with Knowle West teenagers fulfilled their objective.

On arrival at Knowle West Media Centre, a boy greeted me with a hug. We were told the rules for the evening by the project's Canadian leaders: we must all talk to each other, and we mustn't die. I felt kindly towards my hugging boy – they had obviously decided that hugging audience members would be a good way to start, but he looked a bit scared of some of the cool hipster types, and I suspect I was closer to his granny's age than I might like to think. There were some warm-up exercises where we were expected to sing nursery rhymes (with actions) and play various drama games (mostly involving touching bits of people you hadn't met before), and I felt relieved when we set off on the walk. The narrow alleys and graffiti-covered garages had their own atmosphere in the cold, dark February night, and my hugging boy and his mates were amiable company. The walk's rhythm changed when the line of people stopped short in front of a barrier across the path, and I heard a Canadian leader issuing loud instructions that everyone (EVERYONE) had to limbo under it. Limbo dancing is not really my thing. I hung back, waiting for the enthusiasts at the front to take the attention and hoping that interest in the quality of limbo-ing would have waned by the time it was my turn. As the performative walk progressed, I became familiar with its dramaturgical rhythms; we were coaxed and cajoled into playing on the monkey bars or dancing on a hillside, offered a fantasy world of imaginative storytelling, shooed into running along the paths and backstreets of Knowle West and allowed time for more unhurried conversations. We were introduced to the estate's real-live pet duck who posed for selfies. In the rhythms of the walk along the tarmacked alleys and muddy paths, I was reminded of Tim Ingold description of 'wayfarers', a term he uses to describe the ways in which life is always lived in motion:

> Along such paths, lives are lived, skills developed, observations made and understandings grown. ... To be, I would now say, is not to be *in* place but to be *along* paths. The path, and not the place, is the primary condition of being, or rather of becoming (Ingold 2011: 12).

Whatever my resistance to some of the more contrived participatory elements of this event, understood in this way the performative walk becomes a metaphor for living, a way to attend to the everyday ecologies of human and nonhuman encounters that shape experiences and identities.

In *Night Walks with Teenagers* the affective atmosphere was generated by engaging in its nonhuman elements – the cold, damp weather, the nighttime darkness and the urban landscape – as well as by the movement of people along the streets. The philosopher Germot Böhme argues that atmosphere exists 'between environmental qualities and human sensibilities', suggesting that it is both produced organically and manipulated theatrically (Böhme 1993: 117). Part of the promise of *Night Walks with Teenagers* was to explore a different side to the city and, rather than seeing the streets and public spaces as an inert backdrop to the walk, the young people had attended to its affective potential with real imagination. One section of the walk illustrates their approach to reanimating their neighbourhood. We were invited to pause and look carefully at a particular gnarled tree by the side of a path. Later, standing in a field, two of the teenagers recounted a ghost story that unravelled the tree's secret – it had been witness to a bloody murder and was now haunted by the victim in a particularly gruesome way. Our attention was quickly diverted from the story by a change of mood, and we were led to a muddy hillside high above the city with spectacular views of Bristol: magical and unexpected in the dark. On the Sunday night when I attended, the view was a distracting backdrop to the walk as audience members sought landmarks familiar to them – Clifton Suspension Bridge, the harbourside and the cathedral – and responded only slowly to the young people's exhortation to dance. Retracing out steps, however, we were invited to revisit that tree and to attend to its atmosphere now that we knew its story. This delightful fabrication indicates the young people's working processes. As well as inventing the story, they had found the tree and observed its qualities, developing what Jane Bennett describes as 'sensory attentiveness' to its affective potential. This attentiveness, Bennett suggests, encourages the kind of playful participation in the contemporary world that she calls 'enchantment':

> Enchantment is something that we encounter, that hits us, but it is also a comportment that can be fostered through deliberate strategies. One of these strategies might be to give greater expression to the sense of play, another to hone sensory receptivity to the marvellous specificity of things. (Bennett 2001: 4)

For the audience this moment of enchantment might be fleeting – I am not sure that I could find that tree again – but for the teenagers, the tree will always be marked by the memory of the story they invented for the walk. The environmental memories of participants may have been different, but the affective labour of the shared encounter was amplified by walking at night and, for the audience, by handing over control of time and space to the teenagers who were our storytellers and guides.

Over hot chocolate at Knowle West Media Centre I returned to the question of authorship and how power had been distributed between local teenagers and Mammalian Diving Reflex in the workshops. Performative walks are very much associated with contemporary performance art rather than youth culture, and the conceit for an immersive walk in the dark was already established before the project started. *Night Walks with Teenagers* is a brand, and the marketing for every project – whether it takes place in Bristol, Manchester or elsewhere – carries the same strapline: Share footpaths and futures. Take a poignant, rebellious walk on the wild side.[8]

This promise reiterates the familiar trope that teenagers are rebellious, and I was curious to know how far this idea had been imposed on the young people and shaped the work's aesthetic. I asked a girl – only just in her teens – how many of the ideas were generated by them and how much had already been decided in advance. 'It was all our ideas', she answered emphatically, 'all of them', and described how Mammalian Diving Reflex had defined the parameters for the project, but that the creative ideas for the walk itself had come from them. This was easy to believe; there was an energy in the walk that suggested local knowledge. It was less clear whether the young people shared the company's social ambition, described by Darren O'Donnell, creator of *Night Walks with Teenagers*, in the following terms:

> They will feel the city in a different way, they will be in the city in a different way, they get to socialise in a different way. ... A big part of it is freedom, but the other part is sharing a casual social space with adults who they do not know. This is a completely unusual dynamic in our paranoid societies and it's a dynamic that a lot of young people love. Our societies segregate young and old and only allow them to socialise under very strict and highly scrutinised circumstances.[9]

When interviewed on film, the young Bristolian participants echoed this interest in breaking down social division. There was, however, a subtle distinction between their perspectives. Rather than wanting adults to entertain their rebelliousness and share their 'disruptive potential', they hoped that the walk would gain adult approval. One boy, wearing a neat school tie, explained that they did not want to be judged as if all teenagers were the same. 'We're not all naughty', added a girl.[10] The ways in which these witty, creative and thoughtful teenagers subtly reframed the company's values raises questions about the biopolitics of creative practice with young people. Teenagers are often experts in assimilating atmospheres and conforming to adult expectations – even to the extent of performing rebelliousness on a walk.

Night walks with Teenagers highlights the central paradox in the relationship between affective labour, participation and performance: its negotiation of biopower. The young people learnt how to produce and manipulate affect for an adult audience, gaining agency in the process and yet still conforming to the theatre company's mission. I learnt from the young Bristolians that their affective labour needed to be witnessed – to gain agency, they required different publics to experience their enchanted alleyways and paths; it was only through witnessing and being witnessed that familiar places might be newly inhabited and identities newly framed. The project also demonstrated the sociability of affective labour, as we walked together and talked in the Bristol streets, capturing the conviviality of shared experience in its newly imagined spaces. But not everything about this project felt politically egalitarian, and there were different shades and levels of participation from the teenagers' fellow adult wayfarers. Affective labour, however socially generative in the performative moment, did not erase the material inequalities between disadvantaged suburb and the creative city, and at times the experience felt disturbingly divisive.

Cultural participation and the politics of ordinary affects

This chapter critically responds to a particular cultural moment in which the affective labour of cultural participation is being redefined and onto-logical divisions of labour are being unsettled. Neither twentieth-century clarification of theatre-making as amateur, professional, voluntary or community, nor twenty-first-century hybridised terms associated with neoliberalism (prosumer, pro-am or artrepreneur) offer an accurate repre-sentation of this way of working. Participation is immanent to affective labour and generates social networks, but as I have argued, the asso-ciation between affective labour and neoliberal knowledge-based econo-mies places relational art and participatory performance in a politically ambivalent position. My intention in this chapter is to acknowledge these tensions and to challenge simple binaries that position participation in live performance as either a manipulative and coercive symbol of neolib-eral self-entrepreneurship or as a sure route to democratic forms of social participation.[11]

Throughout this chapter I have sought to reimagine the dynamic between affective labour and cultural participation in ways that resist the commodification of participatory experience. All the projects I discuss in this chapter, *Like Mother, Like Daughter; Dad Dancing;* and *Night Walks with Teenagers,* were devised by professional artists working in partnership with untrained performers; all three performances, in different ways, were constructed in response to deep relation-specific connections between people and places – either inter-generationally with family members or as local residents. In each case the process was referenced in performance, giving the work an improvisatory quality, a sense that it was temporar-ily authoring unfinished and ongoing relationships. Conjoining the social and the artistic offered opportunities for participants to attend to the sensory and affective qualities found in the quotidian and habitual spaces of everyday life and to find ways to frame their experiences in performance. Rather than seeking the spectacle of theatrical illusion, the performances invoked in this chapter share an interest in what Kathleen Stewart describes as 'ordinary affects', and this 'ordinariness' carries its own political imperatives and potentialities.

Stewart describes ordinary affects as the kind of sensations, impulses and 'habits of relating' that are integral to everyday life. Ordinary affects are continually in motion and do not necessarily appear as coherent narratives, nor do they always have an obvious 'meaning'. Rather, she suggests, their 'significance lies in the intensities they build and what thoughts and feelings they make possible' (2007: 1–3). Stewart's book, *Ordinary Affects*, captures the fragmented qualities of her subject matter; it is a series of vignettes, autobiographical encounters and imaginings that juxtapose the daily stuff of life (such as waiting for the TV repair man) with the weight and emotional power of 9/11. Understood in this way, ordinary affects underscored all the productions discussed in this chapter; each animated the textures, attachments and encounters of everyday life in ways that invited audiences and participants to respond to the affective intensity of life's ordinariness. Two of the performances discussed in this chapter drew on inter-generational family relationships, and this was captured powerfully in the layers of participation involved in both *Dad Dancing* and *Like Mother, Like Daughter*. The performance of *Like Mother, Like Daughter*, for example, mapped domestic life through a series of juxtaposed conversations between mothers and daughters, glimpsing the intensity of everyday attachments and holding them still for moment. *Like Mother, Like Daughter* re-animated domestic politics by attending to the singularity of ordinary affects – to its flows, narratives and trajectories – which are, according to Stewart, 'more directly compelling than ideologies' (2007: 3). Ordinary affects are future oriented, she suggests, inviting 'potential modes of knowing, relating and attending to things that already somehow present', and all the performances and projects discussed in this chapter invoked relationships beyond the immediacy of the performance, albeit in different ways.

Attending to the ordinary affects of life and the affective labour of artists offers one way to understand the contemporary significance of cultural participation. Resisting the commodification of participation in performance, I suggest, involves not only rehabilitating the conventional role of the artist as social critic but also recognising that new ways of thinking and feeling can be produced affectively, perhaps particularly on the modest scale of ordinary life. As such, not only do the experiments in participation discussed in this chapter generate affect as a *product* of labour, but they also invite participants to become attuned to the everyday, an experience that McCormack describes as 'an opportunity for stretching experience, for modifying senses and sensibilities' (2013). Such creative experiments might work against commodified consumer culture, generating affective encounters that affirm life's enchantment.

Endnotes

1. See, for example, Liz Adkins 'Social capital: The anatomy of a troubled concept', *Feminist Theory*, 6, (2005), 195–211.
2. www.dad-dancing.org [accessed 12 August 2015].
3. Interview with Rosie Heafford, Alexandrina Hemsley and Helena Webb conducted at Battersea Arts Centre 16 January 2015.
4. See Teresa Brennan, *The Transmission of Affect* (Ithaca and London: Cornell University Press, 2004).
5. http://ibt15.co.uk/ [accessed 10 February 2015].
6. Knowle West Media Centre, *Manifesto 2015: A Call for Change*, http://kwmc.org.uk/about/manifesto2015/#sthash.ENc8J5Xt.dpuf [accessed 1 June 2015].
7. Mammalian Diving Reflex, *The Mammalian Protocol for Collaborating with Children*, http://www.mammalian.ca/pdf/publications/MammalianProtocol.pdf [accessed 12 August 2015].
8. See http://ibt15.co.uk and http://www.contactmcr.com/nightwalks [accessed 19 August 2015].
9. http://www.rifemagazine.co.uk/2015/01/think-know-bristol-come-dark-side-nightwalks/ [accessed 9 August 2015].
10. http://www.rifemagazine.co.uk/2015/03/nightwalks-with-teens-taking-on-stereotypes-by-being-silly/. Extracts from the performative walk can also be accessed on this website [accessed 14 August 2015].
11. Of course, participatory forms of theatre have long been applied to educational and community settings, but this is not the primary focus of my attention in this chapter. See Helen Nicholson, *Applied Drama: The Gift of Theatre* (Basingstoke: Palgrave, 2005/2014) for my contribution to this debate.

7 Sometimes the Quieter the Revolution, the Louder It Is Heard

Craftivism, Protest and Gender

Dawn Fowler

Craft and protest share a long and inextricably linked history. The act of individually or collectively making an expressive object in the form of a banner or artwork often performs a fundamental role in protest movements. A striking image or summarising slogan can help to articulate an argument and unite protesters. The emergence of the term craftivism in recent years, however, demonstrates a conscious effort to combine and theorise the complex relationship that craft (particularly in the form of knitting, sewing and weaving) has with social and political activism.[1] While craftivists operate within interchangeable modes of participation that traverse a middle ground between craft practitioner and activist, there are several factors that unite participants within a wider, established movement.[2] When crafted objects are recognised as craftivism, the radical potential of the work is valued as much – if not more – than its artistic completion, which shifts 'traditional emphasis away from polished, professionally made craft objects themselves and toward a political and conceptual focus, positioning, and deployment of the work involved in making them' (Black and Burisch 2011: 205). In many cases the finished craft object is used instead of the physical presence of the protester to perform an anonymous act of opposition, and craftivists often choose to display their work in specifically targeted public or civic spaces.

For the craftivist, making or displaying a work of craft as an artwork or to achieve aesthetic enrichment of an environment combines with the specific activist intention behind the work. Because the work is often painstakingly created over time, slowness, quiet and absence become performative gestures of this activism, which arguably attempt to wrestle back a sense of aesthetic ownership and self-authorship within increasingly despondent urban and political landscapes. As Jen Harvie argues, performative analysis 'through everyday acts of self-articulation and self-creation' within the urban environment provides a challenge to 'inescapable material circumstances' (Harvie 2009: 45). With this resolve, according to Fiona Hackney, knitting has become 'a valid and effective means to critique capitalism, protest against war, peak oil, and exploitative labour practices, and forge alternative identities, communities and ways of living' (2013: 170). If the work of the craftivist 'performs' the protest on behalf of its creator, however, this complicates the notion of participation within the movement and raises questions about the competing ideas of activism, performativity and gender. From an activist perspective, what are the implications if nothing is spoken, there is no physical presence and the craft itself becomes a carrier of the protesting 'speech act'? From a feminist perspective, how can the predominantly female participants in craftivism reconcile effective activism with quietness and absence? This chapter considers a range of practitioners and projects to analyse how in some quarters the creation of craft objects and their method of produc-tion are being used in place of the voice to provide activists (or potential activists) with distinct routes to participation in craftivism. It questions the extent to which slowness, quiet and absence can be powerful forms of social performance that provide alternative communicative possibilities which resist loud, fast and physical forms of protest.

Craftivism as quiet protest: Feminist histories

Geraldine Harris states that female performance art 'always potentially carries some sort of 'political' message because, in being 'authored' by women, it inevitably implies a critique of the politics of representation' (Harris 1999: 22). This view is important here because participation in craftivism requires a re-examination of gendered stereotyping that historically downplays a significant proportion of skilled artisans. Craft practitioners and feminists have long argued for increased recognition of historical female involvement in domestic crafting within academic and design contexts, and while there has been a significant revival of inter-est in crafting in the last decade, there has also been a concerted attempt to reclaim or, perhaps more accurately, rebrand its image.[3] Janis Jeffries, recognising the rise of participation in artistic and hobby crafting due in part to the popularity of artists/crafters such as Tracy Emin or Grayson Perry, states that '[c]raft has become the new cool' (Jeffries in Buszek 2011: 224). Certainly, 'the new cool' aspect of crafting in general, which has been readily adopted by marketing companies, is worth differentiating as it sits uneasily against the proposed or perceived protest intended by the work labelled as craftivism. What does calling oneself a craftivist *do*, and when and how does a work of art become activist?

Some answers to these questions can be found by contextualising contemporary craftivism against a wider history of crafting as a form of feminist protest. Jack Bratich and Heidi Brush argue that 'the organizing cell for the first phase of feminism was the sewing circle, the quilting group, or ladies' charity organization', and one key motivation for participants within contemporary craftivism is the repeated argument that crafting specifically allows for engagement in a form of prolonged activism, which is historically connected with predominantly female participation (Bratish and Brush 2011: 243). Craftivism, it should be recognised, is not a singularly female pursuit, and the increase in men pursuing an interest in sewing has spawned its own buzz-term: 'manbroidery'. There is also a fascinating history of crafting as male protest which deserves a full-length study.[4] What is particularly interesting here, however, is the noted significant rise of female participants within the resurgence of craft activism in Europe and North America and the attraction of slow, quiet activity that appear to be the central tenets to the movement.[5]

Betsy Greer, the American knitter who coined the term craftivism in 2003, for example, directly references a desire to remain quiet and let her craft do the talking: '[Craftivism] meant something more akin to creativity plus activism. Or crafty activism. It was about using what you can to express your feelings outward in a visual manner without yelling or placard waving' (Greer 2011: 183).[6] She recalls a previous women's rights march where she 'remember[ed] walking on the protest route, yelling and holding up some sign that was handed to me, not entirely sure what I was contributing to the world' (2011: 177). The desire to protest in a self-expressive way merged with learning to knit and the process of connecting with fellow crafters in knitting circles. The removal of the voice as the dominant method of protest is, in this sense, a rejection of loudness but also a rejection of forms of activism that reflect, and perhaps ultimately reinforce, dominant ideologically driven behavioural structures that demand that we must be aggressive, forward-moving and decisive.

Greer's account of the birth of craftivism recalls the work of Ann Pettitt, a founding member of the Peace Camp at Greenham Common. On 12 December 1982 nearly 30,000 women gathered to surround and decorate the nine-mile perimeter fence of the US military base in Berkshire, protesting for nuclear disarmament. In her memoir Ann Pettitt describes the scene:

> It was an eerily quiet demonstration. There were no loud hailers or marshals or shouting or people telling anyone what to do. There were banners a plenty but no chants or even slogans. There was no marching up and down, and no one to confront. Only the clattering of police and press helicopters broke into the midwinter stillness. (2006: 149)

Pettitt remembers how large numbers of women each bought items to decorate the fence, 'leaving behind intricate tapestries spelling the message in myriad ways', while watched over by British and American soldiers (2006: 224). Pettitt notes the diversity of the women who participated, including 'political feminist women' but also women who 'would have avowed, if asked, that they did not care two hoots for feminism or politics' (2006: 150). Kirsty Robertson contends that Greenham demonstrated how:

> [T]he very feminine qualities that were used to dismiss textiles as art forms were ironically reversed to demonstrate the peaceful nature of the protests versus the brutality of (masculine) police oppression and the wider threat that had brought the threat of nuclear war. (in Buszek 2011: 185)

The presence of weaponry would not make them replicate militaristic behaviour and take up arms. The tactile nature of craft in this case acted as a conduit to allow the protesters to actively perform a nonviolent stance.

Robertson addresses the potential rejection of crafting as a serious means of protest, arguing that it often gets situated against the historical devaluing of craft as a domestic female hobby:

> In the dismissals of activist knitting there is often an underlying critique of knitters – even those actually at the protest – that their tactics are so nonconfrontational as to be completely ineffective. Knitting, in other words, is seen as a safe form of activism (if it is activism at all), both for those practicing it and those covering it in the media. (in Buszek 2011: 188)

Craftvism arguably still suffers from an association with historical gender biases that infect seemingly positive reporting. Even after adding political intent to the mix, participants can still be dismissed as practising a discipline, which has been seen for too long as novelty, sentimental or twee. Even the way crafting physically makes the body hunch over, the head go down and the crafter become still has been criticised as a demonstrably passive stance. This view has been challenged by Rozsika Parker in her robust defence of embroidery, *The Subversive Stitch: Embroidery and the Making of the Feminine* (1984), and the work of revisionist feminists in the 1970s and 1980s that reconsidered artistic hierarchies in order to celebrate female creativity (Lippard 1978).

The feminist critic Lucy Lippard advocated an overhaul in the attitude towards crafting, where 'the idea is no longer to make nothings into some things but to transform and give meaning to all things. In this utopian realm, Good Taste will not be standardized in museums, but will vary from place to place, from home to home' (Lippard 1978). Craftivism enters itself into this debate in an intriguing way that may reveal more about the motives of participants. Greer said that one of the key factors in the early days of craftivism was to engage with historical female narratives and to feel a sense of solidarity with past and present generations of women. If the personal is political, then craftivism attempts to take that political position out of the home and display (and perform) it in the streets as Lippard envisaged. By effectively turning the established order of things on its head via reclamation and reappropriation of the past, there is arguably an attempt to find a shared political space that has been lacking.

Slowly/quietly/collaboratively: *Pink Tank* and *The Craftivist Collective*

The so-called revival of crafting may be a fallacy of practitioners who have displayed qualities of artistry, ingenuity, collaboration, patience and skill for thousands of years, but the specific attempt to create an alternative means of activism by using these methods speaks to a wider issue, it seems: protest need not be a singular moment or even represent a decisive position. Many craftivists describe how the collaborative and creative potential of art-making acts as a symbolic, performative alternative to violent and distressing situations, as well as an aesthetic response to it. David Revere MacFadden, chief curator at the Museum of Arts and Design, which presented a radical lace and subversive knitting exhibition in 2007, asserts that

> [i]t is not surprising that the reappearance of knitting and other so-called domestic handcrafts followed soon after the events of September 11

2001 and craftivism, as Greer has stated, became a global movement that responded specifically to a sense of impotency caused by military interventions and ensuing wars. (MacFadden 2008: 8)

As images of technologically enhanced warfare filled television screens one of the most celebrated anti-war crafting pieces, Marianne Jørgensen's project in association with the Cast off Knitters group, *Pink Tank* (2006), was created. A giant pink cover consisting of over 4000 squares for a World War II military tank, *Pink Tank* has become the oft-cited example of modern craft's association with pacifism:

> The main impression of the knitted tank is that it consists of hundreds of patches knitted by many different people in different ways: single coloured, stripes with bows or hearts, loosely knitted, closely knitted, various knitted patterns. As such, it represents a common acknowledgement of a resistance to the war in Iraq. (Black and Burisch in Adamson 2003: 611)

An important aspect of the creation of *Pink Tank* is the collaboration of diverse ranges of participating global crafters, which made the final piece a celebration of individual creativity operating within an overriding collective ideology. Individually a separate handkerchief or square of material is unassuming, but together they represent a united voice. The shades of pink feminise and obscure the object of war, removing its militaristic power and undermining the violent potential of weaponry by rendering it absurd. The tank finds a new identity; it becomes tactile, amusing and unthreatening.

This method of symbolically collaborative participation uses global crafters to perform a collective pacifism that widens the field of participation. The individual crafter becomes part of a collective work which is stronger in numbers. In this sense, the pieces are collective, but they are also driven by individual responses to war and conflict. Discontent is marshalled to traverse countries, reinforce connections and respond specifically to world politics. What is perhaps most significant is the idea that materiality potentially performs the pacifist role on behalf of the crafters. The creation of a large work of craft not only demonstrates that a lot of people care but forms its own tactile physical barrier against the issues that it confronts.

Sarah Corbett of The Craftivist Collective is perhaps the most high-profile craftivist in the UK. On moving from a deprived area of Liverpool to work in London as a keen crafter and campaigner, Corbett describes herself at this point in her life as 'a burnt out activist' who was 'actually thinking whether I would have to give up fighting for a better world' (Corbett 2013: 15). She experienced an increasing frustration that a keen sense of social justice was not finding a suitable outlet:

> In 2008, I found myself feeling discouraged and exhausted. Shouting and marching drained me; I didn't like demonising people and telling them what to do. I didn't feel like I fitted into some activist groups. 2013: 3)

Corbett found solace in her hobby of cross-stitching, eventually Googling 'craft plus activism' and discovering Greer's craftivism website. Greer's definition of craftivism as 'a way of looking at life where voicing opinions through creativity makes your voice stronger, your compassion deeper' appealed to Corbett, and with Greer's permission she borrowed the term for her blog *A Lonely Craftivist* (Harris 2013).

In 2013 Corbett gave a speech at TEDx Brixton, in which she contextualised craftivism as its own particular form of cultural participation.[7] She spoke of her exhaustion with activism that takes the form of collecting signatures, sit-ins or marching, and she cited her introverted personality and meditative view on the world as being at odds with the perceived anger and immediacy of public protest. Corbett argued that an imposed idea of how an activist should perform when participating in protest movements – involving loudness, anger and immediacy – excludes many people from demonstrating their disapproval of existing structures. There was a whole quiet army of activists, she suggested, who felt unable to express themselves meaningfully. An alternative route, Corbett offered, is to use the very mechanisms of crafting to physically slow down the protest and create an object that is made over time in the hope that this will allow the activist the space to fully consider and clarify their position. She terms this process 'slow activism':

> Most activism is fast: sign this petition, click here, march there. Craft is naturally slow. Therefore, it forces you to make time to stop and reflect on what the issues mean, whom injustice affects and how we can be part of a solution. Craft connects your heart, head and hands, and when you relate that to justice issues, it can be world-changing personally and politically. (Corbett 2013: 3)

Longevity as a form of protest is not a new concept, as movements such as Occupy would attest. The intricate process of stitching in this sense, however, is intended to reflect symbolically that the crafter who has made the work feels deeply enough about the issue at hand to have laboured over its creation.

Another element, as Bratich and Brush argue, is that '[c]rafting creates slow space, a speed at odds with the imperative towards hyper-production' (2013: 236). When the act of object-making combines with self-expression, it can speak, writes Maria Elena Buszek, 'of a direct connection to humanity that is perhaps endangered, or at the very least being rapidly reconfigured in our twenty-first-century lives' (2011: 1). Buszek addresses the point that globalisation and the capitalist system means that the shifting of industrialised crafting to developing countries has created a disconnect between people and their possessions. Andrew Jackson writes that this has created a sense of 'alienation inherent in mass production and its corollary, mass consumption' (2011: 266). In response, public events in the form of knitting or crafting performances have also attempted to initiate community discussions and promote intimacy and cohesion, which allows spectators to consider alternative behaviours.

Corbett states that the slowness of crafting prevents outward displays of sudden anger which she believes diminish constructive dialogue because they create offensive and defensive positions that override useful solutions. The finished product, which could take a range of forms from mini-protest banners, embroidered handkerchiefs to Barbie dolls holding feminist placards, can then be displayed anonymously in public spaces under the signature of The Craftivist Collective. A key factor in Corbett's argument is that this non-confrontational method of activism appeals to a personality type that is quiet in nature. The Craftivist Collective stresses that if participants are openly crafting, they should not impose themselves on a space or annoy the public:

Don't initiate a conversation, wait for people to decide to engage with you. This type of craftivism is an introverted activism. It's not about performance or vying for attention, it's about offering people the chance to engage. (2013: 31)

This is an approach that is celebrated among members. Craftivist Sarah Tarmaster asserts that '[c]raftivism allows me to express myself without having to have the confidence to get up in front of loads of people' (2013). Messages left on social media support this: 'You don't know whether one whisper in someone's ear is going to make more of a difference than ten thousand shouting on the street' (2013).

The Craftivist Collective, then, as it is described here, is a community of individuals using the form to make interventions with a whisper rather than a loud-hailer. The motivations of participants imply that quiet becomes part of the activism itself, but against what? The message is that loudness is part of the problem and that people need to be reminded to stop and think before they open their mouths, but does loudness itself contribute to the social inequalities the movement denounces? Here emerges a lack of cohesion to the specific aims that craftivism and its offshoots wants to achieve. This is not a criticism of the specific craftivists or projects I have mentioned; it is more an observation of the generalised sense of dissatisfaction that can emerge in the narratives surrounding this movement. Lacey Jane Roberts has noted the 'identity crisis' in contemporary craft and advocates urgent action to 'shape our own progressive discourse' (2011: 244). Global poverty, pacifism and human rights injustices are worth standing up for, but what those injustices are can be interpreted differently by different people. Greer has addressed this point, stating that whenever a term is created and goes out into world, it assumes a life of its own and becomes a more generalised concept that offers the chance to participate actively in what Diane Elam terms a 'notion of ethical activism or the politics of undecideability' (Elam, qtd in Harris 1999: 178).

Craftivism, however, still has a way to go to clarify its own position among hobby, art and activism. In its aversion to yelling and marching, there is a sense, all too common in female narratives, of not 'making-a-fuss' or 'causing bother' in the descriptions surrounding this movement, which, while rightfully challenging preconceived notions of activist behaviour, somehow do not sit comfortably with the ideas of outward-looking feminism, or revolution (even if it is quiet revolution), that the movement prescribes. However, the view that being quiet is synonymous with passivity is an oft repeated mistake which deserves to be challenged, as does the weary and outdated view that crafting is anti-feminist. In this respect, craftivism as a contemporary movement arguably attempts to directly dispute methods of protest that use loudness, large numbers and physical movement.

Anti-physical participation

A politicised form of crafting offers the opportunity to perform an act of radicalism or protest and attempt to connect with others through a mediating object without, as both Greer and Corbett state, raising the voice. Yet, removal of the physical self from protest runs the risk of somehow diluting the message or leaving a lack of clarification in how to move forward. It is important, as Roberts states, that the celebrated qualities of quietness do not result in a 'muted individuality'. Alongside methods of slowness and quiet, The Craftivist Collective's means of display is one that centres on the individual craftivist as lone participant using urban space as a blank canvas for self-expression. Social media rather than physical space is used to 'gather' participants. Glen Adamson notes that '[t]he new crafter wave is fuelled by an intriguing alliance of the oldest and newest of social technologies, the sewing circle and the blog', and certainly appropriation of technology has reinvigorated the more traditional methods of the crafting movement (Adamson 2010: 586). Corbett's singular blog has now evolved into The Craftivist Collective with thousands of followers on social media.[8] There is no prescribed method of partaking in The Craftivist Collective, and although it has a higher profile spokesperson, the overall sentiment is one of autonomy. Many modern crafting groups actively encourage members to take pictures of their work and send them in to the website for publication. Technology functions to display the work of individual crafters under the aims of the collective movement. The use of social media as a gathering space is certainly not unique to craftivism, but in relation to this movement it does complicate the notion of the craftivist as an individual performing a singular action. The individual participates as a means for self-autonomy in protest but also acts under the guidance, possibly even permission, of the group.

The crafter acting as a lone-wolf protester leaving found objects in various spaces raises questions about physical presence and absence in social dissent. In The Craftivist Collective's handbook *A Little Book of Craftivism*, aspiring craftivists are given advice on stitching methods, templates and ideas to disseminate their work. Fabric footprints are suggested as a way to inspire people to think about environmental issues and their personal impact on the planet. The Barbie Project asks participants to 'buy a second hand Barbie or other doll, then colour bruises and wounds onto her. Make her a placard with a fact, quote or statistic about gender inequality, then tie her up with gaffer tape and display her in a public place' (Corbett 2013: 52–53). Handmade Valentine's Day cards and gifts are proposed to carry an alternative message of 'love not just for a single person, but for the planet, our fellow human-beings and for future generations' and are left near cash points or in shopping centres (2013: 52–53). The attempt to disrupt or subvert public space by giving free and unrestricted access to protest materials has historical context. Kim Solga recognises how:

Urban dramaturgy shaped in the wake of Benjamin, Debord and de Certeau has done much to reimagine the relationship between artist, spectator and an environment in an exchange where pedestrians are embodied practitioners engaged in dialectical, performative encounters. (2009: 12)

This form of situationist street anarchy attempts to find a diverse audience and asks its spectators to have a responsive engagement with their surroundings. The public display of the work attempts to create what Jacques Rancière would term an 'encounter' or 'invitation', where 'the artist-collector institutes a space of reception to engage the passer-by in an unexpected relationship' (2006: 90). The displayed objects are intended to perform several functions. First, they intend to 'catch the attention of passers-by in a respectful and thought-provoking way without forcing our views on them' (Corbett 2013: 36). Here the craftivist aims to engineer an encounter, or personal interaction that has a prolonged effect on recipients through an eye-catching aesthetic. The object is encouraged to 'be' activist by carrying some kind of protest message, in the form of an image, slogan or quotation that encourages a dialogue with its environment. The spectator does not know the creator of the work, and the authorial intent is not always spelt out, but there are imbued performative meanings in the interaction between object and environment that are intended to inform our understanding of it.

Leaving a work of art in a public place for others to find and engage with on their own terms can sidestep the aversion that people can have to aggressive campaigning, being bothered in their daily routines or having to cross the road to avoid the person ahead with the clipboard. The mini banners require physical interaction from the passer-by, and it is their choice to make whether they engage with it or not. One problematic issue, then, is that it is impossible to measure the impact of the intervention. The signatures on a petition or numbers attending a protest can be counted, and governmental response can be monitored. With no way of documenting the effect of the work, it is difficult to measure whether the anticipated social change has been achieved. Moreover, the gentleness of the intervention means that the object can be ignored, ridiculed, vandalised or subject to the dismissive treatment that craft has faced in the past, although I would argue that these kinds of initial responses, even if unpleasant, are as valid as any other when pedestrians are invited to be empowered spectators who can co-author the work through their responses to it.

There is a potential danger in planting objects in random spaces of seeming privilege or of subjugating the responsibility of 'standing behind' one's own opinion. Is it possible to effectively protest via a deliberate retreat from participation? As an act of protest, this self-defined quiet revolution removes all sense of catharsis or resolution for its audience, and a physical relationship cannot be formed with the creator; in some respects it is an anti-performance. However, participants would argue that this is precisely the point. The sense of perseverance performed by the object is intended to poignantly provide the voice and create the relationship for the 'army' of quiet protesters previously unable to articulate their dissatisfaction.

Anonymity: Can non-craftivism be craft activism?

Paul Kingsnorth writes of the success of street-artist Banksy that 'anonymity is the new authorship' (2010: 198). One key component of craftivism that sits uneasily with the idea of participation has been its adoption of anonymity and how the lack of physical participation in protest potentially indicates a lack of confidence in public engagement. There is, however, a relationship between street art, graffiti and craftivism that complicates this picture. Kingsnorth notes that 'taggers' working under an assumed identity have 'utilised the vocabulary of the terrorist' to add an intrigue to their work that marks them out as an 'outsider' – someone who does not obey the law and does not operate within the rules (2010: 197). This also applies to technological activism. Hacktivists, for example, are 'Cyber-warriors' who 'terrorize' governments by performing 'electronic assaults'. Groups such as Anonymous or Lulzsec 'attack' their targets and declare war on organisations. The use of the term yarnbombing or craft attack to describe a piece of craft work that just *appears* in public space follows this trend. There is a clandestine quality to the act that adds to the intrigue.

Cultural geographer Tim Cresswell refers to graffiti as 'night discourse ... subversive messages which appear in the morning after the secretive curtain of night has been raised' (Cresswell, qtd in Kingsworth 2010: 198). The use of increasingly subversive methods in street art and graffiti is a response, argues Nicolas Whybrow, to an increased accessibility:

Not only has its imagery been shamelessly plundered, principally by 'youth culture' orientated corporations, but it has also been 'mainstreamed' as art, appearing in gallery spaces or other sanctioned sites. (2010: 198)

Whybrow recognises the insult that becoming 'mainstream' can be for countercultural movements, and he criticises how urban art is commodified as an act to neutralise its radical potential. 'The new cool' aspect of craftivism has already seen this process start as I mentioned earlier. Whybrow also acknowledges that the anonymity of the artist can fall into the trap of overriding the art itself or becoming the point of the art, thereby a clever sales technique. As Adam Alston explores in his chapter on Secret Cinema in this volume, secrets 'can give rise to communities of people', but secrecy can also be commodified and used as a marketing tool. In relation to anonymous street art, we want to know who the artist is, why they won't reveal themselves, what they have to hide. They become fascinating.

In May 2012 Saltburn-by-the-Sea, a small, seaside resort nestled in the North-East English coastline, found itself the unwitting recipient of a surge of publicity. Using language usually ascribed to a crime thriller, local (followed by national) press described how under the cover of darkness a black-clad, balaclava-wearing figure had scaled the town's traditional Victorian pier, equipped with climbing ropes and a head torch. She had then skilfully attached a knitted scarf depicting scenes and characters from sporting events in anticipation of the London 2012 Olympic Games across the length of the 208 metre handrail. Expert knitters estimated that 'the scarf would have taken up to a year to complete – and most of the night to attach to the pier' (Richardson 2014). There was no identifying signature on the work, and no one stepped forward to claim responsibility. The act was described as 'a classic whodunnit', the town Mayor stating that '[i]t's one of the best mysteries we've ever had in Saltburn' (Rainey 2012). Local residents provided their own moniker for the knitter; an article in the *Telegraph* reported that 'she' was known locally as 'the yarnbomber'.[9]

It was the most audacious act yet from the town's resident guerrilla knitter, who had previously yarnbombed smaller targets such as lampposts, railings, benches and the local library. In May 2013 she had struck again with a tribute to the wedding of the Duke and Duchess of Cambridge, and again in May 2014 to celebrate the World Cup. On each occasion a 'marathon scarf' would appear overnight and without warning, covering the length of the pier and creating a colourful visual spectacle. By this point it was clear that this was not the work of a single person, but a group of dedicated crafters. The group began to sign the work 'SYS' for the 'Saltburn Yarn Stormers' (Richardson 2014).

Despite the now annual expectation that the pier would be yarnbombed, the activity itself was still described as a mysterious covert operation. *The Northern Echo* reported the 2014 'bomb' in such terms: 'Shrouded in darkness, they furtively tied their lovingly handmade figures to a rail before dawn broke on Saturday morning' (Richardson 2014). Despite being described as 'the Banksy of the knitting world', the message of the work, at first glance, is one of celebration, patriotism with a touch of tongue-in-cheek humour. It is inoffensive (even pro-establishment) and does not aim to overtly undermine or subvert existing political or cultural structures. On viewing the work in 2013, admittedly intrigued and drawn into the story by what I had read about this secretive group in the newspaper, viewing members of the British Royal Family in woolly caricature dangling precariously off the side of the pier seemed somehow refreshingly subversive. Yet it is difficult to reconcile the work as craftivism or performative protest when it becomes a popular and loved tourist attraction as many spectacular yarnbombing events do. The anonymity of the creators and the audacity of the spectacle is in danger of overriding the political discourse we might have with the work, if indeed that discourse exists in the first place.

There is also an issue of permanence which recalls the firmly non-confrontational approach of craftivism. A large yarnbomb can hardly be ignored in terms of spectacle. Aesthetically the Saltburn pier was loud, colourful and unapologetically in-yer-face. It is nevertheless temporary. It can be and is removed with no destruction of property or vandalism. While the language of street art and graffiti as urban terrorists is borrowed to describe the creators, the generalised acceptance of them shows that they are not feared and are even celebrated by the authorities who would potentially have denied them the opportunity to display their work. Another differentiation between graffiti or street art and craftivism are again the issues of slowness and quiet celebrated in the movement. There is clearly a slow-burn run of collective group effort leading up to the display of the work, but the anonymity of the participants and the overnight appearance of the knitting on the pier means that the impact is sudden. Here, the term craftivism becomes problematic, as it currently appears to occupy a middle ground between crafting and politically engaged craft, the former being confused as the latter if it is displayed in public space.

There is a background narrative to this tale that involves years of work, skill and planning. Moreover, it reflects the ability of a group to join together in collaboration with the ability to keep a collective secret in regard to their identity. What the Saltburn scarves and the reception of their creators as intriguingly ambiguous female James Bond figures stress is the importance of performance and spectacle in the enactment of public crafting. The risky and physically demanding form of display flouts curatorial rules and turns the event into a participatory community project which invites members of the public to interact with and enjoy or mock a national event happening miles away. It also reflects how the appeal of craftivism has spread to smaller regional communities where crafters can engage with home-grown issues, such as the closure of public services or demonstrating against the actions of local councils.

The Saltburn yarnbomb, while not adopting an overt protest message, serves the purpose of celebrating and reinforcing the community ties in a region hit hard by economic instability. It has now become intrinsic to the identity of the town. Craft shops are opening in the centre, and it has exponentially increased tourism to the area that directly affects the local economy. Perhaps the point is, as Nicolas Bourriaud writes, '[b]y offering small services the artist repairs the weaknesses in the social bond' (qtd in Ranciere 2006: 90). Anonymity is exploited in this case to market the work, creating a sense of accessibility that draws it into the mainstream. To commit extensive labour to an activity; display proficiency, humour and ingenuity in the accomplishment; and require no individual recognition or reward for it is a potentially radical undertaking. The response to this group and their work reveals an interesting disconnect between aesthetic appreciation of the work itself, the performance of and response to spectacle, and the marketability of their anonymous identities that arguably threatens to override any activist intention in their covert actions.

Craftivism, or the idea of hands-on creativity, is being offered as a solution to industrialised methods of production and provides an avenue through which participants can develop a skill that allows for the removal of oneself from dominating activist behaviours, and through this action, it explores the radical potential of their work personally and politically. However, if crafting as activism is an idea, it is a contesting idea that traverses both the isolated individual and the collaborating collective. There will be divergent groups and new theoretical avenues to explore within this particular form of activism. The aims and practices of the women who founded and defined the craftivist identity, encouraging others to follow them, will no doubt converge with changing social and political issues. A deliberate, possibly inevitable, politicising of crafting has perhaps not reinvented but certainly reinvigorated the discipline while recognising that many women have practised subversive crafting in their own way throughout history. Indeed, it is through this direct citation of historical crafting that craftivism becomes a gendered performance of protest.

Craftivism allows its predominantly female participants to actively demonstrate their views by using slowness and quiet as a cornerstone of their activism. The early example of Greenham Common as a large-scale, highly attended spectacle set a precedent that began a slow-moving revision of the potential of craft to activate creative potential and encourage gathering. The later examples of collaborative craftivism movements, anonymous or otherwise, epitomise how feminist discourses on participatory art have reconsidered the ways in which women subversively organise and perform protest. There is a performative identity that can be formed in finding a personal model of activism that accommodates individual personalities and allows for self-expression. Clearly, there is a place for alternative forms of protest that allows participants to display their objection to existing social and political structures in their own way. The opportunity to participate in protest is a necessary part of public life, and it is clear that the slowing down permitted by craftivism allows for a meditative rather than knee-jerk response to complex issues. In the provision of opportunity and encouragement to stop, ponder, react and form a response of one's own, the craftivist ensures that not making a sound does not necessarily mean silence.

Endnotes

1. Maria Elena Buszek's edited collection *Extra/Ordinary: Craft and Contemporary Art* (Durham, NC, and London: Duke University Press, 2011), has a section of essays on craftivism that chart the movement and offers a comprehensive overview of the history of the term.
2. The term craftivism came into widespread use in 2003. Throughout the chapter, I use interchangeable terms such as crafter, practitioner, protester and activist. This is to differentiate historical craft protest from craftivism and to recognise that not all crafters would describe themselves by using this word, although the impartial observer might describe their work that way.
3. See a recent advert by soft drink 7UP, which shows the crafting of a public park with the hashtag #FeelsGoodToBeYou.
4. Hackney, for instance, records the story of how Prisoners of War in World War II would stitch subversive Morse code messages into embroideries that would be displayed in camps by unsuspecting guards, 2013, p. 172.
5. See Bratich and Brush 2013, p. 234 for analysis and sources. I am aware that the geopolitics of craft vary in different countries so I have chosen to focus on documented craftivist cases in Europe and North America, as this is work that, in many cases I have been able to view.
6. Greer began to use the term craftivism online setting up a domain name and appropriating it as a form of activist protest.
7. TEDx Brixton is an annual, independently held event to encourage discourse and social cohesion. Corbett's full speech, 'How a Piece of Fabric Can Change the World', can be viewed at http://www.tedxbrixton/videos alongside the other talks in the 2013 programme.

8. In the UK it is estimated that there are 500 active craftivists and The Craftivist Collective has over 3300 followers on Twitter (Source: Harris: 2013).
9. This possibly takes inspiration from the London based collective 'Knit the City' a group of 'friendly neighbourhood graffiti knitters' who had coined the term 'yarnstorming' in 2011.

8   'Tell No One'

Secret Cinema and the Paradox of Secrecy

Adam Alston

Secrecy has enjoyed the limelight in twenty-first-century theatre and performance. First of all, secrecy has played an important role in the design of audience participation. UK-based companies like Punchdrunk and Coney set tasks and challenges for participating audience members that involve the discovery of secrets or covert forms of audience participation. Second, theatre and performance branding, particularly in the marketing strategies of London-based theatre companies, has embraced secrecy as a trope. Examples include the Lyric Hammersmith's Secret Theatre Company, Secret Theatre London and Secret Cinema, which have all marketed theatre performances to paying audiences without telling them what the performance will be and encouraging those in the know to keep schtum. However, it's odd that secrecy has become so *prominent*. For Sissela Bok, a secret is 'kept intentionally hidden, set apart in the mind of its keeper as requiring concealment. ... The word "secrecy" refers to the resulting concealment. It also denotes the methods used to conceal' (Bok 1989: 5–6). So is secrecy still secrecy once concealment of a secret is coupled with an advertisement of secrecy? What do secrets become once packaged and sold to anyone who is able and willing to afford disclosure?

Theatre – the home of spectacle and of public scrutiny – is surely the last place one would expect to find a turn towards secrecy. This turn, albeit a fairly minor turn – more of a glance, perhaps – is concerned with (1) audiences becoming co-conspiratorial clue crackers and (2) a paradoxical form of marketing that promotes secrecy as a spectacle and as a commodity. In this chapter, I want to address how these two aspects of secrecy inform one another. There are important connections to be made between the design of audience participation and theatre marketing, and secrecy can elucidate some of these connections. More specifically, I will be addressing spectacular and paradoxical secrecy, aiming to establish and unravel the roles and uses of the commodified secret and its relevance to audience participation and immersion in contemporary theatre.

The next section begins by setting out some of the ways that contemporary theatre companies have been promoting secrecy in the design of participatory theatre, before turning to secrecy as a trope in theatre branding and marketing and reflecting on where this turn fits within audience participation studies. The section after that considers what I call the 'paradox of secrecy', which refers to the spectacular presentation of secret content in commodity form. I will be addressing how techniques used to prepare audiences for role playing, interactivity and immersion in Secret Cinema's *The Shawshank Redemption* (2012) give rise to this paradox, paying special attention to the 'keying' of secrecy in theatre marketing and branding. Finally, the chapter assesses the role and uses of commodified secrecy in *Shawshank*, focusing on a complex layering of audience inclusivity and exclusivity and its relevance to the aesthetics and politics of audience participation and immersion.

Secrets and secrecy in contemporary theatre

Coney is one of the most innovative experimenters with secrecy in participation design, by which I mean the dramaturgical and formal crafting of participatory procedures and the management of participation over the course of a live participatory performance, as well as periods of time both after and, especially, before. Coney are a collective of artists and game designers that claim to be run by an enigmatic entity called 'Rabbit', and they base their work on three founding principles: adventure, curiosity and loveliness, although a fourth principle, namely reciprocity, has also been noted by co-founder Tassos Stevens (Machon 2013). Stevens has run workshops as training programmes for 'Playful Secret Agents' (199), which flags the importance of secrecy and playful conspiracy to members of the company, who are clearly invested in exploring their connotations and potential. However, more pertinent to this chapter are Coney's performances for playing audience participants. A good example is *The Loveliness Principle* (2010–12), in which participants, among other similar tasks, are invited to 'reverse pick-pocket' strangers by surreptitiously placing or attaching thoughtful, hand-written messages somewhere on or inside of the stranger's clothing or possessions – slipped inside a jacket pocket, for instance, or in the strap of a bag. In both the workshop and the performance, a playful approach to secrecy in the design of participation is used to explore sociality between people who have not met before.

It is worth noting that another piece by Coney, called *The Gold Bug* (2007), was featured as a performance within a performance in Punchdrunk's influential immersive work, *The Masque of the Red Death* (2007–08). *The Gold Bug* was both an online game and a live theatre experience embedded within *The Masque*. The live component could be accessed either by winning tickets via the online game, which involved clue cracking and commitment to an online narrative, or by stumbling across the interloping performance as a Punchdrunk audience member. Aside from this collaboration, however, where there are clear links between the two companies, Punchdrunk and Coney load secrecy with different meanings and orient secrecy towards different ends. Rather than drawing on secrecy to promote explorations of sociality, Punchdrunk approach secrecy as a vehicle for generating greater audience investment in the world and ideology of an immersive performance. For instance, prior to the launch of *The Drowned Man: A Hollywood Fable* (2013–14), critics were invited to a ten-minute 'live trailer' in a dilapidated shop on Kingsland High Street in East London. The live trailer was also made open to the public, although it was extremely difficult to find out where the trailer was happening, beyond a vaguely defined area, not least because Punchdrunk asked critics to keep the precise whereabouts under wraps. This was a trailer to be discovered by keeping an eye open for something out of the ordinary, which turned out to be the word '*Psychic*' scrawled in glowing pink neon lettering in a shop window.

The discovery of secrets, particularly the secret depths of a performance that might take place behind locked doors, or in hard-to-reach recesses of vast buildings, is also something that characterises Punchdrunk's large-scale work more generally. In *The Drowned Man*, audiences could purchase considerably more expensive tickets that would enable them to experience a prologue and special scenes that audiences who could afford only the cheaper tickets would not be party to, which introduces a connection between secrecy and wealth. If you have the cash to flash, you can put yourself in a better position to learn more about the bewildering and complex worlds of a Punchdrunk work, albeit an investment that may not ultimately pay off.[1] Comparably, diners at The Heath – a fairly expensive noir-themed restaurant on the sixth floor of Punchdrunk and Emursive's revived production of *Sleep No More* (2011–) in New York – are privy to secret encounters and information that are not available elsewhere in the multi-storey immersive environment. Those who can afford the cost of the menu, whether or not they choose to experience the rest of the performance, open up possibilities for intimate interactions with performers mid-meal, and they may also find cryptic notes pertinent to the performance hidden in the food.[2] Punchdrunk's 'Key Holder' funding scheme, which puts a fresh spin on more conventional friendship schemes, is also premised on revealing company 'secrets' in accordance with the amount donated, among other privileges.[3]

Coney and Punchdrunk therefore gear secrecy towards different ends while nonetheless sharing common elements: withholding information from audiences and potential audiences, exploring participation as a process of discovery and revelling in the possibilities of clue cracking and problem solving. However, the connections between theatre aesthetics (participation design) and economics (theatre marketing) are much clearer when secrecy is used as a trope in participatory theatre branding and marketing. Secrecy sells. Secrets are owned and they can be exchanged. As with other forms of property, secrets can be profitable – and not just to the blackmailer. Trade secrets most clearly indicate the inherent allure, tradability and profitability of secrets. Trade secrets usually refer to hidden information of some kind, such as a secret ingredient in a recipe, or a particular kind of expertise, rendering knowledge as a form of intellectual property. However, *secrecy itself* can also function as an alluring, tradable and profitable commodity. This is a kind of secret that flaunts itself as a secret, a spectacular secret – paradoxical secrecy that thrives on implied naughtiness and exclusivity. This is Victoria's Secret, the secret-as-brand, the secret that's out. This is commodified secrecy that welcomes all, at a price.

This kind of secret is the kind snapped up by theatre branders and marketers, and not just of performances that involve audience participation. For example, London's Lyric Hammersmith theatre launched a season of plays in 2013 that it called 'Secret Theatre', in part as a pragmatic response to building works that hindered the Lyric's normal operation. While the site around the Lyric auditorium was affected, the auditorium itself remained largely untouched. In response, as artistic director Sean Holmes put it, the Lyric 'decided to make this auditorium a flexible space hosting whatever audience we could get in through back doors and goods lifts. A Secret Theatre at the heart of a building site' (Holmes 2013). Paying audiences bought tickets that were labelled simply 'Show 1', 'Show 2' and so on, and audiences were encouraged to keep play titles to themselves, with some taking it upon themselves to reprimand one another for revealing content to prospective audiences (Orr 2013). Each of the unspecified plays was performed, directed and designed by a Secret Theatre Company and ranged from productions of classic texts, such as Tennessee Williams' *A Streetcar Named Desire* (1947), to new writing, including Caroline Bird's *Chamber Piece* (2013).

Another example is Secret Theatre London, which launched in the same year as the Lyric's Secret Theatre season, but it has nothing to do with the Lyric and in fact grows out of a North American company called Brooklyn Studio Lab. Their first production in the UK was a 2013 site-generic theatre adaptation of Quentin Tarantino's *Reservoir Dogs* (1992). As with the Lyric's

148

Secret Theatre, audiences of *Reservoir Dogs* bought tickets for an unspecified performance in advance of the event, which was revealed only as the
performance unfolded. Nonetheless, as Nathan Brooker writes, audiences
were still told that they were buying tickets for a Tarantino adaptation,
and while the specific film was kept secret, 'it doesn't take the most powerful brain in London to guess which of his eight films it was likely to be',
seeing as the event was 'marketed as a site-specific production staged in a
warehouse' (2013).

Both the Lyric's Secret Theatre Company and Secret Theatre London
market not-so-secret secrets as an alluring feature of marketing campaigns.
These campaigns appeal to the involvement of prospective audiences as
public secret spreaders who ideally withhold disclosure of a performance's
content but announce to friends and networks that secret content is available.
The aim is to maximise the number of people who are 'in' on a public secret.

Both the Secret Theatre Company and Secret Theatre London create
work in the long shadow of another company that helped to cultivate the
turn towards secrecy in theatre branding and marketing: Secret Cinema.
Secret Cinema is enormously successful in the UK, routinely attracting
crowds in the tens of thousands over the course of a run. The company
was founded in 2007 by Fabien Riggall, although it grew out of two other
companies formed by Riggall in 2003 and 2005, respectively: Future
Shorts and Future Cinema. All three incarnations continue to stage film
screenings inside immersive theatre landscapes that mirror environments
featured in the film. These environments contain actors who perform in
roles inspired by, or directly borrowed from, the film prior to (and sometimes during) the film screening. Audiences are also encouraged to wear
costumes appropriate to each event and to interact with the performers.
Future Shorts screens short films, and Future Cinema screens feature films.
What Secret Cinema does is add another layer to the live feature-length
theatre/cinema experience. As with the Lyric's Secret Theatre Company
and Secret Theatre London, audiences do not know the film and accompanying immersive performance in advance of the event, although they
are given clues (such as a dress code) via email bulletins and other marketing resources. This is unlike another of Riggall's initiatives, namely Secret
Cinema Presents, where the film title is included in theatre marketing.
With Secret Cinema Presents, the notion of 'secrecy' has little currency
as a meaningful concept but a great deal of currency as an initiative that
can build on the successes of both a well-known theatre company and a
well-known film, such as their 2014 adaptation and screening of *Back to
the Future* (1985). The production sold 40,000 tickets at a cost of £53 each
within the first hour of going on sale (Aftab 2014).

What sets Secret Cinema apart from their Secret Theatre compatriots is a more concerted effort to match secrecy with role playing, interactivity and immersion in an event that exceeds the duration of a live theatre performance. Secret Cinema exemplifies how the roles and uses of secrecy in participation design and theatre marketing can complement one another. From the outset of a marketing campaign, the company encourages audiences to collude in an agenda that presents itself as secret, engendering audiences as colluding participants. While the possibility for audiences to make a meaningful intervention in live performance is fairly limited in Secret Cinema's participation design, an audience's role in performance is nonetheless keyed as a part of a 'secret' world. Audiences have a part to play, even though their playing is unlikely to affect the unfolding of a performance all that much, and this part is impacted by a framework for audience participation that joins together live theatre aesthetics and the marketing of a theatre event.

There is a tendency in audience participation studies to approach participatory art and performance either as an intervention in the material networks of capitalism or as a complicit feature or effect of the political ideologies that facilitate capitalist hegemony. For example, in *Relational Aesthetics*, Nicolas Bourriaud influentially explores the 'models of sociability' proposed by relational artists such as Rirkrit Tiravanija and Liam Gillick. Promoting inclusive and convivial forms of audience participation, Bourriaud argues that relational artists 're-stitch the relational fabric' of a capitalist society, suggesting that these artists find ways to oppose processes of alienation by remodelling the sphere of interhuman relations (2002: 36). In *Conversation Pieces* and *The One and the Many*, Grant Kester also examines the value of artists offering up 'models of sociability', focusing especially on dialogic exchange in socially engaged art and performance (2004; 2011). Contrastingly, Claire Bishop's *Artificial Hells* questions the ethical impulses of artists and scholars to celebrate the inclusion of participants in consensual forms of engagement if convivial inclusivity comes at the cost of more radical shocks to the ordering of social relationships (2012). Bourriaud, Kester and Bishop all evaluate participatory encounters in light of non-art contexts. However, while they sketch important connections between aesthetics and these contexts, particularly capitalist economies, more work needs to be done to address the imbrication of economics *within* theatre aesthetics, specifically – and particularly the aesthetics of audience participation in theatre.

These authors have set the terms of debate not just in contemporary art history but in theatre and performance studies as well, which is partly why I choose to survey their work with such rapidity; it is well-trodden territory. Performance scholars Shannon Jackson[4] and Jen Harvie,[5] for instance, have both offered balanced assessments of convivial and dissensual participatory art and performance practice that builds on and challenges this discourse. Jackson and Harvie address how socially engaged performance and relational art can comment on and propose alternatives to material systems of production and support (especially Jackson), and they critique the potential complicity of these artists and performance-makers in the material networks of capitalism (especially Harvie). However, I want to widen an understanding of performance, particularly immersive theatre performances, as opposed to socially engaged performance, so that it includes the moment that a prospective audience member comes into contact with a marketing campaign. In this chapter, it is not so much funding and diverse forms of performance production that piques my interest, necessarily, which play important roles in other studies of audience participation in contemporary theatre and performance, like those of Jackson and Harvie, which tackle the economic conditions of production and reception. Rather, focus is placed squarely on the promotion of performance – how it appears and especially how it is sold to a prospectively participating audience member. This is important when addressing the immersive work of Secret Cinema, because the frameworks that guide audience participation are founded at an early point of encounter with performance: the point of promotion.

Scholars such as Gareth White[6] and Josephine Machon[7] have come closest to this approach, and their work will inform this chapter; however, neither scholar chooses to focus on the relationships between aesthetics and economics, which are important foci when economic concerns, such as commodification, influence theatre aesthetics. Additionally, given their popularity, Secret Cinema has remained curiously unrepresented in studies of audience participation and immersion. This may be due, in part, to their overtly commercial status, but this ought to incentivise, not deter, critical enquiry. The secrecy flaunted and ultimately commodified by Secret Cinema raises important questions about audience agency, inclusivity and immersion that merit scholarly attention. What are the roles and significances of secrecy in Secret Cinema's marketing campaigns? In what ways might these roles and the relationships between them inform the commodification of secrecy? And what is the relevance of secrecy for the study of audience participation and immersion?

The possession of secrets and the paradox of secrecy

Secrets and secrecy can give rise to communities of people, mutual understanding and resistance against intolerance or injustice – for instance, the uses of identity markers and codes by homosexuals in societies that consider homosexuality taboo, particularly via dissimulation and camp. Another example would be the 'craftivist' movement explored by Dawn Fowler in this volume, in which (usually) anonymous individuals and groups covertly insert objects, often knitted and displaying activist slogans and/or content, in public spaces. However, secrecy can also inculcate obedience to the state, noting that 'protection' of a citizenry can also work as a form of disenfranchisement. An example here is the threat of prosecution for leaking information that is otherwise withheld from a public.

The visibility or invisibility of a secret's content can differentiate one person or group from another, and an important source of this differentiation is possession. I might possess a secret that I want to safeguard, and were you to find out about it you may end up in a position of power over me, bringing with it the threat of exposure. For psychological anthropologist T. M. Luhrmann, who draws on Georg Simmel, knowledge is 'a form of property, in that it can be possessed. ... And, like the difference between private and public property, it is secret knowledge that evokes the sense of possession most clearly' (Luhrmann 1989: 137).[8] For Luhrmann, '[p]ossession differentiates. Concealed information separates one group from another and one person from the rest. What I know and you do not demonstrates that we are not identical, that we are separate people' (1989: 137). In other words, there are links to be made between secrets, possession and property, and these links impact on how people relate to one another; they impact on 'interhuman relations', as Bourriaud might put it. You are either differentiated from the rest by being 'in' on a secret or you are excluded from that knowledge. This is one way in which secrecy might foster a sense of community grounded in a shared but exclusive knowledge, especially if that shared knowledge is bound up with an aspect of identity that is common and visible, or noticeable, among secret sharers – in the form of behavioural traits, for instance, or knowing facial gestures. Secrets can also be exchanged through bargaining or being marketed and sold in the same way that one would sell any other commodity.

Instead of secrets that are kept on the down-low, or leaked secrets, I want to focus on the 'paradox' of commodified secrecy. In putting forward this paradox, I refer, in part, to Beryl L. Bellman, who suggests that '[t]o tell a secret is to do secrecy. The methods used in that accomplishment are part constitutive of the phenomenon' (Bellman 1981: 8). For Bellman, the paradox of secrecy is that a secret becomes itself through its own negation. 'The informant who is telling a secret', he writes, 'either directly or tacitly makes the claim that the information he or she speaks is not to be spoken' (1981: 10). In other words, a secret is defined as much by revelation, or the threat of revelation, as it is by its being hidden. For Bellman, a secret is defined by its being announced as that which is not meant to be announced, even if this 'announcement' takes the form of private recognition. However, the paradox of secrecy, as it appears in recent theatre and theatre marketing, is more about making the announcement of a secret, as a secret, as spectacular as possible. The paradox of secrecy in this context is about striving to *involve* prospective audiences, rather than exclude them. The secret itself – such as the title of a performance – does not need to be revealed to achieve the desired involvement; it is enough for the framework of secrecy to be flaunted.

As Jack Bratich acknowledges, secrets are ripe for incorporation within the 'Society of the Spectacle', as Guy Debord famously dubbed twentieth-century consumer society, giving rise to what Bratich calls 'spectacular secrecy'. Bratich highlights how the Debordian Spectacle 'usually signifies a heightening of the visible' through commodification, elaborating that secrecy has now 'become integrated into (no longer expelled from) the spectacle' (Bratich 2006: 495). The resulting 'spectacular' secrets are made hyper-visible as an extension of the Spectacle's thirst for commodification.

Spectacular secrets, once applied to the context of capitalist markets (digressing from Bratich's specific interest in homeland security), are granted an exchange value premised on the exclusive allure of secrets. Spectacular secrets capitalise on the desire of consumers to be included and involved with the knowledge and opportunities that a secret is supposed to hide, which is the basis for the paradox of secrecy. This paradox, in my formulation, is thoroughly bound up with capital as it circulates in the information economy. While secrecy is fundamentally concerned with possession – with possessing a secret – the paradox of secrecy is concerned with possessing secrets in commodity form and displaying secrets hyper-visibly. Commodified secrets in this paradoxical scenario are spectacular, even while the information attached to a secret-cum-brand is hidden.

The paradox of spectacular secrecy is clearly applicable to marketing and branding strategies – such as those of the Lyric's Secret Theatre, Secret Theatre London and Secret Cinema – that appeal to desires to be 'in' on a secret. As such, secrecy's antithesis – publicity – is incorporated into a strategic deployment of secrecy to garner interest and sell tickets. This paradoxical incorporation involves using the spectacular image of secrecy as exclusive information, purportedly available only to a privileged few but actually available to anyone who is able and willing to purchase a ticket while tickets are available.

Interestingly, the secrets of Secret Cinema – the location and title of the film to be adapted and screened – do not really hide that much about what to expect from a Secret Cinema performance, at least for those who have heard about, or experienced, their work before. The same devices for preparing, engaging and immersing audiences are used for each show: role playing and encouraging investment in a character assigned in advance of a live performance; costuming audience participants or asking them to prepare their own costumes; incorporating performer-audience interaction and the chance to eat and drink in themed environments; immersing audiences in locations that derive from a film; and presenting a film screening. These commercially friendly devices provide a fairly standard framework for each show, which mitigates the risk of paying to see a performance that may not appeal to personal taste. While content will vary, the immersive and participatory characteristics of a Secret Cinema performance will vary much less.

Preparing for an immersive experience is an important part of each Secret Cinema performance that builds a sense of anticipation and excitement surrounding the possibilities of secret content. Decoding cryptic clues about a forthcoming experience, especially via project websites, email and social media; developing an awareness and understanding of an assigned character; and preparing a costume all position prospective audiences as participants in the development of an ambiguous aesthetic, which is appealing precisely because its meaningfulness is ambiguous in the lead-up to a live performance. It is therefore important to take these preparatory procedures seriously, as they extend the parameters of participation design and, once scrutinised, reveal important connections between the marketing of an event and the aesthetics of audience participation and immersion within a live performance.

Secret Cinema and the keying of secrecy

Prospective audiences are usually notified of a forthcoming Secret Cinema performance, in the first instance, via email or social media. There is nothing particularly innovative about this, but what sets Secret Cinema's approach apart from a broader field of contemporary theatre marketers is an extension of the 'secret' trope from the company's brand to the language used in theatre marketing. As Machon observes, immersive theatre companies, such as Coney and Punchdrunk, often use language that is 'evocative of the mystery surrounding the event, perhaps similar to that of secret societies' (2013: 54). However, for Secret Cinema the theme of secrecy permeates their marketing materials to a much greater extent. They flaunt secrecy, much as Secret Theatre Company and Secret Theatre London flaunt secrecy. For instance, Secret Cinema e-bulletins about past and forthcoming work are signed off with the tagline 'Tell No One', followed, amusingly, by a postscript that reads 'Join us on Facebook, Instagram and Twitter' (2014). While email and social networks have become dominant marketing media in theatre production, the relationships between marketing form and content in Secret Cinema's tweets and emails is more peculiar. Although audiences are told to 'Tell No One', social media implores them to 'Tell Everyone'.

For comic Daniel Kitson, aside from emailing subscribers to his mailing list, this kind of canny publicity – or indeed most publicity – is shunned, resulting in something far closer to Secret Cinema's principle 'tell no one'. As Dominic Cavendish writes, Kitson 'avoids celebrity and publicity like the plague. ... He seldom, if ever, talks to the press these days, and doesn't invite them to review his stand-up gigs' (Cavendish 2014). But for Secret Cinema, secrecy flows through digital economies of reproduction as an abstract and commodified entity. An audience's first encounter with secrecy in a Secret Cinema performance therefore occurs before the performance proper as paradoxical and spectacular secrecy. The announcement of secrecy is made hyper-visible.

At the point of first contact with a Secret Cinema marketing campaign, a frame for a series of participatory exchanges that are still to come is put into place. This frame, which is the frame of secrecy, is just as important to a Secret Cinema show as whatever film and accompanying performance is to be screened and staged. It defines what audiences are to become: they are to take on the role of a 'Secret Cinema society' member, which is my own term for Secret Cinema's peculiar rendering of the archaic secret society. Unlike secret societies, the Secret Cinema society is not difficult to enter, provided that audiences can afford to do so. It is the antithesis of W. B. Yeats' dream of an 'unpopular theatre and an audience like a secret society where admission is by favour and never too many' (qtd in Freshwater 2009: 44). Secret Cinema dreams of a popular theatre that makes its secret membership spectacular, where admission is by purchase and never too few, so long as a run can accommodate numbers or be extended to do so.

White's *Audience Participation in Theatre* (2013) reminded me of the usefulness of Erving Goffman's *Frame Analysis* for the analysis of audience participation in theatre, particularly with regard to the framing of participation. White uses Goffman's research into social relationality to explore the shared assumptions that make procedures for participation in theatre meaningful. The idea I want to borrow from Goffman, though, is his concept of 'keying', which while addressed by White, still merits explication in the context of this chapter (White 2013: 36–37). For Goffman, keying refers to activities that are recognisably 'bracketed' from the everyday and that temporarily, but systematically, alter how an activity might otherwise be understood (Goffman 1986: 45). Those who are aware of Secret Cinema must surely recognise that the kind of secrecy that they promote is 'bracketed' from less visible, less mediatised, forms of secrecy. Secrecy is in this sense 'keyed'. While it is still possible to feel a sense of exclusivity, of being 'in the know' and able to cash in on the cultural capital affiliated with the immersive experiences provided by Secret Cinema, the hyper-visibility of the company online and in the media, along with their popularity, precludes clandestine activity while promoting spectacular secrecy. Secret Cinema's publicity keys secrecy by commodifying secrecy. On the one hand, this negates secrecy as a clandestine activity. On the other hand, because secrecy is bracketed, it doesn't much matter; prospective audiences are still happy to buy into commodified secrecy.

A forthcoming and unknown film and performance is proposed to prospective audiences as a riddle and as a secret to be kept, so long as the keeping of a secret is retweeted, shared and forwarded. Marketing emails will usually be very brief and may contain a teaser quotation of some sort at its head from a text that has influenced the choice of an as-yet-unknown film, a link to a Facebook page for that particular performance, performance dates, and an ambiguous note stating that the show, for nearly all of their UK performances, will take place in a secret location, and more often than not a secret London location.[9] These publicity emails therefore participate in the keying of secrecy as a paradoxical secret; they mark an organised style of secrecy and frame secrecy as a playful practice attuned to the aesthetic character of a forthcoming performance. These emails are obscurely representative of a performance to come and disclose something of it through cryptic means, but they also ensure that secrecy becomes itself through disclosure – more specifically, through the hyper-visible performance of allegiance to the Secret Cinema society on social media's various stages.

Secret Cinema's keying of secrecy has also extended to the design of tickets for some performances. In their 2012 production and screening of Frank Darabont's film *The Shawshank Redemption* (1994), a downloadable e-ticket included a letter signed off from 'P. Doone – Administrator' that informed the ticket holder, in brash typescript, that they were taking part in a profiling campaign and that their identity had been successfully verified. The purpose of this verification remained a mystery until the performance proper began, but the ticket set up a riddle. It added to the mystery surrounding the live event, cohered with the keying of secrecy set up at first point of contact, and developed audience expectation in advance of the participatory encounters that awaited prospective participants.

For this same performance, audiences were asked to sign up to a 'court summons' that determined their arrival time, usefully doubling, I imagine, as an innovative means of getting large numbers of audience members into a theatre space without it seeming too much like entering an auditorium at the five-minute call. Each individual was given an alias – a role – and was asked to prepare for the event by learning the hymn *Dear Lord and Father of Mankind*; wearing belongings discretely; wearing flat shoes; wearing long hair up, not down; and remembering to follow all instructions immediately once inside the space. Audiences were advised to 'bring cash – you will be able to buy "library cards" to the value of twenty pounds from your lawyer upon arrival' (the only valid currency inside the performance for the purchase of food and drink) and were also asked to acquire and wear suits with long johns and vests underneath. Finally and inevitably, the advisory email concluded that '[c]ourt proceedings and anything that may ensue thereafter are state secrets – Tell no one' (2012). More explicit parts of a participation design than the textual features of theatre marketing are therefore put into place after first point of contact, but still at a time before arrival at the secret location, further defining the terms of Secret Cinema's spectacularly secret activities, as well as forthcoming participatory procedures.

So far I have outlined the keying of secrecy before audiences arrive at a secret location for their live cinema experience. But what of role playing, interactivity and immersion in the live cinema experience itself? Role playing as prisoners has an important part to play in *Shawshank*. First of all, costumed audiences 'complete' the immersive environments.[10] There are two phases of costuming in *Shawshank*. In the first, audiences arrive in a costume (a suit with long johns and a vest underneath) that they have purchased, borrowed or made, which requires a form of participatory endeavour. In the second, audiences are required to change into a different costume, a prison uniform, ensuring even greater degrees of homogeneity that is as little affected by personalised costume design as possible. In using costume to foster role-based immersion, then, Secret Cinema use audience members to complete scenographic design, but only in the periods before and at the very beginning of a performance. Audiences participate in the development of a theatre aesthetic, but in a way that requires very little audience responsibility or agency, beyond the creation or purchase of a prescribed costume that, soon after arrival, at least in this performance, is to be replaced with a homogenised aid for both character and scenographic development. Furthermore, as costumed audiences make their way to a performance, this aid also signals to passers-by that something out of the ordinary is happening.

The costumes double as an advert once those passers-by feel the need to find out why costumed crowds are flocking to a particular site.

Role playing in *Shawshank* also ties into procedures for interactivity. Audiences spend part of the performance lying in bunk beds inside a prison cell, listening to the advice of other prisoners (actors) who address them as new inmates of the prison. This particular part of the performance involves responsiveness on the parts of both willing participants and actors to engage in dialogue as a vehicle for improvisatory, role-based immersion. While they are addressed as prisoners – prisoners in the re-presented film world of *Shawshank* – it is up to the audience to decide whether they accept and run with the imposed role or choose instead to reject the imposition. As Sophie Nield recognises, addressing audience members in this way can give rise to existential confusion because the spectatorial and role-based forms of audience engagement do not always align. Addressing audiences in role presumes recognition of the role. When this recognition fails to happen, the conceit of a theatrical scenario can produce an uncomfortable queasiness or a sense of frustration at being recognised as someone *other* at a time when investment in belief is deficient (Nield 2008: 531–544).[11] Nonetheless, what the imposition of a role through interactivity seeks to achieve is complicity in the world of performance. This makes the early stages of role development in Secret Cinema's marketing important, as it is here that the role starts to take shape as something proposed and, ideally, adopted by prospective audiences of their own choosing, although audiences may just as well reject the invitation to wear a costume and reject attempts to cast them in role. However, even if rejected, Secret Cinema's approach to role-based immersion still flags an *intended* connection between the marketing of theatre and participation in theatre. Ideally, though not for all audiences, the keying of secrecy in advance of a live performance affects how processes of participation unfold. Secret Cinema's marketing prepares participation and immersion in the world of a performance and renders both not as imminent and emergent phenomena, but as phenomena that transcend and frame improvisatory negotiations of a fictive cosmos.

An important aspect of an audience member's immersion in *Shawshank* is therefore role based. For example, one of the many rooms that can be stumbled into in the performance is a prison canteen. Throughout much of the performance, up until entering the canteen, I had been annoyed by the fact that the prisoner trousers I had been given to change into were far too big and had to be held up by hand. However, inside the canteen a performer-inmate took me to one side and, from the corner of his mouth, attempted to sell me what he described as 'contraband'. The contraband in question was a piece of rope that I could use as a belt. While there are grim readings of this particular piece of contraband in the context of a prison, the comedic nature of the exchange was built on a conspiratorial mode of audience engagement that both solved a practical problem and served to draw me closer into the world of the performance.

The bracketing of a conspiratorial form of secrecy as play is clear in this example; the behaviour of the actor/character is not *actually* conspiratorial but is instead a playful engagement with the coding of secrecy (fortunately, despite my reluctance to pay, he gave me the rope anyway). For Goffman, coding 'carries the connotation of secret communication', and in some respects this is what sets coding and keying apart; participants in a keyed activity ought to be aware that the activity is bracketed from the everyday (Goffman 1986: 44). In my exchange with the prisoner, though, secret communication was coded as being *noticeably* and *theatrically* secret. Secrecy *was* present, but only as a product of investment in the bracketing of secrecy set up by Secret Cinema, the heritage of which stretched back to promotional activity. I ended up participating as a co-conspirator and, moreover, as a character within the performance who was addressed as a member of the performance's world and not as an observer standing apart from it.

The terms of creativity are underwritten in Secret Cinema performances by a procedural and aesthetic logic that is embroiled in a marketing campaign that precedes the performance. Of course, all theatre performances are connected to economic frames that sustain theatre production; however, Secret Cinema use marketing as a part of participation design. Secret Cinema engenders audiences as partakers in paradoxical secrecy, as 'tell everyone' secret spreaders who disclose the presence of undisclosed information, and this engendering carries forward into a live performance, the subject of which – an as-yet-unknown film – is to be decoded as the performance progresses. Prospective audiences are asked to prepare for a live event by participating as a co-designer (preparing a costume) and as a performer (preparing a role), and these tasks further serve the gradual unfolding of a mystery. Why this dress code? Why this role? Marketing, preparation for performance and participation in performance consequently meld in a cohesive project that does not cut off an immersive environment from the economic frames that serve theatre production but rather tie these frames into theatre aesthetics.

Secret commodities and audience involvement

The exclusive allure of secrets within markets is meant to appeal to – or 'include' – as many people as possible, converting appeal into sales. This leads me to consider how the paradox of secrecy, as it appears in theatre marketing, can inform what might be meant by inclusive/exclusive and inclusionary/exclusionary participation. The paradox of secrecy ultimately reveals the limitations of these binaries, as it is clear that inclusion and exclusion are not poles that oppose within frameworks for participation but layers that intermingle. In Secret Cinema's marketing, participants are included in a campaign that positions itself as exclusive. Those who commit to a performance's preparatory processes are included in a participation design that exceeds live performance, but in ways that may exclude those who do not commit to these processes from enjoying the same levels of immersion and interactivity. Furthermore, participants are included in the exclusive Secret Cinema society provided that they can afford to do so and 'Tell No One', which is an exclusionary feature that runs alongside the inclusionary 'Tell Everyone' logic of social media. Inclusion/exclusion and inclusivity/exclusivity are not oppositional, or even clear-cut, categories.

This layering of inclusion and exclusion was especially clear in the advertising of a Secret Restaurant inside *Shawshank*. An email was sent out to ticketholders from 'Philip W. Romney', who invited the recipient to the Official State Dinner Party for Social Reform. For the staggering sum of £100 per head, audiences were treated to canapés, wine and a three-course meal by guest chef Alan Stewart and food designers Blanch & Shock. Only a few would have been able to afford to participate in this aspect of the performance, the cost of which dwarfs comparable meals in the UK's top two internationally acclaimed Michelin-starred restaurants.[12] In some respects, then, another kind of secret is instigated: secrets closed off to those who cannot afford to pay such a vast amount of money for their food. 'Secrecy secures', to borrow from Simmel, 'the possibility of a second world alongside of the obvious world' (Simmel 1906: 463). This idea of a second world chimes with the ambitions of much immersive theatre work to be set 'alongside of the obvious world' in a world of its own, seemingly segregated from the material contexts that embed immersive performances (Machon 2014: 93). However, the Secret Restaurant is an exclusionary world open only to wealthier members of the Secret Cinema society, comparable to The Heath in Punchdrunk's *Sleep No More*. Both the Secret Restaurant and The Heath operate as worlds closed off from a wider audience. These are worlds for the wealthy that glorify the excesses of privilege and that aspire to an even more total immersion, layering extant forms of privilege and immersion within an immersive world.

As Bok notes, the Latin term *secretum* identifies that which is kept hidden or set apart (1998: 6). The Secret Restaurant offers membership to a secret society which is set apart from the Secret Cinema society. While secret societies may well provide sanctuary for radicals, rebels, thieves, the ostracised, the disenfranchised and the persecuted, they have also played host to the

aristocracy in numerous guises, such as the Venetian *nobili*, Swiss secret officials and German aristocratic families, as Simmel points out (1906: 487). By
including the Secret Restaurant within Secret Cinema events and by setting
a £100 barrier to entry, a wealth-based system of privilege is constructed
within a theatre space that escalates the barrier to entry set up at the box
office. To recall Luhrmann, possession differentiates. In this case, the possession of wealth is what first differentiates one group of people from another
inside and outside of a theatre space, which then leads to a second stage of
differentiation based on the secrets promised by the Secret Restaurant. This
evidences a clear translation of wealth into the possession of a secret experience and the knowledge, or memories, that come with such an experience.

For those who want to extend their experience of *The Shawshank
Redemption*, there was also an option to spend the night in a 'Secret Hotel'
at an additional cost of £30. As with Zecora Ura's *Hotel Medea* (2009–12),
Duckie's *Lullaby* (2011) and Rift's (formerly Retz) *Macbeth* (2014), audiences
had the chance to spend all night within an immersive world and to sleep
within that world, which in this case was the *Shawshank* jail dormitories,
accompanied by actors maintaining their role for the duration (in the role
of prison guard, for instance). As the performance's programme explains,
'Secret hotel is for those looking for adventure and mystery. It will transport you into a carefully curated world inspired by our secret production.
We are looking to bring back the sense of experience and spontaneity into
the world of a hotel' (Secret Cinema 2012: 2).

The thing purchased – a bed for the night – remains a secret until
arrival, like a purchasable surprise party. Neither the location nor the
kind of accommodation is known until audience members put on their
prison uniform, whereupon some likely assumptions could be made,
perhaps with some regret in the case of *Shawshank*. In the Secret Hotel,
audiences participate in their sleep. Dozing inmates pay for incarceration, but the kind of incarceration that they pay for is a spectacle that
can be safely snoozed through. It is a spectacle that does not need to be
watched. It is a spectacle that accommodates thrill as well as slumber.
The promised performance is a spectacle not for the spectator but for
the audience participant who does not need to spectate in their sleep.

Conclusion: audience participation and spectacular secrecy

In the programme notes for *Shawshank*, which presents itself as a 'Parole
Book', Fabien Riggall explains his motivation for making immersive theatre: 'The creative world inside these walls reflects the world we would like

to see outside' (Secret Cinema 2012: 1). I have argued that these worlds are not cut off from one another given the aesthetic and economic connections that link the two. A framework for audience participation and immersion is constructed at a very early stage in an audience's contact with a performance. Secret Cinema's marketing campaigns 'key' secrecy by precluding clandestine activity while promoting spectacular secrecy. The company figures prospective audiences as secret spreaders who must 'Tell Everyone' about the presence of a spectacular secret. This is the paradox of secrecy in Secret Cinema's work, which informs role playing, interactivity and immersion in a live performance – as well as popularity – by building on a clue-based participation design that precedes live performance and that is thoroughly bound up with promotional interests. What emerges is a complex layering of inclusion/exclusion and inclusivity/exclusivity that is concerned not just with the openness of an invitation to participate but with degrees of openness that relate to disposable wealth and participation in bracketed, spectacular, and commodified secrecy that both implies and undermines exclusivity.

I cannot help but wonder whether the growth of secrecy in contemporary theatre marketing is meeting a demand for exclusivity and that immersive theatre companies like Secret Cinema are capitalising on this demand. However, secrecy and participation design can work together in a politically progressive mode, without resorting to the aesthetic and economic logic of the commodity. For instance, Coney uses secrecy in participatory theatre to challenge how strangers are viewed and approached. The point of performances like *The Loveliness Principle* is not to present audiences with clearly defined models of sociability; the point is to invite audiences to covertly play with sociability and to investigate what constitutes a social bond and our role, as participants, in negotiating that bond. However, compelling issues arise when commodified secrecy is connected to the design of audience participation and immersion. In work by Secret Cinema, what emerges is immersion in the landscape of an unknown film that is not cut off from the world *out there*; what emerges is immersion in a world pervaded by the aesthetics and economics of commodification.

Endnotes

1. See Keren Zaiontz, 'Narcissistic Spectatorship in Immersive and One-on-One Performance', *Theatre Journal* 66.3 (2014), pp. 413–14.
2. See Barbara Hoffman, 'Dinner at The Heath more dramatic than delicious', *New York Post* (21 Jan 2014) < http://nypost.com/2014/01/21/dinner-at-the-heath-more-dramatic-than-delicious/> [accessed 19 Feb 2015].

3. See Adam Alston, 'Funding, Product Placement and Drunkenness in Punchdrunk's *The Black Diamond*', *Studies in Theatre and Performance* 32.2 (2012), pp. 193–208; see also Jen Harvie, Fair Play: Art, Performance and Neoliberalism (Basingstoke: Palgrave, 2013), pp. 179–81.

4. Shannon Jackson, *Social Works: Performing Art, Supporting Publics* (London: Routledge, 2011).

5. Jen Harvie, *Fair Play: Art, Performance and Neoliberalism* (Basingstoke: Palgrave Macmillan, 2013).

6. Gareth White, *Audience Participation in Theatre: Aesthetics of the Invitation* (Basingstoke: Palgrave, 2013); Gareth White, 'On Immersive Theatre', Theatre Research International 37.3 (Oct 2012), pp. 221–35.

7. Machon, Immersive Theatres; Josephine Machon, '(Syn)aesthetics and Immersive Theatre: Embodied Beholding in Lundahl & *Seitl's Rotating in a Room of Moving Images*', *Affective Performance and Cognitive Science: Body, Brain and Being*, ed. Nicola Shaughnessy (London: Methuen, 2014), pp. 199–215.

8. See also Georg Simmel, 'The Sociology of Secrecy and of Secret Societies', *American Journal of Sociology* 11.4 (Jan. 1906), p. 454.

9. Secret Cinema ventured outside of London with their Brighton production of Ivan Reitman's cult hit *Ghostbusters* (1984) in 2008. In May 2012, The Other Cinema – another sibling Secret Cinema company – took their production of Mathieu Kassovitz's *La Haine* (1995) to Paris before heading to Sound Central Music Festival in Kabul, Afghanistan, in September 2012. Also, Future Shorts has now presented screenings in over one hundred countries. Nonetheless, Secret Cinema, as an organisation tied to, but distinguished from, these other 'arms' of Riggall's work has primarily remained tied to the UK capital.

10. See Josephine Machon, 'Space and the Senses: the (syn)aesthetics of Punchdrunk's site-sympathetic work', *Body, Space & Technology*, 7.1 (2007) <http://people.brunel.ac.uk/bst/vol0701/home.html> [accessed 7 December 2010].

11. See also Nicholas Ridout, *Stage Fright, Animals, and Other Theatrical Problems* (Cambridge: Cambridge University Press, 2006).

12. In the S. Pellegrino and Acqua Panna 'The World's 50 Best Restaurants' list, Dinner by Heston Blumenthal is rated top in the UK, which at the time of writing, offers a three course set lunch for £38. The Ledbury comes next, which offers a three course set lunch for £37.50 and a three course set dinner for £80. There are more expensive tasting menus available, but these offer many more courses in comparison with the Secret Restaurant. S. Pellegrino and Acqua Panna, 'The World's 50 Best Restaurants 1–50', *The World's 50 Best Restaurants*, William Reed Business Media Ltd (2012) <http://www.theworlds50best.com/> [accessed 17 January 2014].

SECTION III

AUTHORING PARTICIPATION

9   The Agency of Environment

Artificial Hells and *Multi-Story Water*

Stephen Bottoms

'If citizenship is about *acting* as a citizen', Helen Nicholson writes in *Applied Drama*, 'with all the implications of performance that this phrase entails, how might practising drama encourage people to become active participant citizens?' (2005: 21). One of the virtues of this question, it seems to me, is that its focus on 'citizenship' usefully displaces 'democracy' as the key rhetorical term pertaining to participatory theatre. It has often been claimed that performance is 'democratised' when spectators are re-positioned as participants. Jonothan Neelands, for example, in a recent essay, reiterates Boal's quasi-historical notion that 'the ideals of a participatory democracy gradually eroded as the people became represented by actors', but that audience participation 'reclaims a theatre for, by and with the people themselves' (2015: 32). Appealingly neat as this theatrical-political analogy might seem, however, I want to begin by positing three key reasons why it remains untenable.

The first objection, well rehearsed since the publication of Jacques Rancière's *The Emancipated Spectator* (2009), is that spectating is itself an active situation (indeed, 'our normal situation' (2009: 17)), and not a passive state of disempowerment to be overcome. It is for this reason that spectators do not, generally speaking, feel 'disenfranchised' if they are not invited to get on stage with the actors. As Bronislaw Szersynski reminds us, '[b]eing a member of an audience, a community of co-watchers, can still be an important element in a person's sense of themselves as being a citizen among other citizens' (Szerszyinksi 2006: 77–78).

A second objection to the democratising analogy relates to the limitations of democracy itself. If voter turn-out is falling in many of the world's purported democracies, one major cause appears to be that many voters perceive their participation as making little real difference to the electoral outcome. Their votes are solicited, but the process seems manipulated, stage-managed, by the 'powers that be'. In much the same way, participatory theatre can often feel 'rigged' in favour of the interests of the artist or facilitator. Within a pre-arranged set of spatial and dramaturgical conditions, participants will be given the opportunity to 'do' things rather than just 'watch' things, but their doing will have been – to a greater or lesser extent – anticipated and factored in, in advance. This is not to deny that participatory dynamics, well facilitated, can lead to genuinely novel and enlightening outcomes, but unfortunately Claire Bishop's description of such performances as 'artificial hells' can be all too apt, all too often.[1] Ontroerend Goed's recent play *Fight Night* (2013) satirically exposes exactly this point, by staging an election process in which spectators vote – in a series of elimination rounds – for their favourite candidate/performer. We are teased and lured into participating but then are gradually made aware of how little power we really have here: 'by voting when invited', James Frieze notes of the piece, 'we have validated the system's piecemeal participatory offer', and yet 'the mechanisms that have allowed us to engage seem to have blocked any chance of changing the terms of engagement' (2015: 220–221).

Fight Night thus dramatises political philosopher Étienne Balibar's point that, while we often still valorise democracy as 'the *constituent* power of the "multitude"', those at the top 'will continually seek to replace this capacity with forms of *constituted power*'. The 'people', that is, become 'incorporated, perhaps even *assimilated*, into the state' (Balibar 2015: 3). For this reason, Balibar proposes, 'the active modality of citizenship [is] insurrection, in its *different* forms' – by which he means campaigning, activism, disobedience and grassroots organisation (2015: 131). Involved citizens, in other words, operate *outside* of – as well as inside – the terms of democratic participation established for them by the state. Rancière makes a similar point in his commentary on Aristotle's foundational definition of the citizen as 'he who partakes in the fact of ruling and the fact of being ruled'. This, Rancière suggests, means 'something rather different to reciprocity. On the contrary, the exceptional essence of this relationship is constituted by an absence of reciprocity' (2010: 31). That is to say, citizens should not simply reciprocate the appeals of their democratic leaders by consenting to participate in the electoral narratives that they have pre-authored. For Rancière, a citizen is a person whose agency persists independently of such structures, just as a spectator is a person whose responses to a performance remain independent of its makers' intentions.

This brings me to my third objection, which is that democracies are always, by definition, exclusionary. The vaunted Athenian democracy of old was constructed by excluding women, slaves and foreigners from having any say in the city's affairs. Today in the UK, we argue about the age at which young people can be enfranchised and construct arcane 'citizenship tests' in order to induct non-natives into the *demos*. So if we are to posit participatory theatre as 'democratic', we also need to ask, who exactly is participating, and *how did they get in*? The chances are that they either paid for the privilege or that – in the case of applied theatre practices – they were brought 'inside the circle' by a beneficent outsider. In either instance, these are curious criteria for enfranchisement.

The circle of democracy, moreover, even in its most enlightened forms, is unlikely to have been drawn wide enough to incorporate nonhuman participants – the voices of our 'environment'. Human activity both depends on and impacts on the nonhuman – especially in the era of anthropogenic climate change. It is for this reason that, in *Politics of Nature* (2004), Bruno Latour memorably proposes a number of possible strategies for 'expanding the collective' to include the interests of animals and plants – by repositioning scientists as their political advocates, in a representative system. This challenging vision, however, would require such a fundamental rethinking of our anthropocentric value systems that it is unlikely to become reality any time soon.

Bearing all of this in mind, I want to suggest that if we are to take seriously the notion of participation in performance – let alone the question of citizenship – we need to think beyond the carefully controlled parameters of pre-planned, 'democratising' interactivity. We need to extend our frame of reference to consider not just the 'inside' of the performance space or the applied theatre workshop but also the wider ecologies within which performance subsists – and the possibility that there might be 'actors' involved who are, rightly and completely, beyond the control of the artist or facilitator. In what follows, I want to instantiate this proposition by analysing a participatory process for which I was myself the primary facilitator. *Multi-Story Water* (2012–2013) was a site-specific, practice-as-research project (supported by the Arts and Humanities Research Council [AHRC]) which sought to explore community awareness of urban rivers.[2] Yet the project's evolution was shaped at all stages by dissensual participants who were very far from being 'ruled' by me. The simple fact of attempting to work alongside and in response to rivers placed us in (forgive me) a fluid situation, beyond the containing parameters of the theatre, gallery or community hall. A river is always in motion, a ribbon or corridor of continuous flow, not a single, contained site. It epitomises Nigel Thrift's observation that 'the fabric of space' is 'performative' insofar that 'its many components continually act back' (Thrift 2003: 2022–2023). This obstreperous, nonhuman participant was not to be tamed, and what we ended up presenting was a long way from what we had set out to present. Yet for Félix Guattari, such mutations are only to be expected when seeking to think ecologically. 'This new ecosophical logic', he emphasises, 'resembles the manner in which an artist may be led to alter his work after the intrusion of some accidental detail, an event-incident that suddenly makes his initial project ... drift far from its previous path' (2000: 52).

What follows is divided into three parts, which seek broadly to map onto Guattari's model of 'the three ecologies' – his intertwined 'ecological registers' of 'the environment, social relations, and human subjectivity' (2000: 28). Section 1 thus asks some broad questions about the 'mental ecology' underpinning our participatory processes. Section 2 examines the substance of the eventual *Multi-Story Water* performances through the lens of 'social ecology', while Section 3 looks at 'environmental ecology' and the question of unpredictable, nonhuman participation. Finally, I will conclude by returning to Nicholson's animating question about citizenship.

Mental ecology (theatre of the doorstep)

The *Multi-Story Water* project arose as a direct result of a provocation from Michael Guthrie – at that time Community and Stakeholder Relations Manager for England's Environment Agency (EA) – who in 2011 generously responded to my invitation to speak at an event at Kings College London.[3] The assembled performance scholars and artists had conducted a series of discussions about the potential of site-specific performance to explore questions of environmental change, but Guthrie's challenge was for us to consider whether this thinking could be put to practical, social use. He explained that the EA's conventional, one-way communication strategies (leafleting, posters, etc.) seemed largely ineffective in persuading homeowners to act on the dangers of flood risk, particularly in urban areas. Could sited performance perhaps provide a more affective, participatory strategy for engaging 'hard to reach' riverside communities with these issues? This proved to be a discussion that several of those present were reluctant to participate in: did we want the arts to be used in such an 'instrumental' manner by a government agency? Such responses were understandable, but they also – I felt – ran the risk of defending the arts as a kind of knowledge silo. As Gregory Bateson argues in *Steps to an Ecology of Mind*, the mental and environmental are inextricably linked: thinking ecologically necessitates a willingness to step beyond the comfort zones of our own expertise and learn from seemingly alien others. 'A certain humility becomes appropriate', Bateson notes, 'tempered by the dignity or joy of being part of something much bigger' (Bateson 2000: 467–468).

The Environment Agency is an organisation dominated by engineers. Its default operational mode is thus essentially technocratic: if you have a problem, apply expertise to fix it. If climate change is threatening to increase flooding incidents, then build better flood defences. In recent years, however, the EA has been obliged to think more actively about communicating its expertise to others: 'The Environment Agency should work with local responders to raise awareness in flood risk areas', recommended the Pitt Report that followed the major UK floods of 2007.[4] The new watchword of 'distributed responsibility' for flood management means that at-risk homeowners must be alerted to their own need to take preparatory action. Yet this call for participant citizenship, to ensure domestic and community resilience, has coincided a little too neatly with severe cuts in public spending following the 2008 economic crisis (including a significant reduction in the EA staff base). As Claire Bishop notes, governmental 'inclusion' agendas too often posit 'submissive citizens [who] respect authority and accept the "risk" and responsibility of looking after themselves in the face of diminished public services' (2012: 14). In Brad Evans and Julian Reid's recent book, *Resilient Life*, the authors take up this line of argument with doctrinaire bullishness, insisting on the need for *hubris* – not compliant humility – in resisting such neoliberal conspiracies (2014: 43). Such familiar, left–right antagonisms, however, conspicuously ignore the nonhuman participants in our changing climate. In the UK, flooding is forecast to become an increasing problem in the years to come, so unless one is going to propose that the state should demand the right to flood-defend, by force, every individual home in the country (regardless of the expense and invasion of privacy entailed), then the fact remains that vulnerable citizens will need to take precautions.

The problem, then, is less the *why* of flood-risk communication than the *how*. The EA tends to hail citizens from a position of superior knowledge, like a schoolmaster addressing recalcitrant pupils. As is clear from a 2012 summary document title *Flood Risk: Understanding and Communicating with our Customers* (henceforth, *FRUCC*), the EA has segmented its potential 'audiences' (that word is used repeatedly) into five broad constituencies, but in each case the underlying assumption is that a greater or lesser degree of ignorance must be overcome: 'information and services need to be pushed' (Environment Agency/Blue Marble Consulting, *FRUCC* 2012: 5). What *FRUCC* presents is the so-called deficit model of science communication – a technocratic approach which assumes that, when provided with appropriate information by the state, citizens will reciprocate by taking grateful, rational action. And yet, as Mike Hulme notes, this model has been widely questioned by scholars, not least for its circular logic: 'If the public are resistant to these scientific messages, this implies that the public are exhibiting a lack of necessary knowledge – a deficit which needs remedying by science communicators' (2009: 217).

'As you arrogate all mind to yourself', Bateson cautions, 'you will see the world around you as mindless (2000: 468)'. The *FRUCC* document indulges in precisely that fantasy, paradoxically anticipating the failure of its own strategies by insisting that the public is hampered by cognitive blocks ranging from 'complacency' to 'deep-seated denial' (2012: 12); 'at a psychological level, [there is] widespread denial of, detachment from and underestimation of flood risk' (2012: 3). Ostensibly based on social-scientific research findings, these reductive claims have the performative effect of shifting all blame for communication failure onto the receiver, without questioning the way the message is presented. This self-defeating approach is only compounded by the use of terminology such as 'hard-to-reach urban communities'. This familiar political euphemism for those living in lower-income areas posits, in its very wording, a gulf of communication that is difficult to overcome. According to *FRUCC*, those living in 'rural, tight-knit communities' are typically 'independent-minded' and 'proactive' in their response to flood incidents, but those at risk in urban areas are 'living in less cohesive communities', belong to 'lower socio-economic grades' and are 'bitter because they feel they are victims' (*FRUCC* 2012: 15–16). One might as well post a sign: 'don't go there'.

What should we make, then, of Michael Guthrie's suggestion that we might use performance to engage such communities? It is easy to be cynical, of course, but my experience of Guthrie himself, and indeed of most of the EA employees I have met since, is that they are concerned, open-minded citizens, more than willing to acknowledge that the Agency's conventional approach is insufficient to address the challenges it faces. As Guthrie wryly put it,

> I'm personally one of those people who, if told 'You're at risk of flooding', will say, 'Give me all the data, I will make a decision based on that'. And I will work through a very logical pattern. And that's probably why I work for the Environment Agency. Whereas other people, I fully appreciate, are not going to be engaged in that way (Guthrie 2012).

Guthrie's challenge to the Kings College gathering was thus a genuinely open-ended invitation to do something differently. Indeed, he suggested, the 'measures of success' for any performance research project could not simply be the crudely numerical ones usually employed by the Agency – such as whether more people complete Personal Flood Plans (PFPs) as a result of a particular intervention. Such participation is, in any case, impossible to judge accurately, unless all those who complete a downloadable PFP template also opt, voluntarily, to inform the EA that they have done so (a reciprocal gesture for which there is no obvious incentive). Thus, Guthrie suggested, *we* might need to tell *him* what the measures of success should be for this proposed project. In short, he was inviting us to engage in a process that might mildly trouble the EA's established 'mental ecology'.

I was curious to explore Guthrie's challenge in practice, and the AHRC proved curious enough to fund us. Staff from the Environment Agency responded by proposing two case-study areas – Eastville, in Bristol; and Shipley, in Bradford – where they felt more work needed to be done to communicate flood risk, but which were not high priority for the EA themselves (thus, we did not risk treading on toes). This chapter focuses on the Shipley case study, for which I was primarily responsible, but the initial research strategy in both contexts was the same.[5] Rather than perpetuating the EA's one-way messaging strategies, our plan from the outset was to pursue a two-way, participatory approach which invited contributions from local residents. An initial research stage would be used to explore the degree of awareness that at-risk residents had of their local river, and to collect ideas and stories arising in relation to it. Through this process, we also hoped to identify local volunteers who might participate in a series of performance workshops, using the collated research as raw material in a devising process. Finally, performance events using these volunteers as performers would be presented to the wider community, in order to bring the river to the forefront of local consciousness.

In practice, however, these draft plans proved flawed, primarily because we had failed to factor the river itself into the equation. The first challenge we faced was determining who exactly the 'riverside communities' were, whose participation we were seeking. This is not usually a problem for applied theatre projects, which typically work within contained contexts, with pre-existing groups as participants: prisoners, schoolchildren, old people in residential homes and so forth. A determination is usually made, from the outset, to focus on *those* people, in *that* space. But given Guthrie's emphasis on residential flood risk, we felt obliged to start by engaging with people living in homes that might be affected by high water. EA flood maps were used to determine, street by street, which houses were considered close enough to the river to be 'at risk'.[6] Having made our selections, we worked from door to door, using simple survey questionnaires as a means to initiate conversations with householders. Where people proved particularly responsive on the doorstep, we also asked permission to return for longer, interview-style conversations.

In Shipley, through which the River Aire flows on its way towards Leeds, the residential areas proximate to the river are dispersed over about a mile and half and disconnected from each other by waterside mill buildings, government offices, a park, a cricket pitch and so on. We therefore faced difficult judgements as to where to focus our limited resources. We considered focusing solely on the most populous of these areas, namely the Higher Coach Road housing estate, but these homes are separated from the river by a green flood plain area and sit on raised banking – so the flood maps designated them mostly as medium to low risk.[7] Conversely, the homes deemed to be at highest risk turned out to be in Victoria Mills, a recent high-end development that had been designed precisely to lift its apartments out of harm's way, leaving only car parking spaces at flood level (a factor that our 2-D maps had not revealed). We decided not to attempt engaging with these relatively prosperous residents, ostensibly on the grounds that our brief was to address 'hard to reach' communities. But the irony is that the spatial circumstances gave the lie to the terminology: our avoidance of Victoria Mills residents also reflected the fact that they are especially hard to reach. The apartment blocks have security entrances, preventing ready access to front doors, and many of the residents are commuters into Leeds and thus are rarely at home. By comparison, door-knocking on a housing estate was straightforward.

In the end, we selected a number of areas to survey and found varying degrees of responsiveness in each. Many residents, of course, had no wish to talk to us, even if they were at home when we called. At some stage it dawned on me that if someone were to knock on *my* door asking the questions we were asking, I would probably be among those too busy to participate. Context, I realised, is a key incentive in the decision to involve oneself in any arts or research process: if I were a prisoner, for example, and someone offered me a drama workshop to relieve the tedium of staring at my cell wall, I might be up for it. But if someone knocks on my front door, I can quickly shut it again if I have better things to do. The 'participatory theatre' in this door-knocking scenario thus hinges on the first few seconds. The homeowner makes an instant, spectatorial choice about whether the performer framed before them is worth the time of day. First impressions are vital, and if you fluff your first sentence, you can forget about the second. If it was humbling to find myself so frequently sent packing, it was also humbling – in the Batesonian sense, perhaps – when I found myself invited into people's homes, privileged to participate in their domestic life-worlds, to see them in the 'stage sets' that they had built over time, to hear them 'perform' on their own terms. I gradually began to relinquish the fantasy that 'participation' begins at the point when you have successfully corralled people into the containment area of a drama workshop or performance. If people choose to speak to you in their homes, this is absolutely a choice to participate in something. The key difference is that, in this context, I need the humility to relinquish control over the terms of this participation and to negotiate with individuals on a case by case basis.

The Shipley team eventually completed around 60 questionnaires (a reasonable sample size for qualitative research) and over a dozen in-depth follow-up interviews.[8] The respondents were, of course, self-selecting in the sense of being those willing to talk to us, and this will have affected the range of responses we received. Even so, it became clear that the residents surveyed 'minded' considerably more about their local river than EA expertise assumes. Michael Guthrie had warned us to expect 'a disconnection that people have from their local environment', particularly in urban areas: 'they just aren't aware of the water around them' (Guthrie 2012). But while this might apply elsewhere, it certainly did not in Shipley. Asked to gauge their own degree of attention to the Aire, fully 50 per cent of our respondents claimed to be 'very aware of it' or to 'think about it a lot', by self-scoring at '5' on the 1–5 intensifier scale used on our questionnaire. Another 30 per cent scored themselves at '4'. This finding, persistently confirmed by verbal responses, was particularly striking when compared with much more mixed responses to other questions, such as whether or not there was a 'good sense of community' in the local area.

It should be acknowledged that, like many former mill towns in Yorkshire, Shipley exists in a borderzone between the urban and the rural: heavily built up in parts, it also offers rapid access to moors and woodland areas – 'natural' spaces that are cherished by locals from all backgrounds. It follows, perhaps, that they should also take an interest in the river. This caveat, however, underlines the crudity of making generalised distinctions between 'types' of space and people. The picture that emerged from our Shipley research was of a vicinity in which 'multi-story water' was an unexpectedly apt project title. Respondents would frequently bring up the issue of flooding, unprompted, as a memory or concern, but it was almost invariably entwined – ecologically? – with other thoughts about the Aire and its environs. Recollections of Shipley's last major flood incident in 2000, for instance, were often mixed with observations about improvements in the river's water quality, following the closure of local industry during the 1980s and '90s. The social impacts of mill closures have been mixed, we were told, but the environmental effects were overwhelmingly positive: 'it used to be you'd never see a kingfisher around here', one respondent memorably remarked, 'but now you get almost blasé about them.'

This local awareness of the river's short- and long-term changes also translated, in many cases, into a certain scepticism towards the Environment Agency itself. Its automated flood warning telephone calls, for example – a service into which many had found themselves opted by default – were a source of some amusement, due to the perceived inaccuracy of coverage and predictions. Some respondents had found that their own lay predictions of likely water behaviour had proved more accurate, and so they were happy to take (distributed) responsibility for *not* following the automated guidance. Yet they were also shrewdly aware of what they could *not* be responsible for. The key flooding pinch point in the area is Baildon Bridge – Shipley's only road bridge – whose low concrete arches can too easily become blocked by debris in high water conditions, thus forcing the river to seek alternative routes. Too often, it was suggested to us, the responsible authorities (including the Environment Agency) were failing to deal effectively with these risks. Elderly riverside trees, for example, were often left untended until they collapsed into the river channel. We heard some frustration from those participant citizens who had attempted to report such problems, but had simply run into a forest of red tape.

In short, then, what we heard from our respondents offered some validation for Dee Heddon and Sally Mackey's notion (via Rancière) of 'emancipated environmentalism'. People learn about their local environments in the process of living with them, and it is thus important for agencies not to assume ignorance on the part of those they communicate with. It might be better to begin by positing 'the equality of intelligence of the participatory individual in matters of environmental import' (2012: 177). As Rancière himself notes of mental ecology: 'Explication is not necessary to remedy an incapacity to understand. On the contrary … it is the explicator who needs the incapable and not the other way around; it is he who constitutes the incapable as such' (1991: 6).

Social ecology (theatre of the riverbank)

The findings of the project's research stage left us with a number of challenges in developing the site-specific performance outcomes on which our funding was predicated. Not only did our initial notion of encouraging community learning about the environment through a participatory arts process seem to risk condescension. We had also signally failed to identify enough potential participants for such a process from among those we had spoken with. This was partly thanks to having approached people in their homes rather than in some more obvious 'venue' for group activity, such as a community centre. But our respondents also leaned towards the older end age of the age spectrum – perhaps because retirees have more time to spare for door knockers, but also because (as we discovered in Bristol too) people like living beside water and have little incentive to move away. In Shipley, we encountered several people in their nineties who had lived in the same houses since they were built in the 1950s. These older respondents proved to be a treasure trove of stories, memories and local knowledge, which might have remained untapped but for our door-knocking methodology. They were, however, unlikely candidates for involving in site-specific performance workshops.

Rearranging the project budget, I agreed a strategy with director Simon Brewis (initially brought on board with a view to running workshops) to hire three professional actors with whom to create and deliver performances based on the research materials that were gathered. There was some discussion about whether to present a 'static' show at a specific location, targeted at residents of a particular neighbourhood. However, while we did set up an interactive community event on the Higher Coach Road estate (which has led to further activity since),[9] in performance terms the idea of a fixed location seemed to run counter to what the river was presenting us with – a continuum of contrasting but interlinked sites, each of which spoke in different ways to the social and environmental 'ecologies' of the area. The material we had gathered seemed almost to demand a mobile navigation of the course of the river itself, as it flows through Shipley, and as it cuts through contrasting socio-economic zones. 'We must learn to think "transversally"', Guattari suggests: 'Ecological praxes seek to scout out … dissident vectors [that run] counter to the "normal" order of things' (2000: 43, 45).

Multi-Story Water, as performed five times over the course of a long weekend in September 2012, was a cycle of three interlinked journeys (each lasting an hour or so) that could be undertaken as a single sequence or as individual, component parts. Presented free of charge, these tours were advertised both in the riverside neighbourhoods we had researched (we flyered every door we had previously knocked on) and also in the wider vicinity. The trajectories of the routes more or less determined themselves, as we sought to connect up the locations associated with our stronger narrative and research materials. The first and third parts of the cycle – Green Route and Red Route – were walking tours led by our three actors (David Smith, Lynsey Jones and Richard Galloway), who each multi-roled as a series of characters encountered en route, while also providing linking 'narrator' commentary. The intervening segment, Blue Route, consisted of a boat ride on the Leeds to Liverpool Canal (which runs parallel with the

Aire through the Shipley area), and was conceived as a sort of convivial 'intermission' between the walks, complete with proffered cups of tea and semi-improvised conversation. I acted as the on-board host and narrator, while live music (both traditional canal shanties and original compositions) was provided by local singer-songwriter Eddie Lawler, whom we had met during the research process. Canals, of course, are artificial waterways rather than valley-bottom drainage channels, and as such, they present little, if any, flood risk. The Leeds-Liverpool is a key part of the area's 'water story', but the river remained our main focus, and Blue Route – pleasantly atmospheric as it was – was always conceived as an expedient means of bridging the gap between the two stretches of the Aire where we felt we had good stories to tell. It also helped to catch the eye of prospective participants: 'When I first read about the performance', commented an online reviewer, 'I was most excited by the promise of a canal boat tour. ... I was surprised that I enjoyed the walking tours so much more'.[10]

Such comments perhaps vindicate our other key creative decision, which was to develop a performance script based around the interview material we had gathered – often presented verbatim. This approach necessarily limited the opportunity for spectatorial 'participation' within the performances themselves – it being both ethically and practically tricky to improvise around verbatim text. Informal interaction between actors and spectators was thus largely limited to the periods of movement between our various 'staging' positions. I was quizzed on this decision by some of the academic colleagues who functioned in an advisory role on the overall project: might we not have done more to 'involve' people in the performances by soliciting participatory responses? I felt strongly, however, that honouring the participation of our *interviewees* – as shaped into script form – would offer a more layered, involving experience for spectators than would be permitted by opening the performances up to unpredictable, spur-of-the-moment contributions.

This more 'authored' approach to the tours' content enabled us to sustain focus on the theme of flooding, which operated as a kind of irregular bass line through all three segments of the tour (as we recalled memories of past incidents, asked spectators to visualise high water levels and so on). As in our research interviews, however, this theme was interwoven with a number of other ideas: consciously rejecting the advice of EA literature to '[k]eep the language of risk simple!' (*FRUCC* 2012: 9), we sought to reflect something of the complexity of Shipley's social and environmental ecologies by touching on a range of interlinked, river-related issues. For example, Bradford Council's controversial scheme to install a small, hydroelectric power generator on a local weir was contextualised in relation to the global threat of climate change by energy manager Neill Morrison (played by Richard Galloway). Rejecting any suggestion that it wasn't Bradford's responsibility to worry about such things, Morrison insisted, '[t]here is no, "whose responsibility is it?" That's part of the problem. ... You can't use that as an excuse any more. You have to do something!'

Such questions of personal and collective responsibility – of participant citizenship, if you will – formed another recurring thread in the performances. By juxtaposing contrasting perspectives on such issues, however, we also sought to avoid didacticism. Each interviewee's voice jostled for attention without necessarily being prioritised one over another. In *The Three Ecologies* (1989), Guattari anticipates a theme later popularised by Rancière by proposing that, 'rather than looking for a stupefying and infantilizing consensus, it will be a question in the future of cultivating a *dissensus*' (2000: 50). For Guattari, 'hold[ing] complexity in mind so as to counter the homogenizing pressures of the dominant culture' is itself an ecological principle. In our case, however, dissensus emerged almost by default: simply by tracking the river, we found ourselves obliged to structure our walking routes as a series of contrasts or juxtapositions. Red Route, for example, prominently featured Victoria Mills, a former riverside industrial site that had been converted, just before the 2008 crash, into a luxury apartment complex. Here, David Smith performed as Andrew Mason, the property entrepreneur behind the development, lovingly explaining the rationale for his ostentatious design decisions (the whole lower area of the development, Mason notes, is designed to become 'a lovely lake' in flood conditions – or in the EA's terms, 'compensatory flood storage'). Stifling my personal prejudices about developers, I had sought an interview with Mason when it became clear that this former mill site was a key feature in the local landscape. His responses made a compelling case for Victoria Mills as a potential flagship for regeneration in the local economy. At the end of this sequence, however, when 'Andrew' let our audience out onto the river path through the development's back gate (by opening a padlock for which we had procured a copy of the key), they were immediately met by Richard Galloway playing Phillip Moncaster, whose unassuming, semi-detached house – directly across the river – is towered over by the highest-rise section of the Victoria Mills development: 'a thousand prying eyes looking down on me'. Phillip's monologue, as 'he' guided spectators downstream towards the Working Men's Club where he is voluntary secretary, featured not only vivid memories of the 2000 floods (dirty water blasting up through the toilet) but scathing criticism of Victoria Mills's spaceship-like strangeness in the area.[11] There was also bluntly amusing commentary on the failings of the local council and the Environment Agency to address some of the more obvious problems along the riverbank. As we had hoped, spectators subsequently proved split over whether to 'side' with Andrew or Phillip over the best strategy for the area's future (speculative investment or grassroots voluntarism). Gratifyingly, both men had proved happy for their words to be represented in contrast with each other, without us needing to provide a smoothing, interpretive commentary.

Dissensus, let us remember, is a consequence of inclusiveness. For Balibar, this is why ostensibly democratic regimes habitually operate to *exclude* sections of their own populace, through 'discrimination on the basis of anthropological difference: gender difference, age difference, the difference between manual and intellectual capacities' (2015: 15). The Green Route walk necessarily crossed one such threshold of inclusion/exclusion in its journey west along the Aire from Roberts Park. Chosen as a starting point for its ready accessibility, the park is a genuinely shared space, used by all sections of the local population. But it is also a constituent part of Saltaire, a UNESCO World Heritage Site. This model Victorian mill village, in the middle of Shipley ward, mostly lies to the south of the canal (safely out of the flood zone), but its park lies to the north of the river, on flood plain initially thought unfit for building on. Immediately to the west of this nineteenth-century park is the 1950s council housing development known as the Higher Coach Road estate – which, we discovered, is often assumed from the outside to be a stereotypically troubled zone of 'hard to reach' social housing (even though many of the houses are now in private ownership). In crossing the boundary line between park and estate – in order to track the river – our actors playfully proposed that the estate's water-related history might, in its own way, be as worthy of attention as Saltaire's (an argument that, employing both archival sources and our interviewees' long memories, was not difficult to make). Rather than focusing on the area's official heritage discourse – with its insistent focus on Sir Titus Salt, the Victorian entrepreneur who built Saltaire – this 'alternative heritage tour' instead focused on the stories of estate residents such as 92-year-old Billy Glover. Performed by David Smith, while seated beneath a tree right outside Billy's house, this monologue told the tale of Billy's exploits as a teenage footballer with Wolverhampton Wanderers in the 1930s, his time in a Japanese prisoner-of-war camp in the 1940s (he had been among those charged with building the notorious Bridge on the River Kwai) and then of over 60 years of living in this exact spot, as a well-known member of the local community. Woven into Billy's senior-citizen monologue were his eyewitness observations about the different levels of flooding he had seen out of his window over the years.

Intriguingly, our journey along the river in the estate area seems to have prompted a renegotiation of assumptions on the part of some 'incoming' spectators. One email respondent, for instance, voiced the implicitly class-based concerns of a number of people I spoke with, in noting that he had initially wondered 'whether there was a danger of people's stories being "gentrified" or made slightly unreal by being reproduced for "tourists."' Noting the 'power' of personal tales such as Billy Glover's, however, this respondent concluded that 'on reflection of course people like their stories to be told'.[12] Such responses mirrored something of the thought process we had undertaken while making the piece: I too had pondered the ethics of treating this housing estate as a 'stage set' in which to perform to outsiders, as well as residents. And yet, as our community engagement consultant Trevor Roberts pointed out, comparable concerns are never expressed about the regular, costume-guide tours of Saltaire mill village, where there is not so much as a grass verge to separate homeowners' front windows from the street. Our concerns about the estate's residents, Trevor suggested, amounted to a misplaced and potentially exclusionary paternalism, whereas the (already 'gentrified'?) mill village was less controversial simply because it was already *included* in the local heritage narratives.

People like their stories to be told. In the event, we received many expressions of thanks from estate residents for our efforts to share its stories and not a single expression of concern about our brief, theatrical intrusions. Sometimes the performance entourage would happen upon people outside their homes, who would ask what was going on before gesturing assent and continuing whatever they were doing. Local children, meanwhile, would follow us around in curiosity or even, after being given a flyer, reappear at the designated starting time for the next performance, with their parents in tow. Participation takes many forms, and Baz Kershaw's appropriation of the ecological term 'edge phenomena' – in his consideration of the sometimes unpredictable relationship between actors and audiences – seems strikingly apt here: 'Edge effects ... occur when two or more distinctive ecosystems rub up against each other, such as riverbanks, forest perimeters, urban boundaries and so on' (2007: 185). Our focus on tracking an environmental feature had prompted some unanticipated 'edge effects' in the area's social ecology.

Environmental ecology (theatre of vibrant matter)

This brings me, finally, to the nonhuman participants in our process, and particularly to the water that made its presence felt at all stages. Appropriately enough, for a project titled *Multi-Story Water*, it wasn't just the trajectory of the river itself that conditioned what took place but also water on its way to joining that river, coming down the Yorkshire hills and out of the Yorkshire sky. In her book *Vibrant Matter*, Jane Bennett builds on Bruno Latour's conceptualization of non-sentient 'actants', in ecosystems both natural and artificial, to argue that we 'take seriously the vitality of (nonhuman) bodies. By "vitality" I mean the capacity of things – edibles, commodities, storms, metals – not only to impede or block the will and designs of humans but also to act as quasi agents or forces with trajectories, propensities, or tendencies of their own' (2010: viii). Despite that glancing mention of 'storms', Bennett remains silent on the subject of water, but it is surely one of the more obvious forces that influence human behaviour. During our initial door-knocking research, much of which was carried out on wet days in the spring, people were much more inclined to stand and chat on their doorsteps when it was a dry day. Conversely though, on wet days, those residents who had answered the door to us at all proved more likely to invite us *inside*, offering tea and sympathy to the visibly soggy. Some of our richest encounters (such as my first meeting with Billy Glover) emerged through these circumstances.

In September 2012, we had good reason to fear that the weather would rule out any form of participation in outdoor performances. We had just experienced the wettest summer on record, and it rained fairly solidly all week prior to the performances (the actors rehearsing in head-to-toe waterproofs). In the event, we caught a lucky break: give or take a little drizzle, the rain held off for the duration of our five-cycle weekend. The skies opened, though, almost the instant we finished on the Sunday evening. Within two days, the county town of York was in the throes of a major flooding incident. 'It certainly raised my awareness of the water around us', one spectator wrote of *Multi-Story Water* in email feedback, 'and I have often thought about our local river and the flood areas during this week of almost constant rain.'[13] One might almost think of the performances as a collaboration with the sky.

The ground, too, played an unexpectedly vital part in the phenomenology of the walks. Spectators that September often commented on their sharpened awareness of the surfaces underfoot, which the rain had turned into a series of stark contrasts between sodden, muddy grass; slicked tarmac; and uneven rocky footpaths, pockmarked with puddles. The online reviewer for *Culture Vulture* illustrated her account of the experience with an image of wellingtons walking through mud, as well as a weir in full force and an actor standing in a stream.[14] The professional photographer we hired to document the performances proved equally preoccupied with the ground beneath her feet.[15]

These conditions were thrown further into relief when, in July 2013, we presented a second iteration of *Multi-Story Water* – responding to requests for a remount by using a small amount of additional funding to present a slightly revised version of the performance cycle for another long weekend. (Due to availability issues, actors David Smith and Richard Galloway were replaced by Rob Pickavance and Paul Fox, respectively.) The weather on this occasion was relentlessly warm and sunny: It had, in fact, been the driest July on record up to that point (though rain returned later in the month), with the result that the contrasts between walking surfaces seemed much less pronounced; even the grassland was 'rock hard'. To those of us making these pieces, though, it felt eerily appropriate that these two sets of conditions – the excess presence and relative absence of water – had so aptly demonstrated the point made by one of our 'characters', Neill Morrison (interviewed in July 2012):

> You look at how the weather's changed over the last thirty years. ... We're getting more extreme weather, more often. Every year it's the wettest June or the driest January. This year we've had this weird situation where the rivers were really dry in March and April, when they should be stonking – and now in June and July, when they should be at base flow and nothing spare, it's been pumping out here for weeks. I kayak for a hobby, so I notice it.

The details of this speech had to be adapted slightly for live performance in 2013, but its reminder of the previous year's high water seemed all the more pointed in the bone-dry conditions.

The warmer weather also increased the incidence of 'edge phenomena' around the performances, simply because many more people were enjoying themselves outside. Several times that July weekend, our Green Route tour had to negotiate its way around match spectators at Saltaire Cricket Club (the club's pitch lies within Roberts Park, with its pavilion right next to the river), whose long-serving volunteer groundsman, known locally as 'Billy Whizz', was one of our key 'characters'. Since he was often present and watching a match when our entourage came by, the real Billy developed an impromptu routine of calling 'Ey up Billy! How's it going?' to the actor playing him, Paul Fox, who would reciprocate by tipping his cap and calling 'Not so bad, Billy, how are you?' Spectators initially puzzled by this exchange would break into grins on realising that this was the person whom our character was based on.

We should have anticipated, of course, that presenting verbatim theatre within physical proximity of the homes or workplaces of the people depicted might generate some performative side-effects in good weather. The most memorable such moment came when former P.O.W. Billy Glover came out of his house to watch his story being performed by actor Rob Pickavance (the previous September, he had opted to stay dry indoors and watch us through the window). Recognising me among the gathered spectators, Billy grasped onto my waist for support in standing and then proceeded to begin correcting Rob on the details of his monologue – as if re-drafting his own interview transcript. Rob gamely improvised some responses but was clearly thrown by Billy's unscripted participation, so I quietly asked Billy to let Rob finish, which he did. At the end of the scene, though, as people got up to move on, Billy could not resist interjecting with the words, 'Everything he just said – every word of it is true!' This prompted a spontaneous round of applause from spectators who had become understandably uncertain as to where the real 'show' was. Later in the same performance, as our three actors delivered their concluding 'narrator' segment while standing on the riverbank at Hirst Weir, a further unexpected performer made itself apparent in the form a majestic heron – perched dead-centre on the weir's crest, basking in the sunshine, looking out for fish.[16] As the audience applauded the end of the show, the sound startled the heron into taking flight. As if on cue, it soared off down the length of the river, providing a spectacular finale that looked almost pre-rehearsed.

One of our email respondents to the July performances described his experience of the journey as 'really unexpectedly special and magical, with a (good) increasing sense of unreality towards the end'.[17] It is tempting to connect this comment with the heron incident, but this participant had undertaken the full, three-part tour: 'towards the end' thus refers to the closing stages of Red Route. This response, it must be said, was quite unanticipated by us. Red Route was designed to conclude the cycle on a bleakly poignant note of mundane social reality: the final stretch of walking along a neglected, broken river path took participants downstream to Lower Holme, a street of former mill cottages that sits on the flood plain adjacent to what was – in 2012–13 – the fenced-off perimeter of a derelict, demolished mill site. Here, Lynsey Jones, performing as 'Lynda' (a character actually composited, with their permission, from interview material provided by both Lynda and her neighbour Margaret), provided a sardonic catalogue of the ways in which Lower Holme's residents had been abandoned to their own devices by the property developers, the local council, Yorkshire Water and even – in 2000 – emergency services (who could do nothing to pump out the water flooding their basements and lapping at their electricity meters). Though delivered with wit and verve, Lynda's scene was never intended to be 'magical' or 'unreal'.

My recollection of walking towards Lower Holme during the final September performance prominently features a stark, glowering sky of streaky grey (just about to burst) that provided an atmospheric context perfect for the subject matter: I couldn't have designed the lighting better. By contrast, the following July, the riverbank walk was lit by dreamy, golden sunshine and featured a green and purple haze of summer foliage, which walkers had to duck around on their way downstream, as if navigating their way into some magical Yorkshire jungle. (The purple was courtesy of abundant buddleia – an 'invasive weed'.) This build up offset the content of Lynsey's final scene in ways that seemed delightfully incongruous – even 'unreal'. As our respondent further noted, however, the most unexpected twist came at the very end. When our actors finished their concluding three-way narrative, the real Margaret would appear out of the back door of her end-terrace house, in full view of the spectators, dragging a cooler full of beer donated by Saltaire Brewery (whose headquarters were a matter of yards away, across the footbridge). She would then hand them over her low wall to thirsty walkers as if this were an impromptu, post-show bar. When she was in the mood, the real Lynda would also appear on high at her attic window and wave down to the crowd like mock royalty.

In September, of course, the colder weather had meant we didn't need a cooler or interior storage for the beer. Nor would it have felt right to ask Margaret if we could use her house in this way, before she had a full understanding of what the performances entailed. She had, however, proved to be one of the most enthusiastic fans of the Red Route journey, which she had walked twice in September, with different family members, despite personal mobility difficulties. So when we returned the following year, Margaret proved more than willing to participate directly. If there was 'reciprocation' here, though, it was not because we had given her the 'opportunity to be part of something' but because she wanted to thank us for something we had never anticipated. The fact that we had taken the trouble to tell Lower Holme's story to (a very small portion of) the wider world had, she told us, revivified her in her determination not to simply accept the street's abandonment by the authorities. One of the local features drawn attention to in Lynsey/Lynda's tour was the black plastic bin bags that Margaret had habitually hung up with gaffer tape – at the junction of the street and river path – in order that passers-by could deposit the vibrant matter of their dog waste. Lower Holme is a street leading to a footbridge, and as such, it is a much-frequented public right of way, yet it remains 'unadopted' by Bradford Council, which thus refuses to provide amenities such as waste bins. By September 2012, Margaret had become so depressed about the whole situation that she had given up hanging the bags: our stage manager had to fix them up in order for Lynsey's monologue to make sense. Yet the performances, Margaret told us, 'gave me my fight back'. By 2014, she and her neighbours had finally raised the money to secure proper plastic waste bins to the wayside fencing.

Afterword: Participating in place

This small anecdote returns us, perhaps, to Nicholson's question: 'how might practising drama encourage people to become active participant citizens?' Considered in isolation, I am not sure that performance can accomplish any such thing. But there is an ecology of participation that occurs before and in and around and after performance projects, and one of our jobs as theatre makers is simply to embrace the fact that such things can happen, largely beyond our creative control. The process of researching, making and performing *Multi-Story Water* resulted in an authored theatre piece that, for the most part, deliberately avoided structural participation in the sense of requiring audience activity but that nevertheless proved sufficiently porous for all kinds of participants, human and nonhuman, to contribute to the overall 'score' – herons, puddles, cricketers and dog dirt, to name but a few. The law of unintended consequences dictated that the witnesses of our work responded on their own terms rather than ours – choosing to put up bins, for example, rather than look into flood-defences. But then, as Rancière notes, 'whoever emancipates doesn't have to worry about what the emancipated person learns. He will learn what he wants, nothing maybe' (1991: 18).

This might seem to some like an evasion of responsibility. Did our flood emphasis, in the end, achieve anything useful? But Margaret's defiant pride in her street underlines how important one's sense of place can be in galvanising participatory action. Community resilience to challenging conditions will depend on a sense of belonging within a local geographic context, and *place-making* is certainly one area in which performance can make a positive contribution. This much was underlined by the email feedback we received from *Multi-Story Water* spectators. Our handed-out programme had included an invitation for people to send comments if they felt moved to (we consciously chose not to pester people for feedback immediately after the performances), and among the responses we received, the most persistent theme besides general thanks and appreciation was that we had shown people familiar places in ways that had surprised them: 'the whole thing was so interesting, informative, and well thought out, taking us to places we had no idea about'; 'I have lived in Shipley since 1971, but it showed me things and told me things I didn't know'; '[i]t taught me things I didn't know about the area I've lived in 30+ years!'[18] Such statements about longevity of residence recur in the feedback.

This refreshed sense of local perspective was, I think, primarily the result of our decision to navigate a waterside trajectory through the area, rather than taking the road routes that people tend to orient themselves by. Tracking the river almost obliged us to take people along obscure as well as familiar paths. An enhanced sense of place, moreover, was not limited to those who came on the tours. For me, one of the stranger aspects of the work we did in Higher Coach Road, in particular, was the recurrent experience of finding myself being thanked by residents who had no intention of attending the performances. Theatre, they said, wasn't their kind of thing (and indeed, why should it be?), but there seemed to be genuine gratitude that we had taken the neighbourhood seriously enough to share its stories with others.

It is this theme of participatory place-making that has proved most interesting to my new colleagues in Yorkshire's Environment Agency – colleagues with whom I continue to engage three years later, as part of a longer-term AHRC project titled 'Towards Hydro-Citizenship'.[19] Although the *FRUCC* document counsels that 'communications strategy will need to overcome emotional barriers to responding to flood risk – e.g. place attachment' (*FRUCC* 2012: 11), the EA staff I have encountered are well aware that wrapping a river in (metaphorical) hazard tape is likely to be counter-productive and that *positive* emotional attachments are more likely to prompt public engagement with river issues. At the time of writing, I remain actively involved in building participatory partnerships between community members in Shipley and stakeholder organisations, including the EA. Moreover, my own sense of actively involved citizenship in this area remains more pronounced than in the place I actually live – and I expect to continue participating here even after our current project concludes. 'We no longer expect from the future that it will emancipate us from all our attachments', Bruno Latour remarks in *Politics of Nature*: 'on the contrary, we expect that it will attach us with tighter bonds to more numerous crowds of *aliens* who have become full-fledged members of the collective that is being formed' (Latour 2004: 191). Resilience will demand this.

This chapter is dedicated to the memory of Billy Glover (1921–2015)

Endnotes

1. See Claire Bishop, *Artificial Hells: Participatory Art and the Politics of Spectatorship* (London: Verso, 2012).
2. See final project report for full overview. Stephen Bottoms and Lindsey McEwen, *Multi-Story Water: Sited Performance in Urban River Communities* (University of Manchester, 2014). Hard copies available from the author on request; electronic version online at http://issuu.com/martinharriscentre/docs/drama_multi-story_water_report/1 [Accessed 31 October 2015].

3. This was the third and final meeting for members of the AHRC-supported network project, 'Reflecting on Environmental Change through Site-Based Performance'. For details, see http://performancefootprint.co.uk

4. See https://www.gov.uk/government/uploads/system/uploads/attachment_ data/file/69489/2012–01–31–pb13705–pitt-review-progress.pdf [Accessed 31 October 2015].

5. In Bristol, the project was run by the co-investigator, geographer Lindsey McEwen, in collaboration with arts facilitator Jess Allen and others.

6. These maps represent only 'best guess' approximations of where flood water might rise to in various extremities of event.

7. 'High probability' of flood (darker blue on maps) indicates a '1 in 100 or greater annual probability of river flooding (>1%)'. Lighter blue zoning for medium to low risk indicates 'between a 1 in 100 and 1 in 1000 annual probability of river flooding (1% - 0.1%)'. Definitions from http://ambiental.co.uk/riskcentral/ flood-zones/ [Accessed 31 October 2015].

8. For further details, see Bottoms/McEwen, *Multi-Story Water*, pp. 9–10.

9. For details, see Bottoms, 'Higher Coach Road History'. Blog report at http:// multi-story-shipley.co.uk/?p=408 [Accessed 31 October 2015].

10. Katie Beswick, *'Multi-Story Water: A Theatrical Tour of Shipley'*. Online at https:// theculturevulture.co.uk/blog/hometourist/multi-story-water-a-theatrical- tour-of-shipley/ [Accessed 31 October 2015]. The popularity of the boat ride offer necessitated our devising additional boat rides oriented towards children and families, *Junior Blue*.

11. Please note that this essay was written before the still-more destructive floods experienced in the Shipley area on 26 December 2015. On this occasion, Victoria Mills did indeed have a lake in its lower levels (filthy, not 'lovely'), and Philip's home was again seriously hit.

12. The full text of this response is online at http://multi-story-shipley.co.uk/? m=201308 [Accessed 31 October 2015].

13. See 'Feedback' page of *Multi-Story Water* blog, http://multi-story-shipley.co.uk/? p=310 [Accessed 31 October 2015].

14. Beswick, '*Multi-Story Water*'.

15. See online galleries at http://multi-story-shipley.co.uk/?page_id=598 and http:// multi-story-shipley.co.uk/?page_id=752 [Accessed 31 October 2015].

16. See photograph at http://multi-story-shipley.co.uk/?p=660 [Accessed 31 October 2015].

17. See collated feedback at http://multi-story-shipley.co.uk/?p=677 [Accessed 31 October 2015].

18. See collated feedback at http://multi-story-shipley.co.uk/?p=677 [Accessed 31 October 2015].

19. For details of this multi-partner project (2014–2017), see http://hydrocitizen ship.com/ [Accessed 31 October 2015].

10   *One Step Forward, One Step Back*

Resisting the Forensic Turn

James Frieze

Contemporary life affords precious little time and space in which to reflect. Yet even those participatory performances which cast themselves as an escape from or suspension of the buzz and whirr of contemporary life tend to stint on the provision of time and space for genuine reflection. Being invited to handle props, asked to speak and intimately addressed in front of strangers – all common occurrences within participatory performance these days – leave little opportunity to digest what is happening.[1] As Sophie Nield puts it, 'you are using the headspace you would normally be using to analyse and engage with the signs on stage to work out the logistics of just spectating' (2008: 533). With this in mind, I am going to argue for the value of lacunae. Lacunae, as I use the term here, are gaps within a participatory performance event, holes in the event's establishing of a convincing world. These gaps may be accidental – occurring by chance or due to unforeseen consequences of an event's design – or may be deliberately built in by the makers of the event. My argument runs consciously against the grain of much twenty-first-century discourse about participatory performance, which has been about the potential social and ethical value of becoming part of the action and about the personally empowering attractions of immersive interactivity. The promenade, immersive performance by dreamthinkspeak at the centre of my discussion is more than just an illustration or example: *One Step Forward, One Step Back* is, I will suggest, far-reachingly argumentative in itself. It is a performance full of lacunae that bring into view the terms of engagement which propel, but are usually hidden within, most works of promenade, immersive performance.

One Step Forward, One Step Back was enthusiastically received by national newspaper critics. It was selected by Charles Spencer in *The Telegraph* as one of his ten best theatre experiences of 2008[2] and by Susannah Clapp in *The Observer* (and *The Guardian* online) as one of her ten.[3] *The Guardian's* Lyn Gardner closed her review by stating that 'the journey takes about an hour; it will sustain you for a lifetime (Gardner 2008).' All three reviewers focus on the boldness of Artistic Director Tristan Sharps' vision. What they almost entirely neglect to mention, however, are the ambiguities, collisions and interruptions to vision that, I will argue, are crucial to the performance's impact on the participant and to its cultural significance.

If you are one of those who sighed a little when I used the word 'immersive', perhaps thinking to yourself that immersive theatre has had its day, two contrasting pieces by Gardner chime with that reaction. A 2007 review of Punchdrunk's groundbreaking collaboration with Battersea Arts Centre, *Masque of the Red Death*, captures and reflects her excitement about what she heralds not only as a significant new production but as a significant new *kind* of production. She lauds the fact that this form affords the opportunity 'to be both participant and spectator simultaneously' (Gardner 2007). By 2014, Gardner seems to be feeling a seven-year itch in her love affair with the form. Complaining that there is a glut of work tenuously claiming to be 'immersive' when it is not, Punchdrunk are cited as one of the few companies whom she sees as having delivered on the promise of the immersive boom by offering spectators 'genuine agency'. Gardner's pieces bookend a widespread perception of the waxing and waning of the immersive. They highlight the strong association of participatory performance with 'agency', and of both agency and participatory performance with the ambitious adaptation of buildings for a choose-your-own-path experience made famous by, and most associated with, Punchdrunk. It is this discursive linkage of agency, participation and interactive, site-appropriating promenade that dreamthinkspeak and I want to interrogate.

Since their formation in 1999, a year before Punchdrunk, dreamthinkspeak's work has also often involved the ambitious inhabiting of large buildings for invocations of classic texts in which the spectator is cast in detective mode, mining for clues of a narrative or (if they prefer) surveying the scene in a more meandering fashion. In assessing the extent to which this brand of story-trail performance empowers the participant, most critics have focused either on the sensory (as Josephine Machon does) or on the entrepreneurial dimensions of the experiences on offer (as Adam Alston does).[4] Machon argues that immersive forms of communitas 'defamiliarise the familiar to transcend experience' (2013: 38); Alston finds Punchdrunk's collaboration with large corporations, including their willingness to produce advertainment shows explicitly promoting brands, problematically complicit with an experience economy which he wants theatre to transcend. Both these lines of enquiry presume a desire for theatre to rise above the culture within which it is produced. In contrast, my aim is to usher into the debate about participation a fuller consideration of the ways in which theatre *fuels* other domains of culture *and vice versa*.

Participatory performance and the forensic turn

Contemporary theatre, like all of contemporary culture, is obsessed with the detection, verification and display of information. This can be seen in the steady shift from ideologically driven to statistically driven policymaking and in the credibility invested in evidence-based approaches in everything from teacher training to architectural theory to the evaluation of happiness.[5] In these and many other contexts, truth is figured forensically – that is, using approaches that invoke and adapt forensic science. Thomas Keenan (whose work focuses on photojournalism and the staging of evidence in trials), Eyal Weizman (a leading figure in forensic architecture, a field concerned with the role of architectural practice and analysis in relation to human rights) and Allan Sekula (a maker of performances and films, as well as a renowned media and political theorist) are among those across various disciplines who have identified the emergence of a forensic gaze, manifest in a forensic aesthetic. In their short but important book, *Mengele's Skull*, Keenan and Weizman identify the 1985 'trial' of Josef Mengele (the physician who selected victims for the Auschwitz gas chambers and performed experiments on prisoners) as the dawn of a forensic aesthetic. Whereas the 1961 Eichmann trial placed survivor testimony centre stage as a reaction against the primacy of documents and exclusion of witness accounts in the Nuremburg trials, the need to identify an exhumed skull as Mengele's engendered new forms of superimposition, in which images of the living subject were, with the help of the forensic team's theatrical presentation strategies, used to bring the dead to apparent life. These strategies, as Keenan and Weizman detail, instrumentalise the forensic turn's all-deducing approach to truth (2012).

Lindsay Steenberg's study of the application of forensic science in contemporary American popular culture is a book that has much to offer discourse on participatory performance (2012). As Steenberg asserts, an archival, museological drive fuels the forensic turn, an impulse to 'collect, order and display with the intention of creating a clearer picture of the world and demonstrating the owner's superior understanding of it' (2012: 16). A coupling of the nostalgic with the hyper-modern, the archival drive of the forensic is in many ways a return to Enlightenment humanism that 'elides the controversies, anxieties and inconsistencies circulating … in postmodernity' (2012: 16). But its nostalgia is augmented by a postmodern propensity for simulations that animate rather than merely display. These simulations that animate rather than merely display, blurring illusion and reality, are the paradigmatic mode of participation in what is widely referred to as 'the new museum' and its kissing cousin, the story-trail immersive. In both the new museum and the story-trail immersive, the sensation of access to evidence afforded to the viewer-turned-participant is heightened by hands-on, interactive, multimedia design features. Through these features, which bring 'dead' objects and texts back to life, the promise of the archive is itself resurrected.

In a video interview for New York-based, networking think tank FoST (Future of Storytelling), filmed in September 2013, Felix Barrett opposes Punchdrunk's immersive theatre, which he lauds as a sensory, haptic experience that fosters agency, to the 'traditional theatregoing experience' which he denigrates as a disembodied, passivity-inducing spectacle 'that's utterly formulaic'. Just as immersive theatre is constructed as dynamic and progressive, in opposition to traditional theatre, positioned as retrograde, the new museum (as Nick Prior outlines (2006: 509–524)) casts the traditional museum as a mausoleum, a stifling repository of dead culture.[6] Though the intricacies of the relationship between theatre and museums is complex and contested, there is (as both Susan Bennett and Scott Magelssen observe) general agreement that museums have taken a theatrical turn, 'offering exhibits and experiences that equip visitors with learning and invite them to step into roles that require real-time choices based on that learning' – learning that has 'become less about the objects and more about the experience' (Magelssen 2013; Bennett 2013). The *Jurassic Park*-style museum-as-theme-park allows visitors to get viscerally close to material objects and allows curators to commodify visitor experience. The example on which Steenberg focuses is a role-playing exhibit that is an offshoot of the (much franchised) television phenomenon *CSI*:

> The key words appearing consistently across the marketing for *CSI: The Experience* include: immersive, interactive, hands-on, multi-media, and, of course, experience. The experience being offered here is one of role-play and the exhibit frequently addresses its participants directly. … Even if these experiences are mass-produced simulations, they are always unique to the player/participant. Thus, the aura that might be lost from the postmodern artefact can perhaps paradoxically be found in the postmodern simulational experience. (2012: 141)

The impulse to restore materiality to discovery fuels the 'postmodern simulational experience' afforded by Punchdrunk in similarly paradoxical ways.

As Michael Billington observes in his review of *The Drowned Man* (2013),[7] the fundamental mode of Punchdrunk performance is 'simulation' that seeks to 'blur the border between illusion and reality'. For the 2011 (New York) incarnation of their *Macbeth* adaptation, *Sleep No More*, the company went to even greater lengths to blur reality and illusion by making the McKittrick, an invented hotel, seem like a real hotel derelict since the outbreak of World War II. They created websites to 'document' the mythological cachet of the McKittrick arising from its use in filming by Alfred Hitchcock. This cachet is extended within the performance event, which 'restores' the (invented) McKittrick as a multi-storey cabinet of curiosities stuffed to the nines with what might be the most numerous and diverse collection of found objects to furnish any piece of performance in history. Though the idea is that these objects derive from previous eras of the hotel's life, they were actually bought in flea markets to create a set that is a kind of *Wunderkammer*.

Steenberg identifies the *Wunderkammer*, privately owned museums that became fashionable in the sixteenth century, as prototypical manifestations of the contemporary forensic aesthetic. Revelling in the exotic aura of found objects, the *Wunderkammers* are privately owned cabinets of curiosities in which the real and the fake, the made and the organic, are dizzily juxtaposed. Whereas the nineteenth-century museum strives for arrangement, often through taxonomy, the *Wunderkammer* makes 'no distinction between the mythical, the cultural and the natural' (Steenberg 2012: 126). In Punchdrunk's forensic story-trails, we see, as Steenberg suggests, a return to the former augmented by a postmodern propensity for simulations that confuse mythical, cultural and natural.

The blurring of illusion and reality within simulations that fetishise the encounter with evidence informs the design of *OSF, OSB*, as it does the design of *Masque of the Red Death*, *The Drowned Man* and *Sleep No More*. But while these Punchdrunk shows wrap participants *within* a forensic aesthetic, *OSF, OSB* deploys various kinds of lacunae to open a space between participant and aesthetic, a space for reflection on and resistance to forensic logic. In this way, *OSF, OSB* offers an encounter with uncertainty, with not knowing. Instead of making us feel a sense of superior understanding in accordance with forensic logic, *OSF, OSB* creates spaces of *un*knowing that make us conscious of the desires and assumptions we bring to our performance of participation here and elsewhere.

One Step Forward, One Step Back

One Step Forward, One Step Back inhabited the vast interior of Liverpool Cathedral during the post-Easter period of the year in which the city was the European Capital of Culture. The year 2008 was the peak of the enormous wave of regeneration that transformed central Liverpool and that saw the demolition of some listed buildings. A show, as I will detail, that interweaves motifs of spiritual and commercial aspiration, *OSF, OSB* opened at the same time as The Paradise Project was being completed. Now called Liverpool One, The Paradise Project gave the city centre a makeover that featured shiny new shopping complexes. Paradise is not exactly 'lost' for Tristan Sharps in the show he created for this cultural moment, but it is a concept that he wants to rescue from the rhetoric of property development. It is through lacunae, gaps in the fugue of progression in which we are made to step out of and back in time, that we experience the epistemic jolt of seeing the terms of our participation laid bare. I will argue that while Punchdrunk prick our appetite with the promise of access, encouraging us to forget ourselves, dreamthinkspeak want us to remember the relationship of participation to cultural memory and ask, what are we searching for, what propels that search, and what do our searches leave behind?

In the waiting area just inside the imposing arched entrance to the Cathedral, we are grouped into three- or four-strong mini audiences. Each group's first encounter is with a gentleman in Victorian attire who reads with passion the William Blake poem 'Jerusalem'[8] – until he stops, turns to us aghast and shows us his book. 'The words, the words are falling off the page!' As he ushers us out in some distress, we are stopped in our tracks by an extraordinary reveal. In a trompe l'oeil enhanced by the cunning use of a projector, the ceiling disappears and overhead wheel trolleys are pushed by shoppers in a busy supermarket. The shoppers are oblivious to the other drama below. Our bibliophilic gentleman bustles us out towards a dark corridor. We wait.

Someone may knock on the door, or after a while, the door will slowly and slightly open. Peeking inside, we can see a polygonal room. Facing each wall is a red-suited figure. Huddling over portable heaters, the red figures tap away at identical computer terminals in doleful unison. After a while, shyly at first, they start to look around at us. Eventually, we are being stared down by a battalion of bedraggled Santa Clauses. Pausing from their weary typing of (what the more inquisitive observers will detect to be) shopping lists, the Santas seem faintly sheepish at first, then increasingly ashamed. The scene reads as a sardonic betrayal of the magic of Christmas.

The soulless input of the lists seems to counterpoint the words of *Jerusalem* falling off the page in the opening scene, perhaps signalling an enslavement of language to mechanical labour. As these thoughts float around in my head, I am entreated to move on. If observers do not leave this scene quickly, the Santas will become increasingly agitated, their faces becoming as red as their suits; it is clearly not something they want us to witness. They point us further down the corridor.

Figure 10.1   Shoppers overhead. Photograph by Lois Maskell (set designer). Concept and artistic direction by Tristan Sharps.

We make our way to a similarly shaped and proportioned, oddly polygonal room. This one, however, is literally and metaphorically warmer, lovingly furnished in rich, polished woods. Instead of the portable heaters and soulless PCs, there are floor-to-ceiling bookshelves brimming with hardbound books. Two more Victorian gentlemen (referred to by Sharps in an interview as 'failed philosophers') are labouring to piece *Jerusalem*

Figure 10.2   Bedraggled Santas. Photograph by Lois Maskell (set designer). Concept and artistic direction by Tristan Sharps.

back together, each word a fragment of paper that they move around like a jigsaw. Shortly after, we see their companion, the bibliophile figure from the opening scene. Alone by a lamp, he has few words now and seems unable to engage, gesturing more desperately now for us to move on. The room darkens to cue our exit, but as we are leaving, a scene of trolley-pushing shoppers again appears over our heads; this time they are in a park, cherry blossom falling around them like snow. This scene of snow and shopping fades out, and the supermarket from the first scene reappears, except now we are directly below a checkout counter. Pausing momentarily from the production-line repetition of scanning, the checker peers down at us: it is one of the Santas. The philosopher exhorts us to keep moving.

What unites the otherwise oppositional characters (the philosophers and the Santas) is that they collectively point us ever on, ever upwards. The effect of this continual pointing upwards and onwards is disconcerting and palpably paradoxical, clashing with the continual exhortations to pause, to reflect, to take time out and step back. Our journey echoes the poet's epic, allegorical ascent to Heaven in a text which

Sharps cites as a key inspiration for *OSF, OSB*: Dante's *Divine Comedy*. As in the *Divine Comedy*, the focus on guidance is married to a sense of epistemological crisis. Like Dante's, our journey is a comedic but profoundly soul-searching one in which we reflect on our own agency. While Dante is guided through Hell by an ancient – the Roman poet Virgil – we have the philosophers. Through Heaven, Dante is guided by Beatrice, the ideal woman and muse, inspired by a real woman he met in his younger days. Our Beatrice is a similarly worldly and other-worldly presence. After a steady upward journey, we suddenly realise how far we have ascended as we look down hundreds of feet to see a figure in the brightest of blue dresses, a distant yet dazzling vision against the expanse of ochre. She glides a celestial, arcing path towards the altar, turns to us with angelic calm and points skyward before arcing back towards and beneath us, disappearing from view.[9] While there are many moments in *OSF, OSB* that make us stop and think, most such moments are sardonic in tone. The appearance of the Beatrice figure is a different kind of epiphany. After all the cautionary moments, this is a surprisingly joyous, magical and dreamlike one. It is perhaps designed to remind us of the power of wonder. Sharps wants us to dream, but as the final phase of the show will demonstrate, he wants us to reflect on our dreams.

Finally, we ascend the bell-tower (one of the world's largest and highest) to reach the heaviest functioning ringing bells on the planet. Now, though, their ring is eerily silent, as if we have become deaf to their toll. Finally, we are out on the roof, 300 feet above the city. There are tourist-style binocular telescopes promising a better view, vision beyond the cranes. But these ones are trained on particular windows in a building a few hundred feet away. In two of the rooms in the building, we see a library and what looks like our philosophers: one gazing back at us, the other engaged in quiet study. In another window, we see our Santa Clauses working flat out to wrap and label our presents.

Charlie Dickinson, who played the bibliophile of the opening scene in many performances of the show, offered cogent observations about guidance with regard to theme and about Sharps's guidance to the actors in rehearsal:

> The philosophers are searching for knowledge; other more potent minds have seduced them but not given them the full picture. Tristan's interested in the spiritual guides – Milton, Blake and Dante. What links them is love. And the understanding that comes with love. The philosophers don't get this as they are experiencing it second hand.

Dickinson's interpretation is worth underlining: the philosophers are in thrall to 'second hand experience' because 'other more potent minds have seduced them but not given them the full picture'. The idea that 'what links them is love' might seem hazily sentimental, but I read 'love' here to mean that which is beyond the evidential. It means building an understanding of oneself over time and through genuine dialogue with everything one encounters culturally. This, I will argue, could not be further from the forensic logic that aligns interaction with immediate, visceral, spectacular and interactive experience in which the participant surrenders their awareness of themselves.

Search warrant

The experiences facilitated by both dreamthinkspeak and Punchdrunk – offering different kinds and levels of engagement that some participants process with one another outside the event through social media – have often been described as being more akin to video gaming than to watching a play in a theatre. In 2009, intermediality theorist Marie-Laure Ryan felt the need to add a new facet to her influential typology of the kinds of immersion operative in video gaming. Previously, she had conceived three kinds: spatial, temporal and emotional. Now, she added the epistemic, which isolates as a form of immersion the participant's search for knowledge. Ryan states that the 'prototypical manifestation of epistemic immersion – the desire to know – is the mystery story. The player impersonates the detective and investigates the case through the standard repertory of computer game actions: moving the avatar through the game world, picking up tell-tale objects, and extracting information.' As Rosemary Klich testifies, many participants report moving through Punchdrunk pieces something like an 'avatar' and 'picking up tell-tale objects' as they seek to 'extract information' (forthcoming). Klich identifies herself as one of these participants, stating that the 'notion of epistemic immersion particularly resonates with my experience of adventuring through *Masque of the Red Death*, hunting clues to the "hidden story" I had read about beforehand online, or trying to make sense of postcards, drawings and photographs dispersed across different rooms and levels in *The Drowned Man*.' She cites Colette Gordon's pithy observation that 'audience members proceed as if issued with a search warrant' (quoted in Klich, forthcoming).

To Ryan's notion of epistemic immersion, I would add the caveat that, for epistemic immersion to take place, the participant must be allowed to disappear, to lose themselves in their investigation. Punchdrunk's

Artistic Director, Felix Barrett, states that if 'ever an audience becomes aware of themselves as audience, then we've probably slightly failed' (qtd in Machon 2013: 161). Measures taken to help achieve this include the Punchdrunk mask. Experienced by many participants as anonymising and disinhibiting, the mask engenders a degree of disappearance; a further degree is engendered by the darkness of many story-trail performance environments (including Punchdrunk's). Another measure taken is that, in many immersive events (again including Punchdrunk's), we are given a set of rules before we begin about what we are and are not allowed to do. These rules are issued in writing, by a performer/facilitator in front of us or by a voice over a loudspeaker. Such inductions tend to give me the feeling that there is a desire on the part of the facilitators to get the pragmatics over with, so that pragmatic problems do not interfere with our sense of escape.

All of these measures attest to Barrett's desire to 'keep the lid closed so no light from the real world enters in, figuratively or literally!' (2013: 161). Once sealed, there is little guidance for the promenading partici-pant. The mystery story, in these conditions, is experienced as a fugue: a trail of cryptic revelations that spur us on to know more, maintaining our desire to reach a higher level of access without it ever being entirely clear what we are accessing. A sense of access promised and endlessly deferred is essential to the stimulation of desire for knowledge that fuels epistemic immersion. Articulating the particular sense of fugue engendered by the Internet age, Miranda July wryly observes that '[w]e haunt ourselves, googling our own name, perpetually clicking on search – because if we're always searching then we never have to notice that we've found it, we're there, this is really it.' The haunted promise of continually deferred access to something secret, something hinted at and rumoured, is crucial to what is in several respects – including global impact and commercial success – the apotheosis of Punchdrunk's work and of immersive theatre production as both live event and Internet sensation, *Sleep No More*. Bill Worthen details these secrets just out of reach, including the elusive carrot of 'access to the fabled sixth floor' of the fictional McKittrick Hotel in which the event takes place (2012: 95). This privilege and others, such as rare and apparently individually tailored one-to-one performances, are mythologised by blogs and fan sites that extend the event. Drawing on testimony from fellow participants, Worthen conveys how the sense of the occasional one-to-ones performed to chosen spectators are perceived by many as hidden treasures.

While the opposition of Santa Clauses and shoppers to poets and philosophers is a key motif, *One Step Forward* is a story, like *Sleep No More*, in which meaning is not only enhanced but generated by the spaces through which we move. Sharps states that it was the combination of the grandiose and the secret that drew him to the cathedral as a site for the Liverpool performance: 'you cannot fail to be struck by the sense of this huge interior space, but there are also an extraordinary number of inter-connecting passageways that you don't see' on a public tour.[10] As well as the august, open spaces, we are indeed afforded access to confined quarters inaccessible to (ordinary) tour groups. Crucially, though, the things we find there are *in*accessible, frequently stopping us in our tracks and turning our gaze back on itself. We find ourselves in stairwells or corridors, walking over small wooden bridges to nowhere or suddenly shut in by aluminium barriers. These spaces trip us up rather than spur us on. Just as we think we are stuck, glimpses are revealed of worlds lost or buried in time. In one such apparently void space, grey snow falls as we walk across it and a wan light reveals a half-buried building shaped like a question mark but glow-ing in the distinctive orange of a Sainsbury's supermarket. It feels like we have found ourselves in a nuclear winter. By the time we reach a second snowscape, we find beneath us a partly real, partly fantastic Liverpool in faded miniature, replete with what seem to be skyscrapers, shops, offices, eateries and a cathedral. As we walk over a makeshift bridge in an eerily void passageway, a detailed outline map of Liverpool's skyline, in light that is somehow both sepia and neon, lights up beneath us then disappears as soon as we are over the bridge.

The interplay of deliberation (the evocation of a distinct world and a clear thematic opposition between consumer habits and spiritual enrichment/enlightenment) and meandering (the freedom to explore interesting, confusing spaces as we follow or fail to follow what is a narrative in only a loose sense, full of gaps and intriguing ambiguities) is one that characterises many participatory performance events. In *One Step Forward*, how we are compelled to move and how our movement is hampered or deterred are foregrounded in relation to the thematic tensions between static remembering/preserving and fugue-like forget-ting/reinventing. Though we enter the performance in groups of three, there is no desire on the part of the facilitators of our experience to split up (as occurs in some immersive performances)[11] people who come to the event together. As soon as we have left the first segment of performance, we are free to wander at whatever pace we want. Standing out against this background of freedom, the moments where we are shepherded by the Santas and the philosopher register decisively as moments of coercion. Steady movement upwards and onwards provides a sense of propul-sion that is cut by sudden shifts of scale and perspective and by mini time-warps – primordial irruptions and visions of a postapocalyptic future. While there are tropes of showing and revealing, there are equally tropes of burial (snow-covered supermarket) and disappearance (the words falling off the page, the lost city).

The participatory performances that I find most rewarding are those that put participation in crisis. Though I am focusing on Punchdrunk's brand of story-trail performance as my main point of contrapuntal reference in this essay, *many* brands of participatory performance strive to seal off the world of the event from the world outside it. This striving can produce moments in which the thinness, or fragility, of the contract that we enter into as participants of such events becomes awkwardly apparent. Richard Talbot points out the frequency of collisions between the 'play' world and the outside world in performances within the InOnTheAct Festival (Salford Quays, 2012) (forthcoming). Sophie Nield describes how an encounter with a monk in a show by Goat and Monkey made her uneasily aware of her 'not-mediaeval clothes' and 'not-mediaeval bright green handbag' (2008: 531). While such moments are usually suppressed or scuttled around by facilitators, sometimes by improvisation that steers our attention away, ignoring them, the lacunae within *One Step Forward* seem to build *towards* such collisions of the everyday and play worlds. With its motifs of masks (like those of the Santas and the cathedral itself) slipping, *One Step Forward* wants us to feel the thinness of the contracts that we enter into. Talbot describes how the producers of *You Once Said Yes* (Look Left, Look Right) 'try to limit unhelpful "mis-keying" by figures out-of-the-frame: security guards; local police; actors from other shows recognised by audience members; and interruptions from members of the general public.'[12] Such 'mis-keying', in contrast, propels *One Step Forward*, which is a tissue of interruptions and collisions between perceptual frames. Our journey is defined by lacunae as much as by progression. It is through these lacunae that we realise the lessons of our quest precisely at the moment when we thought we had reached a void. This is the opposite of the strangely vacuous emphasis on stimulation and the promise of more that is intrinsic to forensic spectacle. Our egress to the roof of the cathedral is an apparent re-emergence into the world that soon leads us back, through the doctored telescopes, to the tricks of illusion. We are actively staged as a spectacle for passers-by as we stand on the roof of the cathedral facing in the same direction. Judging by the telephone call to which Merseyside Police responded early in the run of *OSF, OSB* that reported an imminent mass suicide attempt, the participants that night looked to someone like they were planning to jump off.

Momentum and regression

As its title suggests, there is a dialogue between momentum and regression in *One Step Forward, One Step Back*. The title might be a commentary or a prescription. As commentary, it suggests the need to be careful about progress, asking us to consider what we lose in the name of regeneration dressed up as glossily futural. As prescription, it exhorts us to take a step back, to retreat and to dig, to actively revisit the products of previous generations, not to live in the past so much as take a broader, epochal view.

One Step Forward is the first part of what would become (rather than being preconceived as) a trilogy of works about regeneration. All three pieces interrogate how we carry forward or obliterate the pasts that generate our present as we try to shape the future. *One Step Forward* was followed in 2010 by *Before I Sleep*, a meditation on Chekhov's *Cherry Orchard* using a derelict co-op building in Brighton; and in 2013, *In The Beginning Was The End* came, which took place in London's Somerset House. As Brighton-based arts journalist and dreamthinkspeak buff Bella Todd notes, both of these pieces take advantage of a historical moment in which buildings with rich histories have been stripped down in readiness for renting out. Escorting Todd and her *Time Out* interview crew 'down a dark alley between Somerset House and what were the King's College science labs, Sharps points to a signpost that reads "Designated Contaminated Waste Route" and reflects that "the faster the pace of regeneration, the faster the pace of degeneration"' (2013). As we confront the snowscapes of *OSF, OSB*, Sharps wants us to consider the value of historical knowledge in planning the future.

It is not regeneration in itself that he sees as the problem but cultural amnesia; he is calling for an honest dialogue between the imperative for new development and the value of preservation. It is fitting that 'Jerusalem' is a poem that invokes conflicting images of regeneration. Amid the poem's paradisiacal imagery of hope and triumph harnessed to the project of building 'Jerusalem in England's green and pleasant land', the 'dark Satanic mills' bespeak the spiritual and physical horrors that are the undertow of the onward surge of industry. These same dark Satanic mills are, one might add, the kinds of space being renovated for immersive theatre events. Zealous preservers, the philosophers trying to restore the text fail because they are too cloistered. There cannot be many poems more iconic in contemporary English culture than 'Jerusalem'. Its resonance is the result of its ritual/partisan use as a hymn, a suffragette rallying cry, a fixture at the Labour Party Conference and at major sporting events. Blake's writing is very powerful, and the emotion that accrues from these applications of the poem in performance add to that power. Here, though, the philosophers fail to restore that power because they pick the poem apart pedantically, treating it as evidence to be restored.

The twist that develops from the opposition of the philosophers to the shoppers is that they are equally myopic. While the shoppers are addicted to the convenience of their trolley dashing, the philosophers fail to see the bigger picture because they fail to leave their room, refusing to engage with the rapidly changing culture around them. Blake's strident short poem and Dante's deeply complex, epic poem are inspirations to Sharps in that they both take an openly palimpsestic approach to the world around them, acknowledging the present while holding the past and the future in view. Mixing an idealistic view of human nature with a square-eyed sense of cruelty and suffering, they embrace change but reject both starry-eyed nostalgia and blind modernisation.

Sharps is not the only immersive theatre-maker to use derelict buildings as sites of immersive theatre. As Gareth White observes, the kind of 'maze-like' spaces appropriated by Shunt and Punchdrunk are 'ready-made exploratory landscapes', but they are also 'redolent of other histories' (2012: 223). Though the performance event is architecturally site-sympathetic, there is a (con)fusion of what is found with what is invented so that the history of the site is over-written by the event. dreamthinkspeak's site-appropriation is conscious of the site's history and self-conscious about the work's engagement with that history. In *One Step Forward*, some of the cathedral's glass display cases containing bibles, robes and regalia are strategically highlighted to evoke the efforts to preserve and inspire through the building of tradition – laying down cultural and spiritual roots. Others are cannily and uncannily transformed – one becoming a block of flats, minute scenes of contemporary life just perceptible through the tiny windows.

Reconstruction and deconstruction are the forensic expert's means of processing evidence. Encountering a scene, the forensic investigator peels back layers that obscure the truth, imagining how the scene came to be in the state that s/he finds it. In this way, s/he builds a picture of what created the scene and why. While the reader-agent of immersive theatre routinely engages in this forensic process of deconstruction and reconstruction, it is less routine for that process itself to be deconstructed in the course of the immersive event. From the opening efforts of the bibliophile to piece narrative together to the closing gag of the telescopes that aid but trick our vision, we are confronted at every playful turn with echoes of our own efforts to make sense of the evidence. Along the way, the augmentation and peeling back of the Cathedral architecture alternately suspends us in illusion and detaches us. Maps and models of city and Cathedral – a city and Cathedral like but not quite like Liverpool – emplace and jolt us at the same time, locating us uncannily. I found myself thinking about those listed buildings bulldozed by the developers of Liverpool One, but also – a bit like Dante – about my desire for illusion. Sharps exploits the Cathedral's resistance to appropriation as much as he exploits its aura. The show's tropes of revelation and obfuscation invoke dialogue between adaptation and refusal to adapt.

There are strong thematic and conceptual parallels between *One Step Forward* and Umberto Eco's *Name of the Rose* (1980). The ludic text-spaces created by Eco are themselves literary equivalents of immersive theatre – reflexive, unfinished stories that call playfully on the reader to complete them. Action and meaning in Eco's novel are generated through a lost and possibly suppressed text – Aristotle's book on comedy. The reader must generate meaning for themselves by acting as detective. The key site is a library (conflating lost and mythical libraries from Borges and elsewhere), and there are poisoned pages from which the words disappear. The two hexagonal rooms in *One Step Forward* recall the complex of hexagonal galleries that make up the library in *Name of the Rose*. Eco states in his postscript that he chose the title 'because the rose is a symbolic figure so rich in meanings that by now it hardly has any meaning left' (1984: 502). Something similar could be said of Santa Claus. As in Eco's novel, the palimpsestic nature of the *One Step Forward* philosophers' efforts to form text mirrors the palimpsestic nature of the event that we are participating in, our own efforts to form/restore text.

Immersion in the wake of the divine

There is another reason why both the *Divine Comedy* and *Name of the Rose*, with their respective emphases on spiritual questing in relation to theo-logical institutions, are useful reference points. In siting *One Step Forward* in a cathedral, Sharps brings into view the related functions of immersive theatre, museums and places of worship. The characterisation of tradi-tional Western museums as mausolea, or shrines, is summarised by Janet Marstine:

> One of the longest-standing and most traditional ways to envision the museum is as a sacred space. ... In the paradigm of the shrine, the museum has therapeutic potential. It is a place of sanctuary removed from the outside world. Museum collections are fetishized; the museum as

shrine declares that its objects possess an aura that offers spiritual enlight-enment as it inspires Platonic values of beauty and morality. (2006: 9)

One Step Forward invokes the 'therapeutic potential' of the museum and the auratic nature of objects from both spiritual (sacred) *and* material (sacrile-gious) perspectives. As Bruno Latour has argued, there is something deeply sacrilegious about the museum that is traditionally repressed. Although the 'critical acumen' deployed in setting up the museum 'depends on a clear distinction between what is real and what is constructed', the museum positions the objects it collects as cultural, not natural – fetishes, idols, vanities – usurping nature in what Marstine calls 'Platonic' fashion (Latour 1997: 63). The problem for the museologist, as Latour asserts, is that they must act as God. It is a problem intensified within the paradigm of the new museum, where all kinds of trickery is used to blur the virtual and the actual, resurrecting the dead through simulation. In *One Step Forward*, this traditionally repressed problem is brought into view: the notion of acting in place of God is hard to miss as we discover buried supermarkets, minia-ture offices and cathedrals looking like models of cities suspended in time. The pathos of our production and consumption clashes with the effortless aura of the sacred space. We are frequently reminded, nonetheless, that this sacred, awe-inspiring space was actually constructed by human hands. The dialogue between dreamthinkspeak and the Cathedral is propelled by hope: the transmission of culture, and how we choose to legitimate that transmission, is entirely in our hands.

In the death of grand narratives that led us to the uncertainties of post-modernism, the death of God is fundamental. It is perhaps not surprising that the aura 'lost from the postmodern artefact' is restored through simu-lations in, say, disused warehouses that offer a sense of wonder and power that might previously have been felt in a cathedral. Long before there was 'neoliberalism', capitalism had been compensating for and accelerating the death of God by promising godlike empowerment through simulation. In former Trappist monk Thomas Merton's 1948 autobiography, *Seven Storey Mountain* – the title of which refers to the *Divine Comedy* – he rails against the appetite for the spectacular stimulated and indulged by modern capitalism:

We live in a society whose whole policy is to excite every nerve in the human body and keep it at the highest pitch of artificial tension, to strain every human desire to the limit and to create as many new desires and synthetic passions as possible, in order to cater to them with the products of our factories and printing presses and movie studios and all the rest. 1999: 148)

205

'Synthetic' is an interesting word. It has two definitions that evolved in tandem: (*in reference to substances*) imitation of the natural through human agency; (*in reference to propositions*) having truth or falsity determinable with recourse to experience. These definitions make Merton's use of the word 'synthetic' seem prescient, resonating as they do with the claims made by some critics and makers for immersive performance. According to these claims, submerging oneself in a simulated reality paradoxically allows the participant to recover a state of embodied agency that has been eviscerated by a cultural diminution of experience. Agency, according to this logic, is revived by deduction through experience. Sharps takes a more Mertonian line. The shifts of perspective, epistemological jolts, epiphanal moments and other lacunae that he builds into his product aim to open a space *between* desire and product. This space offers a chance to reflect on the paradoxes of the forensic age, a stage of capitalist desire fulfilment in which experience is about closing down space, about moving through it in a fugue-like bubble.

From a Mertonian perspective, the products catering for today's 'synthetic passions' might include interactive, multimedia experiences offered in contemporary museums and immersive performance events by the likes of Punchdrunk. Ironically, but logically in Merton's scenario, 'movie studios' are (like 'factories and printing presses') fast becoming things of yesterday, their products increasingly nostalgic. These passions of yesterday are 'synthetically' recovered within new museological, interactive, multimedia experiences. Movie studios feature in several Punchdrunk shows, including *It Felt Like a Kiss*[13] and *The Drowned Man*. The latter is set within and around Temple Pictures, a fictional British outpost of real, Hollywood film corporation Republic Pictures.

While we are literally and metaphorically masked within Punchdrunk's blurring of illusion and reality, we are repeatedly unmasked within *One Step Forward*. All of the images we encounter – including the shamed Santas ordering and wrapping our gifts and the philosophers struggling to make sense from the scraps of culture – conspire to reflect back to us the consequences of our desires, aspirations, vanities and struggles. How we interpret those reflections is up to us, but at least we have time and space *to* reflect and are guided to consider meaningful questions about desire, preservation and regeneration. *OSF, OSB* is the kind of diversion of the forensic turn that can, in a modest but important way, both catalyse civic responsibility and enrich critical thinking about performance and participation. It challenges us – as citizens, makers and consumers – to illuminate what makes us reach, what constrains our reach and what our aspirations leave behind.

Endnotes

1. I echo here comments made by Julian Maynard Smith (artistic director of Station House Opera) during the discussion phase of a presentation by me in a symposium (at the Royal Central School of Speech and Drama, London) titled *Immersive Theatre Experiences*, 12 February 2013.

2. Charles Spencer, 'Ten best theatre nights of the year 2008', *The Telegraph*, 17 December 2008 <http://www.telegraph.co.uk/culture/theatre/3814366/Ten-best-theatre-nights-of-the-year-2008> [accessed 7 February 2015].

3. Susannah Clapp, 'Donmar is a credit to the British stage', *The Guardian*, 14 December 2008 <http://www.theguardian.com/culture/2008/dec/14/2008-in-theatre> [accessed 9 February 2015].

4. See Machon's *(Syn)aesthetics: Redefining Visceral Performance* (Basingstoke: Palgrave Macmillan, 2009) and *Immersive Theatres: Intimacy and Immediacy in Contemporary Performance* (Basingstoke: Palgrave Macmillan, 2013) and Alston's essays, the most frequently cited of which is: 'Audience Participation and Neoliberal Value: Risk, Agency and Responsibility in Immersive Theatre', *Performance Research*, 18.2 (June 2013), 128–38.

5. The emergence of a forensic approach to the perception of emotions is charted by Oliver Burkeman in an essay entitled 'Science of Happiness': <http://www.theguardian.com/lifeandstyle/2011/may/07/science-of-happiness-oliver-burkeman > [accessed 10 October 2014]. For accounts of the emerging dominance of evidence-based approaches to teaching, see Geoff Petty (ed.) *Evidence-Based Teaching: a practical approach* (Oxford: Oxford University Press), 2009.

6. The museum-as-mausoleum motif is central to George C. Wolfe's iconoclastic (and now, ironically, canonical) 1986 satire *The Colored Museum*. Satirising not only realist classics such as Lorraine Hansberry's *A Raisin in the Sun* but also experimental/avant-garde work such as Ntozake Shange's neo-Brechtian, feminist choreopoem *for colored girls who have considered suicide when the rainbow is not enuf*, Wolfe insists that all forms of text are stifling if we regard them as sacred objects.

7. Michael Billington, '*The Drowned Man: A Hollywood Fable – review*', 17 July 2013 <http://www.theguardian.com/stage/2013/jul/17/drowned-man-hollywood-fable-review> [accessed 15 June 2015].

8. The anthemic 'Jerusalem' originates from the Preface to Blake's epic poem, *Milton*, first published in 1808. It reads: 'And did those feet in ancient time/ Walk upon England's mountains green:/And was the holy Lamb of God,/On England's pleasant pastures seen!/And did the Countenance Divine,/Shine forth upon our clouded hills?/And was Jerusalem builded here,/Among these dark Satanic Mills?/Bring me my Bow of burning gold;/Bring me my Arrows of desire:/Bring me my Spear: O clouds unfold!/Bring me my Chariot of fire!/I will not cease from Mental Fight,/Nor shall my Sword sleep in my hand:/Till we have built Jerusalem,/In England's green & pleasant Land.' William Blake, *Milton* (Boulder, CO: Shambhala Press, 1978), p. 62.

9. There were actually three actresses playing the Beatrice role, working in a loop so that one was always in view of the audience as each slowly describes their arc. I thank Chris Tomlinson, who was assistant director to Sharps, for detailing this and other logistical aspects.

10. These comments are made in an interview with Shehani Fernando, 'Milton on Merseyside' (online video feature), *The Guardian*, 2 May 2008 <http://www.theguardian.com/arts/video/2008/may/02/one.step.forward> [accessed 9 February 2015].

11. A recent example of this is Coney's *Early Days (of a better nation)*, first staged in 2014, in which we are each cast as a representative of one of three regions of a fictional country in crisis. Each region works and sits separately within the emergency parliament in which the needs of each region are negotiated in relation to the country's resources. Those who arrive at the event in pairs or groups are given cards of different colours that signify the different interest groups, so that friends are divided across the three regions.

12. Despite these efforts, Talbot reports, an Edinburgh performance of *You Once Said Yes* 'was halted by police as the heist scene involved a driver in a balaclava' and 'in Camden, a participant went off on a long walk with a non-player convinced they were an actor.'

13. *It Felt Like a Kiss* was a Punchdrunk collaboration with filmmaker Adam Curtis and musicians Damon Albarn and The Kronos Quartet which took place in 2009, in the disused former home of the National Probation Office.

11   Authority, Authorisation and Authorship

Participation in Community Plays in Belfast

Alison Jeffers

This chapter investigates questions of participation and authority in community plays. The example that I invoke is that of the community play *Crimea Square*, which took place in the Shankill Road area of Belfast, Northern Ireland, in 2013. This project raised some complex political issues because Belfast exists in what geographers Brian Graham and Yvonne Whelan call an 'unagreed society' (2007: 467), which is a useful way to capture the failure of the 1998 Good Friday Agreement (GFA) to address the legacy of the past in Northern Ireland, despite bringing the conflict to a formal political conclusion. This conflict, sometimes known as 'the Troubles', began in the late 1960s and claimed the lives of 3700 people (McKittrick et al. 2012: 13). Often seen as having its roots in British colonial policies of the sixteenth and seventeenth centuries, it has played out in the twentieth century as a war of attrition and sometimes violent confrontation between nationalists (often linked to the Catholic population) and unionists (often linked with Protestant communities).[1] Despite the success of the GFA in setting up a power-sharing government based on an understanding of the legitimacy of both unionist and nationalist views, many issues remain unresolved. These include '[t]he question of how to deal with the legacy of the past' and the fact that 'division remain[s] an unfortunate fact of life' McKittrick and McVea 2012: 305). Under these conditions, where 'ethnonationalist and sectarian constructs of society … reify an essentialist identity in which an individual is defined by the community into which he or she is born', ideas about participation become very loaded (Graham and Whelan 2007: 467). Creating any cultural product through participation becomes a highly charged activity, made especially acute by the key role played by questions of culture and identity in this 'post-conflict' era.

My goal is to demonstrate that participation alone is no guarantor of the necessary redistribution of authority that may lead to positive social change. Participation in arts activities may be 'fun', may add to an individual's skills and may open doors to other activities, but on its own, without questioning ideas about authority and authorship, it is a pale imitation of any activity that is likely to induce change at a more fundamental level. To make this argument I will first examine the influence of ideas linking arts, social capital and participation that emerged in the late 1990s. I will then go on to point to contemporary thinkers from a range of disciplinary perspectives who are interested in authority and will use their ideas to examine how thinking about participatory theatre practices might be challenged and refined. Specifically, thinking about authority creates a challenge to cause-and-effect narratives that link participation to change in overly simple ways and reawakens the calls for cultural democracy that were iterated by the community arts movement in the early 1980s. I will argue that the process of researching and writing, of authoring, *Crimea Square* revealed different regimes of knowledge and expertise which throw up questions about who has the authority to write a community's stories, the levels of expertise needed to craft those into a dramatic narrative, who can authorise the telling of a community's stories in a public arena and what stories remain untold.

Locating *Crimea Square*

The Shankill Road is an arterial route running west out of Belfast, but it also denotes a geographically and politically boundaried part of the city. Leaving the city centre and walking up the Shankill Road, it is hard not to be surprised by the proximity of the green hills of Antrim straight ahead. During the day, the traffic is busy and the small shops and bakeries are full of people undertaking everyday errands. The map outside the Shankill graveyard (which contains gravestones going back several hundred years) shows the usual sites of churches, leisure centres and schools but also the locations of the various murals that support the Protestant Orange Order and Loyalist paramilitary organisations, as well as other pieces of public art commemorating those who died as a result of the recent political conflict in Northern Ireland (see Figures 11.1 and 11.2). Off the small side streets to the south sits a peace line, one among many 'monuments to mistrust and communal wariness' that remain in Belfast, a large wall that marks the boundary between the Shankill and the Falls Road areas (McKittrick and McVea 2012: 306). On one of my visits we drove through the open gates of the peace line to eat at a local cultural centre knowing that those gates would be locked at dusk. It is hard not to be struck by the terrible ordinariness of

Figure 11.1   View of the Shankill Road from the room in Spectrum Centre where the writers met to create Crimea Square.
Photograph by Alison Jeffers.

a location where people negotiate the everyday alongside the repercussions of following the violence of this protracted sectarian conflict.

Elements of this complex and troubled history were discussed, negotiated, authored and, finally, presented in the form of the community play *Crimea Square*, performed 11 times in October 2013 in the theatre at the Spectrum Centre on the Shankill Road. Initially attracted by a six-week writing course run by writer and community artist Jo Egan, four local people formed a group to research and write the script over a period of about 18 months before the production process began. In common with the community play model, which I will discuss in more detail below, a cast of 35 local people were recruited as actors. They were supported by a small cast of professional actors; a professional production team (including Egan, who also directed); sound and film artists; set, lighting and costume designers; and a stage management team of four. The resources needed for a project on this scale are considerable, and public money came from Peace III (the common name for the EU Programme for Peace and Reconciliation in Northern Ireland and the Border Region of Ireland) as well as National Lottery money through Arts Council of Northern Ireland. One of the main goals of Peace III is to 'reinforce progress towards a peaceful and stable society and to promote reconciliation', so the fact that these funding bodies were prepared to support the project to such an extent suggests that funders saw some potential for participation in the project to play a part in generating the conditions needed to move away from conflict.[2] *Crimea Square* was part of the programme for the Ulster Bank Belfast Festival at Queens University, which had the effect of attracting much more attention and a wider audience than might be expected for a community play.[3] This 'raised the stakes', placing a very high level of expectation on the artists and participants, something which I will return to below. The by-line for the play was '100 Amazing Years of Shankill Road History', and the narrative ran chronologically from 1912 to the present day. Set in three houses in the fictional Crimea Square, it focused on the different generations of the imagined families that lived there over this period.

Figure 11.2   Map of the Shankill area outside the Shankill graveyard.
Photograph by Alison Jeffers.

The modes of enquiry for this chapter include viewing the production of *Crimea Square*; attendance at a public workshop with the writers, director and 15 actors; and subsequent interviews with the director, the writers, 12 cast members, sound designer and the (then) manager of the Spectrum Centre. This analysis embraces Bill McDonnell's writing on the ethics of representation in 'the many popular theatres which arise at times of acute political and social crisis' (2005: 128) – especially his observation that many such practices are written about by outsiders who can safely walk away from the difficult situations in which they have been temporarily hosted. McDonnell's call 'to be very precise about our belonging' presents an ethical responsibility to speak to my connection to the practices under question and to acknowledge my relationship to the participants of the community play on the Shankill Road (2005: 134).

My relationship to *Crimea Square* moves beyond acknowledging what McDonnell calls the 'asymmetries in power, resources, and status between the outsider and the host community' because, as well as being an academic from an affluent university in England, I spent my childhood and teenage years as part of the Protestant tradition in Belfast during the Troubles in the 1970s (McDonnell 2005: 132). So in some senses I 'belong' in the location that I am researching, but it is a tenuous belonging, partly because I left Belfast and partly because the very means of my leaving, going to university in England, followed a route which was mainly open to well-educated, middle-class young people at the time. I should also add to this a practitioner's commitment to the potential of people's involvement in creative activities as a result of working as a community artist for most of the 1980s. The dates are important because authorship was a central tenet of the community arts movement in a way that has not been so evident in participatory arts practices since the 1990s, and this is a key part of my argument. Part of my task here then is to balance out this layered pattern of relationships, beliefs and experiences within the necessary and beneficial strictures of analytical thinking and critical reflection.

Participation and the arts

Participation has played a pivotal role in arts and cultural discourse in the UK since the late 1990s when New Labour championed a social inclusion agenda based on notions of social capital that was emerging at that time. Soon after their election victory in 1997, the new government set up the Social Exclusion Unit as definitions of poverty were widening out beyond the material to encompass social, cultural and educational elements

(Belfiore 2002: 92). A series of 17 reports on different aspects of social exclusion, and how to tackle it, followed, and Policy Action Team 10 (or PAT 10 as it became known) produced the report on arts and sport. In the foreword, Secretary of State for the Department of Culture Media and Sport (DCMS) Chris Smith stated that

> art and sport can not only make a valuable contribution to delivering key outcomes of longer-term employment, less crime, better health and better qualifications, but can help to develop individual pride, community spirit and capacity for responsibility that enables communities to run regeneration programmes themselves. (Policy Action Team 10 1999)

According to the report, economically and socially disadvantaged people needed to be encouraged to participate in their locality, thus increasing their sense of investment and building their capacity to be engaged citizens. One key to the success of this venture was 'participation in arts and sport', which it was hoped would lead to increased levels of participation generally and to communities 'having the power and taking the responsibility to make things better' (PAT 10 1999: 2). The committee for PAT 10 was made up of representatives of DCMS, The Arts Council, Sport England, local government representatives and a number of community artists for whom this seemed an exciting opportunity: sitting in consultation with top government officials, offering examples of good practice from work that they had been doing, largely unnoticed at this level, for many years. Their belief in the power of participation, in the making of art rather than consuming it, was not only being recognised; it was beginning to form a major plank of government policy: in Eleanora Belfiore's words, it was the first time that the government seemed to 'take the arts and the cultural sector seriously' (2012: 104).

Building on this surge of interest Francois Matarasso (who headed the Best Practice subgroup for PAT 10) carried out the first large-scale attempt in the UK to find evidence for the social impact of participating in arts activities. In his report *Use or Ornament? The Social Impact of Participation in the Arts* and in *Vital Signs*, based on research into participatory arts in Belfast (1998), he noted very similar patterns of findings and outlined '50 Social Impacts of Participation in the Arts'. These he grouped under six headings: personal development; social cohesion; community empowerment and self-determination; local image and identity; imagination and vision; and health and well-being. In aiming his report at policymakers in local government and voluntary sector organisations, he hoped that it could become a tool for advocacy for participatory arts work or 'harnessing the forces of art for social democratic purposes' (Matarasso 1997).[4] Participating in the arts, being involved in the making of art rather than being a viewer, observer or visitor, was promoted as an important way to 'support personal and community development' (Matarasso 1997: v).

Community plays are a specific art form that rely on the participation of non-specialists. Baz Kershaw notes that the rhetorical conventions of the community play include an emphasis on scale in terms of the numbers of participants and of historical subject matter and notes that 'participation is paramount in all aspects of community play production' (1992: 193). The community play form emerged from the work of the Colway Theatre Trust in Devon in the early 1980s when playwright Ann Jellicoe sensed the potential of a large-scale theatrical project to generate a powerful sense of emotion that she felt was missing from professional theatre at that time (1987: 6). As the community play movement developed, the emphasis on historical content and the participation of large numbers of community members as actors became hallmarks of the form. There was a strong belief in the power that could be generated by a common sense of purpose and Howard Barker, who wrote *The Poor Man's Friend* for Jellicoe in 1981, noticed a 'bonding experience' among participants (Barker, qtd in Jellicoe 1987: 18). Equally, the Dorchester Community Play Association empha-sises drawing in as many people together as possible in order to 'unite the community in a common artistic enterprise' (Burton 2011: 13).

At least ten community plays have been staged in Northern Ireland since the late 1980s presumably partly because of this belief in the power of the form to unite participants behind a common goal.[5] However, the early plays had to be 'single identity' projects that involved communities from only one side of the sectarian divide. For example, *Dock Ward Story* (1991) developed in a working-class Catholic area in the north of the city with a reputation for nationalist politics, while *The Mourning Ring* (1995) took place in Ballybeen, a housing development in the east of the city with a reputation for being a Loyalist area that housed mostly Protestant fami-lies (Carr 1987). *The Wedding Community Play Project* (1999) was the first attempt to create a 'cross-community' project, bringing participants from these two groups together in a narrative surrounding a 'mixed marriage' – which drew stark attention to participants' differences, both on and off the stage. The play was formally experimental, based on community artist Jo Egan's idea of using different sites in the city and moving the audience between them (Moriarty 2004: 13–32).[6] To view the play, small groups of audience members were instructed to meet in the city centre, a politically neutral location, and were then driven to two terraced houses in different parts of the city to view the wedding preparations of a Protestant family and a Catholic family. This entailed audience members' going into areas of Belfast that they may never have visited, before being taken to a church in the city centre for the ceremony and a riverside pub for the reception. In the early stages of the project, such were the levels of nervousness about the two groups meeting that it was agreed that there would be a series of 'single identity' workshops at the beginning of the project to create a 'safe space' for the participants to discuss ideas, thoughts and emotions.

Having brought the Protestant and Catholic groups together, *The Wedding Community Play Project* still contained a number of tensions, and at one point the Protestant cast members considered withdrawing because they felt that the representation of the Protestant characters by the professional playwrights was 'clichéd, dated and stereotyped' (Moriarty 2004: 20). The writers had been authorised to represent both communities, but the Protestant cast members felt that the writers did not have the authority to do this accurately in their case. As actors they were concerned about their limited powers of self-representation in producing characters that they felt undermined the community they represented. At the same time, if they refused to participate, they were worried that they would be seen to be fulfilling a number of cultural stereotypes of intransigence, small-mindedness and negativity. To understand the strength of their feelings, it is important to understand that Loyalist Protestant communities 'have long been pilloried for their siege mentality [and] resistance to change' (McKittrick and McVea 2012: 290). Edna Longley suggests that artistic culture is 'seen in some quarters as a Catholic thing' (Longley and Kibeard 2011: 29), and in relation to community theatre projects specifically, David Grant has discussed the need to lower 'resistance to drama in working-class Protestant areas' (1993: 41). Writer and director of *Crimea Square* Jo Egan corroborated this when she spoke of 'the "old chestnut" that Protestants don't "do" culture', an idea to which I will return below (2013).

What these examples repeatedly bring up is ideas around authority and authorship and, closely connected to these, authorisation. Authority is often based on experience – people become 'authorities' on something because they appear to have a superior level of knowledge, training or experience. This is not innate but generated through relationships to each other and often to realities beyond our control. Thus, when an important decision needs to be made, or certain actions undertaken, we often defer to the individuals or groups who appear to have a higher level of authority, authorising them to act on our behalf. Authoring in an obvious way might gesture towards the writing of a play but *authorship* is a much more far-reaching term which involves 'naming, describing and affecting the world around us' and claiming 'the right to participate meaningfully in the making and defining of culture' (Morgan 1995: 26). In emphasising authorship, community artists are concerned to delve back into questions of authority: who sets up the apparently immutable status of experts, and in whose interests is this perpetuated? Is it really not possible for 'non-experts' to develop levels of expertise that would allow them a greater degree of control over their lives? What role might the arts play in this endeavour? I would now like to place some of these ideas into the discussion on participation and examine some of the ways in which participation might be said to 'redistribute' authority, using the specific example of *Crimea Square*.

Participation and the redistribution of authority

Recent critical thinking about participation has developed in the fields of community and international development, and it is helpful to draw on some of these voices to develop a more complex view of some of the claims made for participation. According to Erhard Berner and Benedict Phillips, the case for participation is usually made on three grounds – first, as an end in itself because the freedom to make choices is a driver for well-being; second, as a method of generating a sense of ownership and thus a greater chance of longevity or impact; third, as a generator of efficiency whereby communities are mobilised to make their own contributions. The same scholars raise serious questions about the complexities and challenges of participation, particularly in the present political and economic climate, focusing on the fine line between generating strong and resilient communities and a model of self-help which could lead to a withdrawal of state support. They argue that participation was 'once radical and controversial [but] has become mainstream management theory'[7] and point to the rhetoric of organisations like the World Bank who value participation as a money-saving model of self-help. Also in development studies, Bill Cooke and Uma Kothari investigate what they see as a 'tyrannical' trend in the over-use, or misuse, of participatory methods in development settings.[8] Naomi Millner suggests that 'participation today is being adopted into policy-making and planning in ways which further disempower those with a stake or interest in a particular problem'.[9] Margaret Ledwith's critique of what happens when key concepts like participation are 'reduced to buzzwords [that] can dangerously flip transformative practice into placatory practice' (2005: 29) could be applied to participatory arts and ongoing debates about their instrumental use in social policy. Indeed, reflecting back on Chris Smith's statement that increased capacity in communities will enable them to 'run regeneration projects themselves' can be seen as an example of such thinking.

While these critiques serve to draw attention to the instrumentalisation of participation, they also suggest ways in which participation interacts with authority on a number of levels, and it is this strand of thinking which I intend to pursue. Claire Blencowe uses the concept of authority as a way to get beyond the assumption that simply 'identifying and denouncing power' will lead to any kind of change (2013(a): 9–28). The value of thinking about authority is that it allows us to identify and examine different *types* of power and the role of knowledge and relationships in developing these. Blencowe's ideas about uneven distributions of authority have been influential to this discussion because she highlights the ways that authority is granted to 'experts' and opens up the question whether 'participation practices can be technologies for redistributing authority' (2013(a): 41). Blencowe suggests that 'analysing authority can help us to understand the range of possibilities and limitations with respect to transforming or engaging in specific situations of power' (2013(a): 10). What happens if we take Blencowe's ideas, developed in political science, and apply them to questions of participation and community plays?

I argue that the participatory arts activities of the 1990s conform largely to what Blencowe calls a 'widening participation' model whereby 'participatory processes can expand access to the kinds of experience that are normally the preserve of experts and those with means to achieve specialist status' (2013(b): 41). The emphasis is on experience, getting involved, 'having a go'; it can make a difference in the lives of those individuals who participate, but it leaves existing power structures fundamentally unaltered. Its other downside is that it also has the potential to 'confirm the importance and authority [and] add even more authority to the existing élites', in this case the artists, theatre makers, curators and others who are working with 'non-expert' groups (Blencowe 2013(b): 43). This may have been the case for some of the 35 community actors who got involved in the project. They were able to have an experience of acting for the time that they were involved. Some spoke of getting 'the acting bug', but without access to the specialist structures that would allow them to develop this skill, it is unlikely that many will be able to pursue this ambition. However, a different model operated for the writers, one which enabled them more clearly to create 'alternative reference points for authoritative relationships, voices and claims' (2013(a): 26) and which Blencowe might call 'transforming reality' or 'changing perceptions about what is important – what makes things happen – and thus changing ideas about who has participated in such happening' (2013(b): 44). This is closer to the community arts practices of the 1970s and 1980s, which emphasised the importance of 'cultural democracy' (Kelly, Locke and Merkel 1986), shared

authorship and the shift in the balance of power between artist and participant (Webster and Buglass 2005: 21). This practice was more concerned
with a fundamental redistribution of power, initiated by developing an
understanding of existing power structures and distributions of authority.

Community plays are usually authored by a professional playwright;
The Wedding community play, for example, was written by playwrights
Martin Lynch and Marie Jones. In a significant departure from this model,
Crimea Square was written by community members Sally Cochran, John
Dougan, Albert Haslett and Jacqueline Nicholson, who worked in close
collaboration with Jo Egan.[10] The writers of *Crimea Square* will be viewed
as 'experts by experience', an idea developed in mental health settings
whereby self-help groups become, as Noorani calls them, 'crucibles for
learning' (2013: 60). The growing authority of the 'expert' community
writers allowed them to examine their troubled and contested history in a
critical way as they developed confidence in their abilities as local histori-
ans or authorities on their own history. The conditions within which the
play was produced, in the midst of ongoing protests about that community's identity, could have led to a retrenchment of the 'siege mentality'
mentioned above and a hegemonic version of the historical narrative.[11]
Taking this project back to a 'single identity' model could be seen as a
regressive step after the apparently progressive move of bringing both
communities together in the case of *The Wedding*. Paradoxically, I argue
that *limiting* participation in the creation of a 'single identity' project
allowed the writers' confidence in authoring their history and narrative to
develop and grow, to the extent of allowing them to authorise some challenges to their traditional historical narrative.

As well as being a playwright, Egan has many years' experience in
making theatre in a community arts context, but it is equally important to
understand that she was born in London, brought up in Dublin and identifies as a socialist and a feminist from a Catholic background: almost directly
opposite to the participants in *Crimea Square*, who were mostly born and
brought up in the Loyalist Protestant tradition, which is generally politically conservative and often patriarchal. One of the writers explained some
of their differences: 'I would be challenging Jo on the writing. She's not a
Loyalist, she's not a unionist, not a [Protestant], not for the Queen.'[12] He
explained, as a way to illustrate their political differences, a moment during
the writing of the play when the group were looking at a photograph of
a young boy at the annual Protestant Twelfth of July bonfire celebrations:
'There was a photograph of a wee lad at a bonfire and I would look at him
and his wee face and how happy he looks – and Jo looks at the photograph
and says "Why's he got no shoes on?"'[13] Viewing the same image and

interpreting it as both one of celebration and inequality depending on the perspective of the viewer illustrates in microcosm something of the political distance between Egan and the other writers. However, in allowing her to work with them on this project, the writers authorised the challenge of working with an outsider who might disrupt their historical narratives and political positions. In the process of researching and writing the play, all the writers bartered their respective sets of authorial knowledge – Egan offering insights into theatrical form and technique as well as a possible challenges to the community's narratives and the four community writers bringing characters and ideas based on the shape of their lives and histories on which the play was based. This informal barter of technical know-how for lived experience meant that Egan and the community writers depended on each other: she could not work without their authority, and they could not craft the stories so effectively without her professional expertise. In their collaboration a complex relationship between professional and lived authority developed, one that sits in the heart of any transformative potential that this project may have had.

The community writers were all members of the Shankill Area Social History group (SASH) set up in 2011 to 'record, compile, archive & educate ourselves & others about the History of the Greater Shankill Area.'[14] Writing about the proliferation of such groups against the background of a remarkable rise of interest in local history in Northern Ireland since the late 1990s, Catherine Nash argues that local history in Northern Ireland is strongly associated with 'loaded concepts' like heritage, tradition, culture and identity (2005: 47). However, she suggests that exploring these in historical terms 'encourages senses of confidence within "communities" that can lead to more critical explorations of identity, in a context where dominant expressions of collective identity are often based on defensive and anxious assertiveness' (2005: 48). The opening of the Public Records of Northern Ireland (PRONI) in 2011 in a prestigious new building, under the authority of the Department for Culture, Leisure and the Arts, signals the importance that is placed on family and community histories; PRONI records are freely available online, encouraging active participation in historical research. One of the writers explained how they had made extensive use of the archives available through PRONI to research many of the characters in the play. Most of the participants claimed that they had never been taught their own history at school where lessons had been dominated by 'English history, all kings and queens and stuff like that'[15] as one told me, although several of the male participants, both writers and actors, also confessed that their attendance at school had been poor as they had got caught up in paramilitary activity in the 1970s and 1980s. One of the

writers explained her impulse for writing the play based on their historical research: 'I don't think people know about their history, but they're
beginning to want to learn and I think if you know your history you do
begin to take a pride in your area', and this was echoed in different ways
by all the writers involved.[16] However, the process of writing this history
into such a public dramatic narrative involved both celebrating *and* challenging certain cherished historical narratives of identity, and integrating
these challenges to received narratives of identity into the play placed the
whole endeavour firmly in the public eye.

The sense of ownership and pride on both levels – beginning to know
and understand their own history through growing expertise in handling
archival material, as well as their authority over their own stories – was
palpable in discussions with the writers. The process of dramatising this
material enabled them to appreciate that their history was more fragmented
than they might have imagined before they began their own minute investigation, embedded with contradictions and paradoxes, and this troubled
their authority in a productive way. In the process of becoming 'experts'
or authorities in their own histories, and in being able to perform that
expertise to a wider community through the play, they not only developed
a sense of personal confidence but also played a part in generating a social
confidence, creating a space in which their expertise allowed them to look
out beyond the usual received histories and which also gave them access
to cultural opportunities from which they would otherwise feel excluded.
Three examples from the play will show how the community writers
authorised and authored some challenges to their history, as well as where
and how they worked out the limits to these challenges.

Given the importance of Loyalism in the Shankill, it was not surprising
that *Crimea Square* opened with a scene discussing the signing of the Ulster
Covenant in 1912 when nearly half a million men in the north of Ireland
signed the Covenant, registering their protest against Home Rule from
Ireland and pledging their support and allegiance to the British Crown.[17]
However, the opening scene presented unexpected subtleties and political
complexities surrounding this canonical narrative. The writers had uncov-
ered a range of 'characters' who contradicted traditional narratives surrounding the historical events presented. One such, George Devlin, unearthed
from the PRONI records, was a policeman and a Catholic who lived on the
Shankill Road and who refused to sign the Covenant. It would have been
easy for the writers to pass off his anxieties about signing by pointing to his
religion, as those who opposed Home Rule were predominantly Protestants:
but his motivation is explained partly by his pride – 'I'll freeze in hell's halls
before my mother-in-law'll dictate to me'[18] – and is partly attributable to his

belief that his job as a member of the Royal Irish Constabulary makes a big enough statement about his sense of belonging. Pointing to his uniform, he says, 'D'ya see that? That's as loyal as it gets. Any fool can sign a name, what does that stand for? This [he points again] stands for a whole lot more.'[19]

In the neighbouring house, Jack Campbell refuses to sign because, as a religious man, he believes his covenant is with God. One of the writers explained that she had struggled politically with showing a character who had not signed the Covenant, explaining that although she was also religious like him, she identified strongly with her country and had felt ambivalent about showing someone who valued religion over politics. Later in the interview she conceded that Jack and his son, who was frustrated by his father's intransigence, eventually became her favourite characters because of the turbulent relationship that the writers had built up between them: 'I liked that very much. It gives me goose bumps even now thinking about it.'[20] This visceral reaction a year after the performance of the play is telling, but more important is the fact that, despite her reservations about showing characters who were less than loyal, she was prepared to face up to the complex emotions that she felt in having her fiercely guarded history challenged in such a public way.

Even in the 'loyal' Starling house, where they all intend to sign, the writers draw attention to the fact that only men were allowed to sign the Covenant, while women signed a separate declaration, drawn up by a group of women who 'were not satisfied thus to be cold-shouldered', as James Winder Good commented in 1919 (Craig 1999). The daughter Evangeline is teaching her mother how to sign her name and has the following exchange with her father, Jim:

EVANGELINE:	When you sign your name'll be on the Covenant for the rest of time – for all to see.
BIG JIM:	It won't Miss Evangeline know all. The women signs the declaration. Only men signs the Covenant. Don't be leading your mother into wild ways. Next thing she'll be out in strike like them lunatics in Gallagher's.
EVANGELINE:	Oh aye, so they're lunatics because they want paid properly and better working conditions!!
BIG JIM:	Look at her. In like a gander. Better working conditions? And what do you know wee girl and your mummy still brushes your hair. I told you. What did I tell her? Stay out a' that mill union. You'll get the reputation for a big mouth.[21]

222

Labour relations, multiple identity positions and putative feminist poli-tics are not usually at the heart of the story of Home Rule as told from a conservative, Loyalist position. This early scene acts as an indicator that the play will both celebrate and challenge local and national histories.

The second example is taken from the scenes around 1916, a highly significant year in Irish history, commemorated by nationalists as the date of the Easter Rising in which a group of Irish nationalists occupied a number of government buildings in Dublin, claiming independence from the British State. A Loyalist commemoration of this date stresses the Second World War and the importance of the Battle of the Somme, which plays a prominent role in Loyalist history and mythology (Brown 2007).[22] Much of its significance is gathered from the close ties between the UVF (Ulster Volunteer Force), a military force established to support the anti-Home Rule unionists, and the 36th Ulster Division of the British army, who lost so many men in that battle. The writers clearly felt an enormous sense of responsibility to the memory of the men who died in the First World War, and there is a strong community narrative which emphasises their bravery and the fact that they have developed a reputation for, as one of the writers put it, 'pushing further and harder than any other divi-sion within the British army that day'.[23] In the same conversation, which took place in a public arena in front of an audience of American university students and staff, the suggestion from Egan that they might have known that they were 'cannon-fodder' received a gentle but firm response from one of the writers: 'I don't know that they knew they were cannon-fodder, but they were definitely the bravest that day'.[24] It was interesting and surprising to observe this lack of deference to Egan as the artist in this public setting, but it seemed that this was one of the lines that could not be crossed. Time plays a role in shifting the perspective of a community's 'founding events', as Ricoeur has suggested (1999: 9), and this delay may have made it more challenging to look at this and other long-held and cherished community narratives in a more critical light. However, the writ-ers' position on the First World War was not entirely uncritical. They had discovered in the archives the story of a young boy called Walter Sterling, who tried to join the British army twice while underage. This 'charac-ter' was written into the 1916 scene, and in an argument between his parents about his behaviour, his mother challenges the boy's father, who, she says, encouraged him:

You filled his head with stories. You filled their heads with soldiers on horses and king and country like it was some adventure, some fairy story. Well it's not a fairy story now.[25]

Listeners to this dialogue may hear allusions to King Billy, a seventeenth-century Protestant hero who defeated the Catholic King James, typically pictured in many murals as riding a white horse (see Figure 11.3). Here again is a sense of challenge to the authority of the traditional Loyalist narrative, in such a way that another gentle critique is embedded in a scene from a completely different period of history.

Finally, it proved understandably challenging for the writers to explore the period of the Troubles, commonly dated from the late 1960s to the late 1990s. Some of the group had been involved in paramilitary activities, and all continue to live with the profound impact of the violence that

Figure 11.3 Painting of William of Orange on the wall of the Orange Lodge on the Shankill Road.
Photograph by Alison Jeffers.

dominated this period, including emigration, physical and mental health problems, the loss of friends and family, personal injury and suicide, all of which were dealt with in the play. Egan spoke of how they wanted to reject the 'seduction of the Troubles' and the other writers stressed repeatedly that they did not want the play to be dominated by stories of political violence (2013). Two episodes of violence are notoriously linked to the Shankill in particular: in 1993, in an incident sometimes known as 'the Shankill bomb', a bomb went off in Frizell's Chip Shop on the Shankill Road, killing ten people, including the member of the IRA (Irish Republican Army) responsible for planting it. The Shankill is also often linked with the so-called Shankill Butchers, a group of UVF members who were responsible for 'probably the most notorious sequence of killings in Northern Ireland' (McKittrick and McVea 2012: 134). Clearly, the writers could not ignore the Troubles, but given the potential of political messages to divide in such a volatile time and fragile location, there was a clear steer away from possibly contentious examinations of aspects of history concerning the Shankill Butchers, for example, and a strong desire to 'tackle' the Shankill bomb of 2013. It would be easy to criticise the group for representing the people of the Shankill as victims rather than perpetrators of violence, but given the already high stakes of representing such a painful and still raw history, this seems understandable. Even the representation of the explosion was seen as 'risky', and all the interviewees stated that this was the scene they were most nervous and concerned about placing in front of an audience, not least because the production coincided with the twentieth anniversary of the event.[26] Regarding the visuals, the scene was staged in darkness, with the focus on the acoustics of the specially recorded interviews of some of the men who had encountered the immediate aftermath of the bomb that day. All the interviewees were adamant that this was the scene that had affected the audience most in post-show conversations.

Risks and stakes

Having outlined the potential of the project in the redistribution of authority and in creating a place where histories can be shared, explored and challenged, where apparently stable identities can be questioned, I conclude by reflecting on metaphors of risk and high stakes. Jellicoe alluded to these at the inception of the community play movement when she suggested that the risk of trying to build cohesion through a community play in an inner-city area was too great (1987). Moriarty also used them in connection with *The Wedding* (2004), and Egan repeatedly invoked the metaphor of the stakes being high in relation to *Crimea Square*. The strong sense of risk inherent in these high-profile participatory theatre projects is acute. Failure might reinforce negative perceptions of the communities involved in the 'unagreed society' of Northern Ireland where minute examinations of success and failure in community projects are exacerbated by the ongoing sectarian divide. But risk is vital if authority is really to be claimed, because if participation 'does not incorporate some openness to calamity and creativity, to the world pushing back' (2013(b): 43), then there is nothing at stake and the experience of claiming authority will have proved hollow.

Originally hammered into the ground as a boundary indicator, a row of stakes or a pale indicated what was within and considered safe and what was outside. The stake and the pale have a particular resonance through their role in the colonial history between Britain and Ireland, stretching back to the Middle Ages, The Pale originally demarcating those areas of Ireland that were under English rule. To 'go beyond the Pale', or to move away from this area, suggested unacceptable behaviour because 'to transgress this boundary limit was to betray the tribe' (Kearney 2002: 92). To have a stake in something suggests a strong investment, and for the writers, it was vitally important to place a working class social history on stage for a wider audience. But this was a risky endeavour because they were in danger of challenging a fiercely guarded history and of potentially betraying their 'tribe'. However, precisely because there was so much to lose, the process of researching and writing that history proved invaluable in encouraging the participants to move outside the pale, to edge beyond the traditional narratives that have reinforced a monolithic identity position.

In writing the play, the writers became authorities on their own history, enabling them to develop a sense of confidence in projecting and communicating a complex set of narratives, not only to their audience but also to themselves. They were not simply learning how to write a play, which might conform to a participatory arts agenda, but potentially creating a new cultural, social and political reality, one in which they had a stake in cultural activities from which they had previously felt excluded. Some of the writers and actors have subsequently been involved in setting up a small theatre company called The Heel 'n' Ankle (rhyming slang for the Shankill) to create and perform their own work. At the time of the interviews, two actors had begun working on their own play, and many were attending ongoing writing workshops in the Spectrum centre. One of the writers summed up the cultural impact of being involved in the play:

This whole community feels that the Lyric [theatre] isn't for them. They get the idea that it will be full of Catholics and nationalists and middle class people – and that's fact, that's the way it is. I still think that but now it wouldn't stop me from being involved in it. I have the confidence to go now.[27]

This is a good example of the ways in which an understanding of where authority seems to lie can cause a shift in perception which, as a result, can possibly cause a real shift. This writer understands that he will feel like an outsider in this particular cultural setting, but this understanding gives him the confidence to enter the doors and participate in the activities on offer. This, in turn, may open up new horizons and opportunities. Limiting participation in the single identity model gave the writers of *Crimea Square* permission to probe and question their own and their community's identity within the security of 'the pale', managing, or at least diminishing, the risk inherent in their activities. The process of writing the community play involved constant negotiation as to the limits of the challenges that they had authorised, at the same time as learning the skills of authorship and how to craft that history into a dramatic narrative. Through their growing engagement with their own historical narrative, the writers developed sufficient confidence to authorise a series of small but significant challenges to their history, and a shifting sense of identity emerged. The final risk, taking the play out of the relative safety of the writing process and placing it on stage in a public arena, demonstrated something of that achievement to an audience and may also have caused them to ask questions of their own history and identity. Finally, the academic interest in the project, manifested in the research process and analysis taking place here, has served in a small way to reinforce the value of the project in the eyes of the participants and hopefully beyond.

Endnotes

1. I acknowledge that the emphasis on religious and cultural differences creates a narrative that diminishes the influence of the state players in the political analysis of Ireland's conflict. Readers wanting more information on this in relation to theatre practices should look at Hughes (2011) and McDonnell (2005 and 2008).

2. http://www.seupb.eu/programmes2007–2013/peaceiiiprogramme/overview. aspx (accessed 3 July 2015).

3. Julie Andrews, Manager of the Spectrum Centre (Interview with the author, 18 October 2014).

4. Matarasso cautions that 'these are not waters to be casually stirred' in his report, and 'Use or Ornament' landed him squarely in the debate about the instrumental value of participatory arts. Readers wanting to pursue this should look at criticisms of Matarasso's study by Paola Merli (2002) and Eleanora Belfiore (2002) in *The International Journal of Cultural Policy* as well as Matarasso's response (2003) in the same journal.

5. Gerri Moriarty, personal communication (2 January 2015). There is no single source for this information, and some is drawn from Lynch (2004) and Grant (1993), as well as from conversations with artists who have worked on these projects.

6. Egan's experience of working on *The Wedding* is partly what drew her to the single-identity play *Crimea Square* (Interview with the author, 28 November 2014).

7. Erhard Berner and Benedict Phillips, 'Left to their own devices? Community self-help between alternative development and neo-liberalism', *Community Development Journal* 40 (2005), pp. 17–29 (p. 18).

8. Bill Cooke and Uma Kothari (eds) *Participation. The New Tyranny?* (London: Zed Books, 2000).

9. Naomi Millner, 'Involving others: from toolkit to ethos for a different kind of democracy', in Tehseen Noorani, Claire Blencowe and Julian Brigstocke (eds), *Problems of participation. Reflections on authority, democracy, and the struggle for common life* (Lewes: ARN Press, 2013), pp. 21–36 (p. 26).

10. The writers were all named on the programme, but under the ethical guidelines that guide this project, they will not be individually named here.

11. The play was performed against the backdrop of riots and protests after distress among Loyalist communities at the decision to fly the Union flag at Belfast's City Hall only on designated days. In the interviews one of the writers described their fears that local protesters might march on the venue where the play was being performed when they heard that the Lord Mayor of Belfast was attending a performance that evening.

12. Playwright (Interview with the author, 20 October 2014).

13. Playwright (Interview with the author, 20 October 2014).

14. http://www.shankillhistory.com/about-us/ [Accessed 12 July 2014]. The sash has political overtones that will resonate differently on both sides of the sectarian divide because of its iconic status in the Protestant Orange Order, who wear orange sashes at public events and parades.

15. Playwright (Interview with the author, 20 October 2014).

16. Playwright (Interview with the author, 20 October 2014).

17. http://www.proni.gov.uk/index/search_the_archives/ulster_covenant.htm (accessed 17 March 2015).

18. Act 1, scene 2. All quotations from the play are taken from the unpublished script of *Crimea Square*.

19. Act 1, scene 2.

20. Playwright (Interview with the author, 20 October 2014).

21. Act 1, scene 1.

22. See also Richard S. Grayson, *Belfast Boys. How unionists and nationalists fought and died together in the First World War* (London: Continuum, 2009).
23. Event at Linenhall Library, Belfast (18 September 2013).
24. Event at Linenhall Library, Belfast (18 September 2013).
25. Act 2, scene 6.
26. This coincidence was unintentional and came about because an earlier funding application had been rejected. Jo Egan (Interview with the author, 28 November 2013).
27. Playwright (Interview with the author, 20 October 2014).

References

Adamson, Greg (ed.), *The Craft Reader* (Oxford: Berg, 2003).

Adkins, Liz, 'Social Capital: The Anatomy of a Troubled Concept', *Feminist Theory*, 6 (2005), pp. 195–211.

Aftab, Kaleem, 'Secret Cinema *Back to the Future*: Interactive Cinema Experience Finally Arrives', the *Independent*, 31 July 2014.

Ahmed, Sara, *The Cultural Politics of Emotion* (Edinburgh: Edinburgh University Press, 2nd edn, 2014).

Ahmed, Sara, *Willful Subjects* (London: Duke University Press, 2014).

Alston, Adam, 'Funding, Product Placement and Drunkenness in Punchdrunk's The Black Diamond', *Studies in Theatre and Performance*, 32:2 (2012), pp. 193–208.

Balibar, Etienne. *Identity and Difference: John Locke and the Invention of Consciousness*, trans. by Warren Montag, ed. by Stella Sandford (London: Verso, 2013).

Balibar, Étienne. *Citizenship*, trans. by Thomas Scott-Railton (Cambridge: Polity, 2015).

Bateson, Gregory, *Steps to an Ecology of Mind* (Chicago, IL, and London: Chicago University Press 2000 [1972]).

Baudrillard, Jean, *Simulacra and Simulation*, trans. by Sheila Faria Glaser (Ann Arbor, MI: University of Michigan, 1994).

Bellman, Beryl L., 'The Paradox of Secrecy', *Human Studies*, 4:1 (Jan.–Mar. 1981), pp. 1–24.

Bennett, Jane, *The Enchantment of Modern Life: Attachment, Crossings, and Ethics* (Princeton, NJ: Princeton University Press, 2001).

Bennett, Jane, *Vibrant Matter: A Political Ecology of Things* (London: Duke University Press, 2010).

Bennett, Susan, *Theatre and Museums* (Basingstoke: Palgrave Macmillan, 2013).

Berlant, Laura, *Cruel Optimism* (London: Duke University Press, 2011).

Bessel van der Kolk, Onno van der Hart and Charles R. Marmar (1996), 'Dissociation and Information Processing in Posttraumatic Stress Disorder', in *Traumatic Stress: The Effects of Participation*, ed. by Claire Bishop (London: The MIT Press, 2006).

Beswick, Katie (2012) '*Multi-Story Water*: A Theatrical Tour of Shipley', https://theculturevulture.co.uk/blog/hometourist/multi-story-water-a-theatricaltour-of-shipley/ [Accessed 31 October 2015].

Bishop, Claire (ed.), *Participation* (London: The MIT Press, 2006).

Bishop, Claire, *Artificial Hells: Participatory Art and the Politics of Spectatorship* (London: Verso, 2012).

Blencowe, C., (a) 'Biopolitical authority, objectivity and the groundwork of modern citizenship' *Journal of Political Power*, 6:1, 2013 (9-28).

Blencowe, C., (b) 'Participatory Knowledge matters for Democracy' in T. Noorani, C. Blencowe, J. Brigstocke eds. *Problems of Participation*, (Lewes: ARN Press, 2013) (37-47).

Böhme, Gernot, 'Atmosphere as the Fundamental Concept of a New Aesthetics,' *Thesis Eleven*, 36 (1993), pp. 113–126.

Bok, Sissela, *Secrets: On the Ethics of Concealment and Revelation* (New York: Vintage, 1998).

Boltanski, Luc and Eve Chiapello, *The New Spirit of Capitalism* (London: Verso, 2005).

Boon, Suzette, Kathy Steele and Onno van der Hart, *Coping with Trauma-Related Dissociation: Skills Training for Patients and Therapists* (New York: W. W. Norton & Company, 2011).

Bottoms, Stephen and Lindsey McEwen, *Multi-Story Water: Sited Performance in Urban River Communities* (University of Manchester, 2014) http://issuu.com/martin harriscentre/docs/drama_multi-story_water_report/1 [Accessed 31 October 2015].

Bourriaud, Nicolas *Relational Aesthetics*, trans. by Simon Pleasance and Fronza Woods (Dijon: Les Presses du Réel, 2002).

Bradby, David and John McCormick, *People's Theatre* (London: Croom Helm, 1978).

Bratich, Jack, 'Public Secrecy and Immanent Security: A Strategic Analysis', *Cultural Studies*, 20:4–5 (2006), pp. 493–511.

Bratich, Jack Z. and Heidi M. Brush, 'Fabricating Activism: Craft-Work, Popular Culture, Gender', *Utopian Studies*, 22:2 (2011), pp. 233–260.

Brennan, Teresa, *The Transmission of Affect* (Ithica, NY, and London: Cornell University Press, 2004).

Brogan, Linda and Polly Teale, *Speechless* (London: Nick Hern Books, 2010).

Brooker, Nathan, 'Secret Theatre: Reservoir Dogs', *Exeunt Magazine*, 2013.

Bull, Michael and Les Back (eds), *The Auditory Culture Reader* (Oxford: Berg, 2003).

Buszek, Maria Elena (ed.), *Extra/Ordinary: Craft and Contemporary Art* (London: Duke University Press, 2011).

Butler, Judith and Athena Athanasiou, *Dispossession: The Performative in the Political* (Cambridge: Polity, 2013).

Carter, Paul, 'Ambiguous Traces, Mishearing and Auditory Space', in *Hearing Cultures: Essays on Sound, Listening and Modernity*, ed. by Veit Erlmann (Oxford, New York: Berg, 2004), pp. 43–63.

Caruth, Cathy, *Literature in the Ashes of History* (Baltimore, MD: The Johns Hopkins University Press, 2013).

Cavendish, Dominic, 'Daniel Kitson: The Reluctant Hero of British Comedy', the *Telegraph*, 24 February 2014.

Connolly, William, *A World of Becoming* (London: Duke University Press, 2010).

Connor, Steven, 'The Help of Your Good Hands: Reports on Clapping', in *The Auditory Culture Reader*, ed. by Michael Bull and Les Back (Oxford: Berg, 2003), pp. 67–76.

Corbett, Sarah, *A Little Book of Craftivism* (London: Cicada Books Limited, 2013).

Couser, G. Thomas, *Signifying Bodies: Disability in Contemporary Life Writing* (Ann Arbor, MI: University of Michigan Press, 2009).

Craftivist Collective, (n.d. [2013]), 'Homepage', http://www.craftivist-collective.com [accessed 16 September 2014].

Crouch, Tim, *My Arm* (London: Faber and Faber, 2003).

Crouch, Tim, 'The Theatre of Reality…and Avoiding the Stage's Kiss of Death', the *Guardian*, 18 June 2014.

De Nooy, Juliana, *Twins in Contemporary Literature and Culture: Look Twice* (Basingstoke: Palgrave Macmillan, 2005).

Debord, Guy, *Society of the Spectacle* (Detroit, MI.: Black and Read, 1984).

Deleuze, Gilles and Claire Parnet, *Dialogues II* (New York: Columbia University Press, 2007).

Devisch, Ignaas, *Jean-Luc Nancy and the Question of Community* (London: Bloomsbury, 2013).

Dobson, Andrew, 'Democracy and Nature: Speaking and Listening', *Political Studies*, 58 (2010), pp. 752–768.

Dobson, Andrew, *Listening for Democracy: Recognition, Representation, Reconciliation* (Oxford: Oxford University Press, 2014).

Doyle, Jennifer, 'Untitled', *Social Text*, 32:4 121 (2014), pp. 27–31.

Duggan, Patrick, *Trauma-Tragedy: Symptoms of Contemporary Performance* (Manchester: Manchester University Press, 2012).

Eco, Umberto, *The Open Work*, trans. by Anna Cancogni (Cambridge, MA: Harvard University Press, 1989).

Edensor, Tim, Deborah Leslie, Steve Millington and Norma M. Rantisi (eds), *Spaces of Vernacular Creativity: Re-thinking the Cultural Ecomony* (London: Routledge, 2010).

Elam, Keir, *The Semiotics of Theatre and Drama* (London: Methuen, 1980).

Evans, Brad and Julian Reid, *Resilient Life: The Art of Living Dangerously* (Cambridge: Polity, 2014).

Fiumara, Gemma Corradi, *The Other Side of Language: A Philosophy of Listening*, trans. by Charles Lambert (London: Routledge, 1990).

Fletcher-Watson, Ben, 'Seen and Not Heard: Participation as Tyranny in Theatre for Early Years', *Research in Drama Education: The Journal of Applied Theatre and Performance*, 20:1 (2015), pp. 24–38.

Florida, Richard, *The Rise of the Creative Class* (London: Basic Books, 2002).

Fraser, Nancy, 'Behind Marx's Hidden Abode: For an Expanded Conception of Capitalism', *New Left Review*, 86 (Mar./Apr. 2014), pp. 55–86.

Freshwater, Helen, *Theatre & Audience* (Basingstoke: Palgrave Macmillan, 2009).

Frieze, James, 'Beyond the Zero-Sum Game: Participation and the Optics of Opting', *Contemporary Theatre Review*, 25:2 (2015), pp. 216–229.

Gallagher, Michael, 'Listening, Meaning and Power', in *On Listening*, ed. by Angus Carlyle and Cathy Lane (Axminster, Uniform Books, 2013), pp. 41–44.

Gitten, Anthony, 'Resonant Listening', *Performance Research*, 15:3 (2010), pp. 115–122.

Goffman, Erving, *Frame Analysis: An Essay on the Organization of Experience* (Boston, MA: Northeastern University Press, 1986 [1974]).

Grau, Oliver, *Virtual Art: From Illusion to Immersion*, trans. by Gloria Custance, (Cambridge, MA, and London: MIT Press, 2003).

Greer, Betsy, *Craftivism: The Art of Craft and Activism* (London: Arsenal Pump Press, 2014).

Guattari, Felix, *The Three Ecologies*, trans. by Pindar and Sutton (London and New York: Continuum, 2000).

Guthrie, Michael, 'Kings College address, May 2012', http://performancefootprint.co.uk/documents/kings-college/michael-guthrie/ [Accessed 31 October 2015].

Hackney, Fiona, 'Quiet Activism and the New Amateur: The Power of Home and Hobby Crafts', *Design and Culture*, 5:2 (2013), pp. 169–193.

Hallward, Peter, 'Staging Equality: On Rancière's Theatocracy', *New Left Review*, 37 (Jan./Feb. 2006), pp. 109–129.

Haraway, Donna, *When Species Meet* (Minneapolis, MN, and London: University of Minnesota Press, 2008).

Hardt, Michael and Antonio Negri, *Empire* (Cambridge, MA: Harvard University Press, 2000).

Hardt, Michael and Antonio Negri, *Multitude: War and Democracy in the Age of Empire* (London: Penguin Books, 2004).

Hardt, Michael, 'Affective Labor', *boundary 2*, 26:2 (1999), pp. 89–100.

Harris, Geraldine, *Staging Femininities: Performance and Performativity* (Manchester: Manchester University Press, 1999).

Harris, Katie, 'Meet the Women Quietly Crafting Their Own Revolution', the *Telegraph*, 13 March 2013.

Harvie, Jen, *Theatre & the City* (London: Palgrave Macmillan, 2009).

Harvie, Jen, *Fair Play: Art, Performance and Neoliberalism* (Basingstoke: Palgrave Macmillan, 2013).

Heddon, Deirdre, 'Turning 40: 40 Turns, Walking & Friendship', *Performance Research*, 17:2 (2012), pp. 67–75.

Heddon, Deirdre and Adrian Howells, 'From Talking to Silence: A Confessional Journey', *PAJ: A Journal of Performance and Art*, 33:1 (2011), pp. 1–12.

Heddon, Deirdre, Helen Iball and Rachel Zerihan, 'Come Closer: Confessions of Intimate Spectators in One to One Performance', *Contemporary Theatre Review*, 22:1 (2012), pp. 120–133.

Heddon, Deirdre and Sally Mackey, 'Environmentalism, Performance and Applications: Uncertainties and Emancipations', *Research in Drama Education: The Journal of Applied Theatre and Performance*, 17:2 (2012), pp. 163–192.

Hoffman, Barbara, 'Dinner at The Heath More Dramatic Than Delicious', *New York Post*, 21 January 2014.

Holmes, Sean, 'Maybe the Existing Structures of Theatre in This Country, Whilst Not Corrupt, are Corrupting', *What's on Stage*, 18 June 2013.

Hopkins, d. j., Shelley Orr and Kim Solga (eds), *Performance and the City* (London: Palgrave Macmillan, 2009).

Horowitz, Sara R., *Voicing the Void: Muteness and Memory in Holocaust Fiction* (New York: SUNY, 1997).

Hulme, Mike, *Why We Disagree About Climate Change* (Cambridge: Cambridge University Press, 2009).

Iball, Helen, 'Towards an Ethics of Intimate Audience', *Performing Ethos: An International Journal of Ethics in Theatre & Performance*, 3:1 (2014), pp. 41–57.

Ihde, Don, *Listening and Voice: Phenomenologies of Sound* (New York: SUNY Press, 2007).

Ingold, Tim, *Being Alive: Essays on Movement, Knowledge and Description* (London: Routledge, 2011).

Ingold, Tim and Elizabeth Hallam (eds), *Creativity and Cultural Improvisation* (Oxford: Berg, 2007).

Jackson, Shannon, *Social Works: Performing Art, Supporting Publics* (London: Routledge, 2011).

Janus, Adrienne, 'Listening: Jean-Luc Nancy and the "Anti-Ocular" Turn in Continental Philosophy and Critical Theory', *Comparative Literature*, 63:2 (2011), pp. 182–202.

Jeffries, Janis, 'Loving Attention: An Outburst of Craft in Contemporary Art', in Buszek, Maria Elena, (ed) *Extra/Ordinary: Craft and Contemporary Art* (London: Duke University Press, 2011) pp. 222–242.

Johnson, Dominic, 'The Kindness of Strangers: An Interview with Adrian Howells', *Performing Ethos: An International Journal of Ethics in Theatre & Performance*, 3:2 (2014), pp. 173–190.

Jones, Hugh, *The Expert's Guide to Marathon Training* (London: Carlton, 2003).

Kane, Sarah, '4.48 Psychosis' in *Complete Plays* (London: Methuen, 2001).

Kartsaki, Eirini, Rachel Zerihan and Brian Lobel, 'Editorial', *Performing Ethos: An International Journal of Ethics in Theatre & Performance*, 3:2 (2014), pp. 99–105.

Keenan, Thomas and Eyal Weizman, *Mengele's Skull: The Advent of a Forensic Aesthetics* (Berlin: Sternberg Press, 2012).

Kershaw, Baz, *Theatre Ecology* (Cambridge: Cambridge University Press, 2007).

Kester Grant H., *The One and the Many: Contemporary Collaborative Art in a Global Context* (London: Duke University Press, 2011).

Kester, Grant H., *Conversation Pieces: Community + Communication in Modern Art* (Los Angeles: University of California Press, 2013).

Kirby, Michael, *A Formalist Theatre* (Philadelphia, PA: University of Pennsylvania Press, 1987).

Klein, Gabrielle, 'Labour, Life, Art: On the Social Anthropology of Labour', *Performance Research: On Labour*, 17:6 (2012), pp. 4–13.

Klein, Gabriele and Bojana Kunst, 'Introduction: Labour and Performance', *Performance Research: On Labour*, 17:6 (2012), pp. 1–4.

Klich, Rosemary, 'Playing a Punchdrunk Game', in *Reframing Immersive Theatre: The Politics and Pragmatics of Participatory Performance*, ed. by James Frieze (London: Palgrave Macmillan, forthcoming).

Knowle West Media Centre, *Manifesto 2015: A Call for Change*, http://kwmc.org.uk/about/manifesto2015/#sthash.ENc8J5Xt.dpuf [Accessed 1 June 2015].

Kuppers, Petra, *Disability and Contemporary Performance: Bodies on the Edge* (Abingdon: Routledge, 2003).

LaCapra, Dominic, *Writing History, Writing Trauma* (Baltimore, MD, and London: The John Hopkins University Press, 2001).

Latour, Bruno, 'How to Talk About the Body? The Normative Dimension of Science Studies', *Body & Society*, 10:2–3 (2004), pp. 205–229.

Latour, Bruno, *Politics of Nature: How to Bring the Sciences into Democracy*, trans. by Catherine Porter (Cambridge, MA, and London: Harvard University Press, 2004).

Laws, Catherine, 'On Listening', *Performance Research*, 15:3 (2010), pp. 1–3.

Lehmann, Hans-Thies, *Postdramatic Theatre*, trans. by Karen Jürs-Munby (London: Routledge, 2006).

Levinas, Emmanuel, *Ethics and Infinity*, trans. by Richard A. Cohen (Pittsburgh, PA: Duquesne University Press, 1985).

Lichtenstein, Olivia, *Inside Story: Silent Twin – Without My Shadow*, BBC1, first broadcast 22 September 1994.

Lipari, Lisbeth, 'Rhetoric's Other: Levinas, Listening and the Ethical Response', *Philosophy and Rhetoric*, 45:3 (2012), pp. 227–245.

Lippard, Luc, 'Making Something from Nothing: Toward a Definition of Women's "Hobby Art"'. Heresies 4 (1978). Rpt. in Adamson, *The Craft Reader*, pp. 483–490.

Longley, Edna and Declan Kibeard, *Multi-culturalism: The View from the Two Irelands* (Cork: Cork University Press, 2011),

Lorimer, Hayden, 'Cultural Geography: Worldly Shapes, Differently Arranged', *Progress in Human Geography*, 31:1 (2007), pp. 89–100.

Luckhurst, Roger, *The Trauma Question* (London: Routledge, 2008).

Luhrmann, T. M., 'The Magic of Secrecy', in *Ethos*, 17:2 (June 1989), pp. 131–165.

Machon, Josephine, 'Space and the Senses: the (syn)aesthetics of Punchdrunk's Site-Sympathetic Work', *Body, Space & Technology*, 7:1 (2007).

Machon, Josephine, *Immersive Theatres: Intimacy and Immediacy in Contemporary Performance* (Basingstoke: Palgrave Macmillan, 2013).

Machon, Josephine, '(Syn)aesthetics and Immersive Theatre', in *Affective Performance and Cognitive Science*, ed. by Nicola Shaughnessy (London: Bloomsbury Methuen Drama, 2013).

Magelssen, Scott, *Simming: Participatory Performance and the Making of Meaning* (Ann Arbor: University of Michigan Press, 2014)

Mammalian Diving Reflex, *The Mammalian Protocol for Collaborating with Children*, http://www.mammalian.ca/pdf/publications/MammalianProtocol.pdf. [Accessed 12 August 2015].

May, Todd, *Nonviolent Resistance: A Philosophical Introduction* (Cambridge: Polity Press, 2015).

McCarthy, Tom, *Remainder* (Richmond: Alma, 2010).

McCormack, Derek P., *Refrains for Moving Bodies* (London: Duke University Press, 2013).

McFadden, David Revere, *Radical Lace and Subversive Knitting* (New York: Museum of Arts and Design, 2008).

McKittrick, David, Seamus Kelters, Brian Feeney, Chris Thornton and David McVea, *Lost Lives. The stories of the men, women and children who died as a result of the Northern Ireland troubles* (Edinburgh and London: Mainstream Publishing, 2012).

McKittrick, David, and David McVea, *Making Sense of the Troubles. A history of the Northern Ireland Conflict* (London: Penguin: 2012).

Millner, Naomi, 'Involving others: from toolkit to ethos for a different kind of democracy', in Tehseen Noorani, Claire Blencowe and Julian Brigstocke (eds), *Problems of participation. Reflections on authority, democracy, and the struggle for common life* (Lewes: ARN Press, 2013), pp. 21–36.

Mollon, Phil, 'Dissociation', in *Remembering Trauma: A Psychotherapists Guide to Memory and Illusion* (London: John Wiley, 1998).

Morgan, Sally. 'Looking back over twenty-five years' in Malcolm Dickson (ed.) *Art with People* (Sunderland: AN Publications, 1995).

Mouffe, Chantal, 'Artistic Activism and Agonistic Spaces', *Art and Research: A Journal of Ideas, Contexts, Methods*, 1:2 (2007).

Mouffe, Chantal, *Agonistics: Thinking the World Politically* (London: Verso, 2013).

Mukařovský, Jan, *Aesthetic Function, Norm and Value as Social Facts*, trans. by Mark E. Suino (Ann Arbor, MI: Michigan Slavic Contributions, 1979).

Murakami, Haruki, *What I Talk About When I Talk About Running*, trans. by Philip Gabriel (London: Vintage, 2009).

Nancy, Jean-Luc, *Being Singular Plural* (Stanford, CA: Stanford University Press, 2000).

Nancy, Jean-Luc, *Listening*, trans. by Charlotte Mandell (New York: Fordham University Press, 2007).

Neelands, Jonothon, 'Democratic and Participatory Theatre for Social Justice', in *Drama and Social Justice: Theory, Research and Practice in International Contexts*, ed. by Freebody and Finneran (London and New York: Routledge, 2015).

Newling, John, 'From My Garden: Being Human in the Anthropocene Era' (2008), http://www.john-newling.com/essays/ [Accessed 15 January 2015].

Nicholson, Helen, *Applied Drama: The Gift of Theatre* (Basingstoke: Palgrave Macmillan, 2005/2014).

Nield, Sophie, 'The Rise of the Character Named Spectator', *Contemporary Theatre Review*, 18:4 (2008), pp. 531–544.

Oliveros, Pauline, *Deep Listening: A Composer's Sound Practice* (New York, Lincoln, NB, and Shanghai: iUniverse, Inc., 2005).

Petkova, Valeria I., and H. Henrik Ehrsson, 'If I Were You: Perceptual Illusion of Body Swapping', *PLoS ONE*, 3:12 (2008) <www.plosone.org/article/info%3Adoi% 2F10.1371%2Fjournal. pone.0003832> [Accessed 25 January 2015].

Pettitt, Ann, *Walking to Greenham: How the Peace-Camp Began and the Cold War Ended* (South Glamorgan: Hanno, 2006).

Plumwood, Val, *Environmental Culture: The Ecological Crisis of Reason* (London: Routledge, 2002).

Rainey, Sarah, 'Darn it, just who is this secret knitter?' the *Telegraph*, 10 March 2012.

Rancière, Jacques, *The Ignorant Schoolmaster*, trans. Kristin Ross (Stanford, CA: Stanford University Press, 1991).

Rancière, Jacques, *Eleven Theses on Politics*, trans. by Marten Spangberg from a lecture by Rancière on 4 December 1996. Available from http://www.theater.kein.org/ node/121 [Accessed 31 August 2012].

Rancière, Jacques, 'Politics and Aesthetics: An Interview', *Angelakai: Journal of Theoretical Humanities*, 8:2 (Aug. 2003), pp. 191–211.

Rancière, Jacques, *The Philosopher and His Poor*, ed. by Andrew Parker, trans. by John Drury, Corinne Oster and Andrew Parker (London: Duke University Press, 2004).

Rancière, Jacques, *The Politics of Aesthetics*, trans. by Gabriel Rockhill (London: Continuum, 2004).

Rancière, Jacques, *Hatred of Democracy*, trans. by Steve Corcoran (London: Verso, 2006).

Rancière, Jacques, *The Emancipated Spectator*, trans. by Gregory Elliott (London: Verso, 2009).

Rancière, Jacques, *Dissensus: On Politics and Aesthetics*, trans. Steven Corcoran (London and New York: Continuum, 2010).

Re-Enactments, written by Liam Jarvis (with contributions from Hannah Barker), devised by Analogue, sound design by Tom Wilson, voice-overs by Morag Cross, Dan Ford and Brian Martin, produced by Ric Watts. Shoreditch Town Hall, London. 9–12 October 2013.

Reinelt, Janelle, 'The Promise of Documentary', in *Get Real: Documentary Theatre Past and Present*, ed. by Alyson Forsythe and Chris Megson (Basingstoke: Palgrave Macmillan, 2009).

Richardson, Lucy, 'Saltburn Yarn Bombers in World Cup Tribute', *Northern Echo*, 25 May 2014.

Ridout, Nicholas, *Stage Fright, Animals, and Other Theatrical Problems* (Cambridge: Cambridge University Press, 2006).

Roach, Joseph, *Cities of the Dead: Circum-Atlantic Performance* (New York: Columbia University Press, 1996).

Roberts, Lacey Jane, 'Put Your Thing Down, Flip It, and Reverse It: Reimaginging Craft Identities Using Tactics of Queer Theory', in Buszek, Maria Elena, (ed) *Extra/Ordinary: Craft and Contemporary Art* (London: Duke University Press, 2011). pp. 243–259.

Robertson, Kirsty, 'Rebellious Doilies and Subversive Stitches: Writing a Craftivist History',in Buszek, Maria Elena, (ed) *Extra/Ordinary: Craft and Contemporary Art* (London: Duke University Press, 2011) pp. 184–203.

Schneider, Rebecca, *Performing Remains: Art and War in Times of Theatrical Reenactment* (London: Routledge, 2011).

Sedgwick, Eve K., *Touching Feeling: Affect, Pedagogy, Performativity* (London: Duke University Press, 2003).

Shaw, Peggy, *RUFF*, Contact Theatre, Manchester, 28 May 2014.

Shuttleworth, Sally, *The Mind of a Child: Child Development in Literature, Science, and Medicine, 1840–1900* (Oxford: Oxford University Press, 2010).

Simmel, Georg, 'The Sociology of Secrecy and of Secret Societies', *American Journal of Sociology*, 11:4 (Jan 1906), pp. 441–498.

Steenberg, Lindsay, *Forensic Science in Contemporary American Popular Culture* (New York: Routledge, 2012).

Stewart, Kathleen, *Ordinary Affects* (London: Duke University Press, 2007).

Szerszyinksi, Bronislaw, 'Local Landscapes and Global Belonging: Toward a Situated Citizenship of the Environment', in *Environmental Citizenship*, ed. by Andrew Dobson and Derek Bell (Cambridge, MA, and London: MIT Press, 2006), pp. 77–78.

Talbot, Richard, 'She Wants You To Kiss Her', in *Reframing Immersive Theatre: The Politics and Pragmatics of Participatory Performance*, ed. by James Frieze (London: Palgrave Macmillan, forthcoming).

Thompson, E. P., *The Making of the English Working Class* (London: Penguin, 1991).

Thompson, Simon, *The Political Theory of Recognition: A Critical Introduction* (Cambridge: Polity, 2006).

Thrift, Nigel, 'Performance and...', *Environment and Planning A*, 35 (2003), pp. 2019–2024.

Tomlinson, Richard, *Disability, Theatre and Education* (London: Souvenir Press, 1982).

Trueman, Matt, 'Immersive Theatre: Take Us to the Edge, But Don't Throw Us In', the *Guardian*, 7 April 2010.

van der Kolk, B., A. McFarlane and Lars Weisaeth (eds.) *Overwhelming Experience on Mind, Body, and Society* (New York: Guilford, 1996).

Van der Kolk, Bessell. A., Onno Van der Hart and Charles Marmar, 'Dissociation and Information Processing in Posttraumatic Stress Disorder', in *Traumatic Stress: The Effects of Overwhelming Experience on Mind, Body, and Society*, ed. by B. Van der Kolk, A. C. McFarlane and L. Weisaeth (New York: Guilford, 2008), pp. 303–322.

Wallace, Marjorie, *The Silent Twins*, rev'd edn (London: Vintage, 2008).

Warhol, Andy, *The Philosophy of Andy Warhol* (Camberwell, VIC: Penguin, 2010).

Watkin, Christopher, 'A Different Alterity: Jean-Luc Nancy's "Singular Plural"', *Paragraph*, 30:2 (2007), pp. 50–64.

Webster, Mark and Glen Buglass, *Finding Voices, Making choices. Creativity for social change* (Nottingham: Educational Heretics Press, 2005).

White, Gareth, 'On Immersive Theatre', *Theatre Research International*, 37:3 (October 2012), pp. 221–235.

White, Gareth, *Audience Participation in Theatre: Aesthetics of the Invitation* (Basingstoke: Palgrave Macmillan, 2013).

Whybrow, Nicholas, *Performance and the Contemporary City: An Interdisciplinary Reader* (Basingstoke: Palgrave Macmillan, 2010).

Zaiontz, Keren, 'Narcissistic Spectatorship in Immersive and One-on-One Performance', *Theatre Journal*, 66:3 (October 2014), pp. 405–425.

Zerihan, Rachel, 'One to One Performance Study Guide' (Live Art Development Agency, 2009). Available at http://www.thisisliveart.co.uk/resources/catalogue/rachel-zerihans-study-room-guide [Accessed 15 January 2015].

Index